Our Two-Track Minds

PSYCHOANALYTIC HORIZONS

Psychoanalysis is unique in being at once a theory and a therapy, a method of critical thinking and a form of clinical practice. Now in its second century, this fusion of science and humanism derived from Freud has outlived all predictions of its demise. **Psychoanalytic Horizons** evokes the idea of a convergence between realms as well as the outer limits of a vision. Books in the series test disciplinary boundaries and will appeal to scholars and therapists who are passionate not only about the theory of literature, culture, media, and philosophy but also, above all, about the real life of ideas in the world.

Series Editors
Esther Rashkin, Mari Ruti, and Peter L. Rudnytsky

Advisory Board
Salman Akhtar, Doris Brothers, Aleksandar Dimitrijevic, Lewis Kirshner, Humphrey Morris, Hilary Neroni, Dany Nobus, Lois Oppenheim, Donna Orange, Peter Redman, Laura Salisbury, Alenka Zupančič

Volumes in the Series:
Mourning Freud by Madelon Sprengnether
Does the Internet Have an Unconscious?: Slavoj Žižek and Digital Culture
by Clint Burnham
In the Event of Laughter: Psychoanalysis, Literature and Comedy
by Alfie Bown
On Dangerous Ground: Freud's Visual Cultures of the Unconscious
by Diane O'Donoghue
*For Want of Ambiguity: Order and Chaos in Art, Psychoanalysis, and
Neuroscience* edited by Ludovica Lumer and Lois Oppenheim
Life Itself Is an Art: The Life and Work of Erich Fromm by Rainer Funk
Born After: Reckoning with the German Past by Angelika Bammer
Critical Theory between Klein and Lacan: A Dialogue by Amy Allen and
Mari Ruti
Transferences: The Aesthetics and Poetics of the Therapeutic Relationship
by Maren Scheurer
At the Risk of Thinking: An Intellectual Biography of Julia Kristeva
by Alice Jardine and edited by Mari Ruti
The Writing Cure by Emma Lieber
The Analyst's Desire: Ethics in Theory and Clinical Practice
by Mitchell Wilson
Our Two-Track Minds: Rehabilitating Freud on Culture
by Robert A. Paul

Our Two-Track Minds

Rehabilitating Freud on Culture

Robert A. Paul

BLOOMSBURY ACADEMIC
NEW YORK · LONDON · OXFORD · NEW DELHI · SYDNEY

BLOOMSBURY ACADEMIC
Bloomsbury Publishing Inc
1385 Broadway, New York, NY 10018, USA
50 Bedford Square, London, WC1B 3DP, UK

BLOOMSBURY, BLOOMSBURY ACADEMIC and the Diana logo
are trademarks of Bloomsbury Publishing Plc

First published in the United States of America 2021

For legal purposes the Acknowledgments on pp vii–viii
constitute an extension of this copyright page.

Series design by Daniel Benneworth-Grey
Cover design by Namkwan Cho
Cover image © Pascal Deloche / Getty Images

Library of Congress Cataloging-in-Publication Data
Names: Paul, Robert A., author.
Title: Our two-track minds: rehabilitating Freud on culture / Robert A. Paul.
Description: New York, NY: Bloomsbury Academic, [2021] | Includes bibliographical
references. | Summary: "Critically examines and revises many of Freud's seminal ideas
about culture from the perspective of contemporary anthropology, psychoanalysis,
evolutionary theory, and literature and the arts" – Provided by publisher.
Identifiers: LCCN 2020033890 | ISBN 9781501370021 (hardback) | ISBN 9781501370038
(paperback) | ISBN 9781501370052 (ePDF) | ISBN 9781501370045 (eBook)
Subjects: LCSH: Psychoanalysis and culture. | Freud, Sigmund, 1856–1939.
Classification: LCC BF175.4.C84 P38 2021 | DDC 150.19/52–dc23
LC record available at https://lccn.loc.gov/2020033890

ISBN: HB: 978-1-5013-7002-1
          PB: 978-1-5013-7003-8
          ePDF: 978-1-5013-7005-2
          eBook: 978-1-5013-7004-5

Series: Psychoanalytic Horizons

Typeset by Integra Software Services Pvt. Ltd.,
Printed and bound in the United States of America

To find out more about our authors and books visit www.bloomsbury.com
and sign up for our newsletters.

CONTENTS

ACKNOWLEDGMENTS

This book would not have come into existence, and certainly not in its present form, without the encouragement, support, and helpful editorial work of Peter Rudnytsky, one of the editors of the *Psychoanalytic Horizons* series. I am deeply grateful to him for his careful reading of several drafts of the manuscript, and also for the many substantive suggestions and comments he has made that have materially improved the work.

I am deeply indebted to Mark Stoholski, my research assistant at Emory, who not only performed excellent technological assistance in preparing the manuscript for publication, but also read the entire manuscript several times and engaged with the ideas in it in insightful and valuable ways.

My ideas about dual inheritance, psychoanalysis, Freud, and culture have been influenced and enriched over many years by conversations with various people to whom I am indebted and to whom I want to express my appreciation here. These include Lawrence Blum, Robert Boyd, Leslee Nadelson, Melvin Konner, Jonathan Lear, (the late) Naomi Quinn, Lars Rodseth, Bradd Shore, Joel Whitebook, and David Sloan Wilson.

The people with whom I have worked at Bloomsbury Academic have been uniformly helpful, gracious, and professional; I am indebted to them for making the production of this book a seamless and gratifying experience. They include Viswasirasini Govindarajan, Rachel Moore, Rachel Walker, Haaris Naqvi, and others with whom I never interacted but who helped produce the book.

Several of the chapters in this book began as papers and journal articles that were prompted by invitations or solicitations from various people, including Mark Auslander, Rachel Blass, Lawrence Blum, Melvin Bornstein, Ellen Schattschneider, Michael Slevin, and Greg Urban. I'm grateful to all of them for their role in instigating the creation of these chapters.

I am also grateful to the following journals for permission to include these materials in the present book:

Chapter 2, Robert A. Paul (2012). Originally published as "*Civilization and Its Discontents* in Anthropological Perspective, Eight Decades On." (*Psychoanalytic Quarterly* 32(6), 582–598). Reprinted by permission of Taylor & Francis Ltd., http//www.tandfonline.com.

Chapter 3, Robert A. Paul (2010). Originally published as: "Yes, The Primal Crime Did Take Place: A Further Defense of Freud's *Totem and Taboo.*" (*Ethos: Journal of the Society for Psychological Anthropology* (38(2) 230–249). © 2010 by the American Anthropological Association.

Chapter 4, Robert A. Paul, "The Genealogy of Civilization" (1998). Originally published as: "The Genalogy of Civilization" (*American Anthropologist*, 100 (2) 387–396). ©1998 by the American Anthropological Association.

Chapter 5, Robert A. Paul (2000) .Originally published as "Sons or Sonnets? Nature and Culture in a Shakespearean Anthropology" (*Current Anthropology* 41(1) 1–9.) © 2000 by the Wenner-Gren Foundation for Anthropological Research. Published by the University of Chicago Press. All rights reserved.

Chapter 7, Robert A. Paul (2010), Originally published as "Incest Avoidance: Oedipal and Pre-Oedipal, Natural and Cultural" (*Journal of the American Psychoanalytic Association*, 58(6) 1087–1112). © 2010 by Sage Publications.

Chapter 8, Robert A. Paul (2016). 'Sexuality: Biological Fact or Cultural Construction: The View from Dual Inheritance Theory." (*International Journal of Psychoanalysis* 97(3). 823–837. Reprinted by permission of Taylor & Francis Ltd., http//www/tandfonline.com on behalf of Institute of Psychoanalysis.

All of these articles have been revised for inclusion in the present book.

Finally, in the spirit of dual inheritance, I dedicate this book to my children and grandchildren – Ari, Eloise, Isaac, Josephine, and Sylvia.

Introduction: The Stream and the Road

In a book entitled *Mixed Messages: Cultural and Genetic Inheritance in the Construction of Human Society* (Paul 2015), I presented a reformulation of what is known as "dual inheritance theory" in contemporary evolutionary thinking. According to that theory, which I will spell out further below, humans and to a lesser degree some animals inherit the information they need to construct themselves as viable organisms through instructions encoded in two separate channels. One is the genetic channel, in which instructions are transmitted across generations in the DNA and associated materials from the two sets of gametes that join to give rise to a new organism. The other channel, rudimentary in most animals, but robust and crucially essential in humans, is the cultural channel, in which much of the information about how to live is transmitted as instructions encoded in symbols, broadly construed. Symbols are elements of patterned matter available to the senses that convey meaning to and among individual humans. Cultural symbols in humans are organized into complex systems (Geertz 1973), of which the clearest example is language. Like the DNA, language consists of messages composed in a fundamentally digital code, which instructs the developing person how to do the things necessary to fulfill the basic biological tasks of sustaining itself as a metabolic system and of reproducing itself. I demonstrated in my earlier book that due to the differing nature of those two channels of communication, the messages each channel delivers are not (necessarily) consistent with each other and, in a wide array of example from the ethnographic record, I explored the social and cultural phenomena that arise from that basic mismatch.

In *Mixed Messages* I needed the space of a full-length monograph adequately to present my particular version of dual inheritance theory and to illustrate the varied and interesting implications of dual inheritance in human sociocultural systems. I also considered that it was quite enough for the scope of one book to bring together concepts from social and cultural anthropology with contemporary thinking in evolutionary biology, because those two disciplinary discourses are so often kept separate from each other. But as I wrote in the preface to that book,

> It will be obvious to many readers that while the present book is focused almost entirely on anthropological concerns, with almost no mention of psychoanalysis, the entire conception is infused with a deeply Freudian perspective. (2015, x)

The present book, representing the results of thinking about the intersection of culture, evolution, and psychoanalysis over several years, now takes up the challenge of placing dual inheritance and psychoanalysis directly in dialogue with each other, in order to expand and illuminate each.

The relevance of these two theoretical discourses to each other is clearest in the simple fact that a key difference—indeed, I would say, *the* key difference—between the two channels of information transmission across generations is that one of them, the genetic one, requires a fertile act of sexual intercourse, while the other one, the cultural or symbolic channel, does not. (I explain below why this is so important and why it leads to conflicts.) The connection to psychoanalysis seems intuitively obvious, given that conflicts around sex form a central feature of psychoanalytic thinking. The substantive chapters that compose this book will each exemplify and spell out different ways in which I understand the theories of dual inheritance and psychoanalysis to inform each other productively. Therefore, in order to facilitate the reader's ability to follow my arguments, in this introduction, I present an outline of dual inheritance theory as I use it and as I have recast it from its original formulation.

Dual inheritance refers to the undeniable observation that humans inherit necessary information about how to form themselves from conception through post-uterine life in two forms, one as DNA and one as learned cultural symbol systems. When sophisticated

Darwinian approaches to the study of human life and society arose in the 1970s, with the over-enthusiasm that often characterizes the opening phases of a new paradigm, many theorists assumed that social and cultural phenomena among humans could be explained using the concepts and methods that had proven so valuable in understanding non-human life in its vast variety. For many, social life and cultural concepts were thought to be reducible to the then-current ideas in the modern synthesis of Darwinian theory, in which behavior could always be shown to serve the adaptive function of optimizing the reproductive success of individual organisms. According to this view, sociocultural systems were to be seen as the collective result of the optimizing strategies of a group of individuals to produce copies of their genes in subsequent generations. The classic Darwinian formulation proposes that adaptive behaviors, including social behaviors, are evolved through natural selection under the existing environmental conditions, acting on inherited variation in populations of individual organisms, not on species or on social groups conceived of as distinct entities in themselves. This process, it is thought, results in organisms adapted to maximizing their own reproductive advantage, with larger groups, such as species or societies, merely representing the aggregates of such individuals.

But even Darwin himself, in *The Descent of Man* ([1871] 2007), saw that human society entails a level of cooperation among members of a group that appears to be at odds with the picture of separate individuals each pursuing the selfish goal of reproductive advantage over competing conspecifics. To address the obvious fact that humans do in fact cooperate in social settings, the modern synthesis added two important new ideas to save the basic commitment to the idea of individuals bearing "selfish genes" while acknowledging their ability to somehow form cooperative groups. The first of these (Hamilton 1964) is the idea of inclusive fitness, operating on the basis of kin selection. On this theory, individuals could still be understood to be operating on the principle of reproductive fitness if they cooperated with other individuals closely enough related to them that helping them would have the effect of perpetuating their own genes. Close kin, such as full brothers and sisters, share enough of the genes each inherited from the same parents so that it is possible that helping each other also serves the reproductive success of each, insofar as some genes passed along by one sibling would be identical to those of the other close relatives. Thus social cooperation and altruistic behavior could be seen as possible among close kin.

The other important contribution is that of reciprocal altruism, as proposed by Robert Trivers (1971). Clearly human societies consist of larger units than just sibling sets or parents and children, or even groups of cousins. To explain how non-kin could cooperate in a way consistent with the tenet of individual reproductive fitness maximization, reciprocal altruism posits that individuals will cooperate with and altruistically help non-related others if there is a reasonable likelihood that those others will at some point reciprocate with aid equal to or surpassing the aid that was given to them. This principle corresponds to the analysis of the gift in the classic formulation of Marcel Mauss ([1925] 2000), whereby one is under the obligation to give, to receive, and to return a gift of equivalent or greater value. As both Mauss and Trivers showed, and as a great many examples from around the world amply demonstrate, this pattern of reciprocity is in fact essential in many social systems at all levels of complexity. Together with kin selection, the principle of reciprocal altruism saved Darwinian theory in the form of the modern synthesis for most evolutionary thinkers who theorized about human sociocultural systems.

However, in 1985 two biologists, Robert Boyd and Peter Richerson, broke with the then-current orthodoxy to argue that culture could not be understood as merely the ideological superstructure of social systems operating according to principles of fitness maximization, kin selection, and reciprocal altruism. Animal observations had shown that cultural learning of various behaviors in many different species plays a role that appears to be independent of genetic inheritance. Thus, to take two of the most well-known examples, sweet potato washing among Japanese macaques and fishing for termites with a twig among chimpanzees are behaviors that were invented and then learned by many other individuals in the group, including ones who were neither kin nor likely reciprocal altruists relative to the individual from whom each learned the new behavior.

In their path-breaking book *Culture and the Evolutionary Process* (1985), using the mathematical modeling techniques that had become canonical in evolutionary studies, Boyd and Richerson showed that the evolution of culture, which they defined as behavior acquired by social learning—that is, learning from another animal or person, rather than from lived experience of one's own—could not only be theoretically modeled in the same way as biological evolution, but also that it is in principle to a large extent independent of the system of fitness maximization that alone (so it was widely thought) prevails in the realm of biological reproduction and genetic inheritance. Whereas E. O. Wilson (Lumsden and Wilson 1981) argued that the genes "keep culture on a leash," Richerson and Boyd (2005) argued that if this is so, it is a very long leash. In their 1985 book, they even suggested quite explicitly that they saw the relationship between genes and culture in humans as in principle capable of being a conflictual one.

Boyd and Richerson further saw that their position is consistent with the Freudian view according to which "civilization" keeps biologically given instincts in check. In a section of their book entitled A "Freudian" Model (2005, 194–7), they describe a process of "genetically inherited propensities pulling the individual in one direction and culturally inherited beliefs pulling in the other"; and they go on to write:

> This model invokes a familiar picture of the human psyche. Many authors ... have portrayed humans as torn between the conflicting demands of an animal id and a socially acquired superego. One is tempted to conclude that because so many observers have found this picture of the human psyche plausible there must be something to it. It is intriguing that this view of human behavior is a natural outcome of a dual inheritance model of human evolution. (197)

That these authors deploy a specifically Freudian formulation to characterize an aspect of dual inheritance provides a clear link to my present project of bringing the two discourses of psychoanalysis and dual inheritance theory together to see where such a synthesis leads.

Boyd and Richerson's theoretical contribution was groundbreaking and seminal; but of course they had precursors, notably Luca Cavalli-Sforza (Cavalli-Sforza and Feldman 1981) and Donald T. Campbell (1975). Here, though, I want to also recognize a much earlier precursor from a very different academic discourse, namely the important American social theorist Charles Cooley.

Cooley formulated the idea of dual inheritance in a metaphor so apt and so beautiful that I have taken from it the title of this introductory chapter:

> The stream of ... life-history, whose sources are so remote and whose branchings are so various, appears to flow in two rather distinct channels. Or perhaps we might say there is a stream and a road running along the bank—two lines of transmission. The stream is hereditary or animal transmission; the road is communication or social transmission. One flows through the germ-plasm [genetic material]; the other comes by way of language, intercourse, and education. The road is more recent than the stream: it is an improvement that did not exist at all in the earliest flow of animal life, but appears later as a vague trail along-side the stream, becomes more and more distinct and travelled, and finally develops into an elaborate highway, supporting many kinds of vehicles and a traffic fully equal to that of the stream itself. ([1902] 1956: 4–5)

The fact that a dual inheritance perspective was anticipated not by an evolutionary biologist but rather by a student of society provides me with an opening to discuss how I, a cultural anthropologist and psychoanalyst by training, have recast dual inheritance theory from the angle of sociocultural systems and individual psychology rather than from that of evolutionary biology.

Current dual inheritance theory as formulated by Boyd and Richerson posits that learned cultural knowledge passes from the brain of one person to the brain of another, where it may be stored until it is again transmitted to yet another person or persons. Human brains, Richerson and Boyd (2005) argue, are the only entities in nature complex enough to serve as the material systems managing the vast amounts of knowledge humans work with all the time. On this formulation, that which is learned, that is, "ideas," such as the idea of washing a sweet potato before eating it, are like genes that are stored and secreted in the sexual organs and exchanged in copulation so as to engender a new incipient person: just so, brains secrete ideas, concretized in behaviors, that can be observed by learners and taken into their own brains so that the idea travels from brain to brain and in this way across generations, thus creating the parallel road of culture alongside the genetic stream. All this seems intuitively plausible on the face of it.

What this formulation misses, however, from the perspective of cultural anthropology, is the reality and importance of sociocultural systems, which are obviously composed of individuals (and their brains), but which beyond them have their own reality as collectivities over and above the people who constitute them. Anyone who has looked at an "org chart" of some social system such as a company or university can immediately grasp the reality of this, but any social system has its own internal organization of roles, functions, and responsibilities that cannot be generated from any one individual, any more than a human organism can be generated from any individual cell that goes into constituting it. This is true not only of companies with written org charts, but of any human society, which, whether or not the ground rules are overtly expressed, nonetheless is guided by concepts and assumptions organizing people into social categories, institutions, and roles and specifying the appropriate connections between and among roles, statuses, and institutions.

The sociocultural system, while surely requiring human brains to operate, does not reside only in them. Rather, the "cultures" (which we can roughly define as the total ideational components of a sociocultural system) at work in any human society form a comprehensive arrangement of systems of symbols, the most important one in humans being language. These organized patterns of matter observable via the senses can be communicated through space or through other symbolic communication channels (such as via smell, touch, and sound). Such systems are in an important sense external to any individual. This fact is most obvious when one recognizes that a symbol system, for example a language, existed as a collective phenomenon in the social system into which any individual is born before the individual came into existence, and must be incorporated in the course of development to produce a fully capable mature person. Before they get into anyone's brain, then, cultural symbols—including not only linguistic symbols but also any gestures, actions, or images that convey meaning—literally exist in the airwaves, as material phenomena that represent things that are heard, felt, or seen. It is, therefore, in my own formulation of dual inheritance, all the sensory media that convey systems of symbols flowing among persons and exist in the shared public arenas they all occupy that are the equivalent of the gene pool in the cultural channel. The encoding of externally originating information in brains is thus a secondary phenomenon. And because the symbols convey information that the new human will need to complete itself as a viable organism and member of society, they are thus coequal with the genes, and certainly quite as capable as genes are of generating a huge amount of information, especially in the distinctively human form of language (Terrace 2019). It is not for no reason that we often talk of the genes as composed of "letters" in a "genetic alphabet," clearly equating the two channels of communication with a metaphor derived from language.

The parallels between the external symbol system and the internal genetic system—internal in the sense that the genes are encased inside the cells of a person's body—are many, but the differences between them are equally important and it is on these that I focused in *Mixed Messages*. These differences cause the conflicts I have posited between genes and culture, on the one hand, and the parts of the mind in psychoanalytic theory, on the other. Therefore I need to lay these differences out here as the basis for the discussions that are to follow in the rest of the present book.

First among these differences is that for genetic information to flow across generations, the reproductive cells must be released from their storage in internal reproductive organs of the body and brought together in an act of fertile heterosexual copulation. I will address the fact that this is no longer true in Chapter 8, where I discuss the implications of new reproductive technologies. However, for all of human evolutionary history until just a few years ago, and then only in a few parts of the world and in a few socioeconomic strata, copulation has been the only means of procreation among humans.

In the cultural arena, however, copulation does not play a role in the transmission of information. Instead, ideas (and by that term I include thoughts, memories, emotions, feelings, and so on) move among persons by being expressed and observed in the realm of sense perception: words are produced and heard; images are made and seen; emotions are expressed through bodily signs seen and understood; rituals are enacted; techniques are demonstrated and imitated. Human learning, thanks to our capacity for culture and our ability to communicate with symbols, is not simply the "social learning" we share with other species. It is critically different not only in scale but in essential characteristics from animal social learning, even that found among our closest primate relatives. Culture, then, is real; it is concrete in that it is materialized in perceptible forms. Ideas do not just float from one mind to another in disembodied form; they only operate by becoming available to the senses, in the form of material entities that have been endowed with meaning and thus serve as signs or symbols to someone already imbued with the symbol system in which they are communicated.

A second difference between the two channels, which follows from the first, is that copulation is the paramount value for the genetic system: genes maintain themselves over time only by inducing the phenotypical organisms which bear them to reproduce, and in sexually reproducing organisms including humans reproduction requires copulation. Therefore humans, like other animals, are evolved energetically to pursue opportunities to copulate in such a way as to maximize their reproductive genetic success. The strategic program of the genome of any individual is to reproduce itself in greater numbers than those of other organisms of the same species, and in that sense it operates "selfishly" and indeed at the expense of competitors among its same-sex rivals. These rivals, according to the principle of inclusive fitness, include everyone else of the same sex except one's very closest kin, as well as potential reciprocal altruists. The human motivation to copulate has been evolved to ensure the reproduction of the genes; but of course it is obvious that this powerful motivation also leads to copulations, as well as to other sexual behaviors, that either are not intended to or cannot by their nature result in reproduction. I will discuss this phenomenon further in Chapter 8.

The cultural system, on the other hand, is a phenomenon that has evolved in humans to allow otherwise competitive persons motivated by the genetic program to form lasting and at least minimally harmonious social groups that depend on some degree of cooperation, mutual aid, and organization in order to survive. And because (heterosexual) copulation, the supreme good from the point of view of the genetic program, must, by the logic of that program, imply or lead to competition and selfishness rather than cooperation, it is not only not the supreme good in the cultural system, it is in fact a threat to its very existence. That is why social groups characterized by long-term cooperation among many non-relatives are so rare in the animal kingdom. It follows from this difference that in humans the cultural system must have some degree of antipathy towards copulation, which it operates to control, regulate, circumscribe, and very frequently devalue. Cultures therefore limit the direct performance or appearance of copulation in the public arena in which symbol communication occurs (except on very rare occasions) in the interests of maintaining the level of cooperation necessary for social life. This conflict between the sexual and symbolic programs has to be calibrated in such a way that biological reproduction does actually occur in sufficient numbers to maintain the society over time and the succession of generations, while also preventing the potential competition generated by the pursuit of genetic fitness from threatening the harmony or even the existence of the group.

A third difference, flowing from the first two, as Richerson and Boyd (2005) argue, is that humans appear to have evolved two different and opposed classes of social instincts. One of these is that which enables groups formed among close genetic kin, in accordance with the principle of kin selection; this typically involves some form of the nuclear family and would include polygamous marriages as well as monogamous couples. The other social instinctual endowment, unique to humans, is what Richerson and Boyd call the "tribal instincts" (2005: 196) that enable humans to live peacefully with each other in groups over and above the family mating units. Other animals, it is true, as well as some insects, have also managed to develop prosocial group living, but the human method, through the elaboration of a vast and comprehensive system of symbols in the cultural sphere, has few if any parallels elsewhere in nature.

This "tribal instinct" has been able to arise among humans and become part of their genetic endowment over the long period of their evolution because those most suited for group living and social life would have been favored as mates. Those individuals exhibiting too much competitive aggression or overbearing self-assertion would have been eliminated from the gene pool, as undesirable mates, by social controls and norms such as ostracism, expulsion, or even, as Richard Wrangham (2019) has recently argued, execution. This is a form of what Darwin termed "sexual selection," in which members of one sex choose mates from among those in the other sex exhibiting characteristics likely to enhance their own genetic reproductive success. By this principle, one chooses a mate with characteristics that will produce progeny which will themselves, having inherited those traits, be normatively acceptable from the cultural point of view. These tribal instincts, together with the norms and values favoring cooperation conveyed in the symbolic system, make possible the wider societies that extend beyond the nuclear family and include non-kin individuals as equivalent members. The principle of reciprocal altruism also plays an important role in allowing this to occur, since exchange is the foundational social interaction in many societies, especially in the exchange of spouses or reproductive mates. The result of this phenomenon is that the genetic program contains a predisposition for both antisocial and prosocial behaviors. Reciprocally, cultures have evolved to enable behaviors that work against social harmony as well as those that enhance it. These complications are important, but do not negate the conflicts that exist between the most salient aims and values of the two whole systems of inheritance.

A fourth difference between the two systems is that whereas in the genetic program the difference between the sexes is crucial, in the cultural system, and therefore in the tribal group that it maintains, the difference between the sexes is not intrinsically necessary. Of course there may be a division of labor by sex, or it may be the case that cultural symbols are gendered on the analogy of sexual difference; but because copulation is not a necessary feature of the life of the symbols in the public arena, the biological categories of male and female are not of existential significance as they are in the genetic program. This means that human societies, as well as the individuals who are evolved to constitute them, are characterized by a conflict between the pursuit of social cohesion based on the principle either of kin selection or of adherence to the wider group, and that their sexual identity and activity are relevant in one form of society but not necessarily in the other.

Furthermore, in the genetic program, there is a difference between males and females in terms of their respective strategies for achieving reproductive fitness, stemming from basic biological differences: males not only produce many more sperm cells than females produce ova, but are in principle able to inseminate hundreds or even thousands of females (as Genghis Khan and his sons are supposed to have done) and father hordes of descendants; while there is a strict and much lower upper limit on the number of offspring a female can produce, given that she must gestate each one for nine months and then nurture it through lactation (at least in the great majority of pre-modern societies) for months or more usually years. In the wider "tribal" society, by contrast, as long as sexual reproduction is successfully managed, and although almost all societies make some form of gender distinction, there is no *necessary* difference between the genders (as opposed to the biological sexes); and instead of the strict duality necessary in the genetic system's mode of reproduction, there is room in the wider cultural symbol system not only for the gendering of various aspects of life on the analogy of the difference between the sexes, but also for other gender arrangements, as well as for the absence of gender distinctions, at least in principle.

What all this means is that there is much more intense mating competition among men than among women—and among humans, in most societies, the men are almost always armed with lethal weapons whereas the women are not. This in turn requires that the social arrangements necessary to organize the potentially more disruptive and homicidal men are different from those required to organize women. And as I showed at length in *Mixed Messages*, it has meant that in a majority of human societies in the ethnographic record, men, having arrogated to themselves the cultural arena, assign to women the disruptive genetic program and hence have dominated and devalued them, seeing them as the agents of biological procreation and so as the supposed cause of competition among the men. (This is ironic of course, given that it is actually the men who, being more competitive and more liable to violence, are the ones who actually need more than women to be controlled and pacified by culture.) But as I showed in *Mixed Messages*, this phenomenon of gender asymmetry favoring males is not inherent in human society, though it is widespread; and I cited various ethnographic examples to show that it need not prevail.

Yet another implication of these distinctions between the sexes and the genders is that the cultural system, more often than not, holding itself to be superior to the biological means of reproduction, develops symbolic means that not only parallel genetic procreation but seek both to minimize its importance and to establish alternative artificial, man-made means of reproducing. These involve not only transmitting symbols instead of genes across generations but often an effort to actually monopolize and seize control of biological reproduction and in some ethnographic cases to mimic it. The manifold practices in the ethnographic record that illustrate this last point include for example such things as the couvade, male rituals that symbolically generate fertility magic or enact parturition, and the ideology in many patrilineal descent systems according to which, as Apollo argues in *The Oresteia,* it is only male semen that produces offspring, the mother's womb serving merely as a receptacle.

Another implication of all these considerations is that there are two different sorts of sexual practices: the one that can in principle result in biological reproduction, and all those that can't. Heterosexual copulation is intimately tied to the logic of the genetic program, while all forms of non-genital sexuality, including both same-sex and opposite-sex sexual practices which do not lead to reproduction, are therefore more closely allied with the cultural program. All acts of non-reproductive sex are carried out, therefore, with another goal, generally that of satisfying a desire for a sensual pleasure (although of course there can be many other motivators as well).

One of the most significant differences between genetic and cultural reproduction yet to be mentioned is that sexual reproduction can only be accomplished between two people, and (usually) only produces one newly created person at a time; and, in addition, that an act of fertile copulation delivers all its information once, as one complete package recorded in the chromosomes bearing the DNA (though this information is only put into effect in segments and over time). But cultural reproduction, by contrast, occurs all the time during persons' lives as they learn new information; and it can deliver its message to many people at once, as for example when a speaker addresses a crowd or audience assembled in the public arena. This can happen in small groups when everyone is physically present and within earshot or sight range; but it can also occur in larger and more dispersed societies in those public arenas created by enhanced media of communication, so that it is now possible to address millions of people at once. The implication of this difference is that cultural reproduction is a far more efficient means of reproduction than is genetic reproduction, at least in terms of numbers, which at least in part accounts for its ability to override and control the powerful selfish proclivities, potential violent conflict, and unruly sexual urgency inherent in the operation of the genetic program.

The genetic program produces individuals who are genetic "kin," in the sense that they have inherited and are informed and instructed by replicas of the same genes; this is the basis for "kin selection." If they exhibit kin solidarity, it is because they are in the genetic sense to a significant extent actually genetically similar or, in the case of identical twins, even identical, so that promoting the reproductive interests of one serves the genetic fitness of all. But in the cultural system too, individuals are united by being informed and instructed by the same means of inheritance, only in this case it is via the transmission of symbols rather of genes. In anthropology it has been customary to refer to a phenomenon known as "fictive kinship," in which, for example, members of a non-related or distantly related group refer to each other as "brother" or "sister." The phrase "fictive kinship" is misleading, however, because it implies that genetic kinship is real and symbolic kinship is merely an imitation of it that is made up and therefore "constructed" and by implication secondary and even insubstantial. A key argument in my formulation of dual inheritance theory is, by contrast, that symbolic relatedness stands on the same level of "reality" as genetic kinship and is equal or even superior to it in the amount of information it conveys to cultural kin. Just as siblings can see each other as closely linked because they share many of the same genes, so genetic non-relatives can see others as closely linked insofar as they each carry the same symbolic system within them.

Thus cultural kinship can make symbolic relatives out of people who share the same cultural symbol system, so that people speaking the same local dialect, or sharing a religion or ideology, can have the same sense of connectedness to and be able to communicate and cooperate with others in the group who are not genetically related at all. This fact, which means one has many more cultural relatives than genetic ones, enhances the cultural system's ability to outperform the genetic system as a reproductive system. With this outline of my formulation of dual inheritance theory as a baseline, the reader will be able to follow the arguments in the chapters that constitute the remainder of this book.

I have stressed the important differences between the genetic and cultural programs because these differences can be seen as produced by or producing conflict between the two systems, in individuals and in societies; and conflict, especially conflict about sex, pro and con, has been a cornerstone of psychoanalytic thinking since Freud.

The chapters that comprise this book will examine in extended detail how the differences and conflicts I have depicted are to be understood in relation to both psychoanalysis and culture.

Our Two-Track Minds is divided into three parts. Part I is called "Dross into Gold: Recuperating Freud's Social Theory." In it I present what I understand to be the main features of Freud's theory of human society, derived from his books and essays dealing with culture rather than with individual psychology; and then I examine aspects of this theory carefully to show what contemporary validity they contain when viewed from the perspective of dual inheritance. Chapter 1, "Freud's Theory of Society," offers a brief synoptic overview of Freud's ideas about how human society is possible given that, as he sees the matter, and as I have outlined it above, society is composed of fundamentally asocial people equipped with evolved unruly drives. The next two chapters are detailed attempts on my part to show how, if reconceived in more contemporary terms, central aspects of his theory are in fact quite consistent with current thinking.

Chapter 2, "Biology and Culture in *Civilization and Its Discontents*," serves first of all to give a clear and coherent account of the main argument of that rather diffuse and often misunderstood essay, and then to reinterpret it in the light of contemporary anthropological and evolutionary theory, and specifically the theory of dual inheritance, so that its essential insights are revealed as quite coherent and persuasive.

Chapter 3, "Yes, the Primal Crime Did Take Place," addresses Freud's story of the overthrow of the primal father by his sons that inaugurated human society, as related in *Totem and Taboo*. Although this supposed historical event is often regarded as fanciful at best, if not just plain wrong—he himself referred to it as a myth—I show that shorn of some of its dated aspects it is actually a quite plausible account of the roots of human social life and of dynamics that inform society to this day, in ways consistent with dual inheritance theory.

Part II is called "Like Rabbits or Like Robots? Sexual versus Non-Sexual Reproduction in the Western Tradition." In it I apply a central idea of dual inheritance theory to aspects of Western culture: the idea that in order to maintain itself, culture as a system of symbols embodying a set of principles organizing a society must exhibit a certain degree of ambivalence and even hostility toward sexual reproduction. To establish and maintain itself across generations, then, culture provides alternatives to sexual procreation in some form of what may be termed cultural or symbolic reproduction. The three chapters in this part each address a different facet of our own Western tradition, and in so doing illustrate different ways in which cultural, non-sexual reproduction has been understood and constructed in our particular cultural system.

Chapter 4, "The Genealogy of Civilization," illustrates the dynamics of the conflict between biological and cultural reproduction as it has played out in the origins and history of our "Western" civilization. Dealing with the transition from the cultural system of the era of the Hebrew Bible to that of the dominance of the New Testament in the West, this chapter shows the historical process by which the value of reproduction via the production of new generations by means of inculcating them with cultural ideas superseded the value of sexual procreation as a means of social reproduction. Here, cultural or non-sexual reproduction is constructed as the enculturation of new biological individuals with a cultural symbol system.

In Chapter 5, "Sons or Sonnets," I propose a reading of the first nineteen of Shakespeare's *Sonnets* according to which they provide a remarkable poetic evocation of the conflict between sexual reproduction and cultural reproduction, leading up to the victory of symbols over the genes. In the progression of these sonnets, the poet moves from encouraging a beloved youth to beget biological heirs to "reproducing" the youth himself through the symbolic form of his own immortal poetry. Thus the poet with his words is cast as the one responsible for the youth's reproduction across the generations, not the youth's genes.

Chapter 6, "The Pygmalion Complex," provides a thumbnail history of some high points in the Western imagination of the ongoing and unresolved conflict between the value of sexual reproduction on the one hand and the opposed higher valuation of the fantasy of the non-sexual reproduction of humans. Beginning with Ovid, the chapter traces the ups and downs of the contending values, ending with considerations of Mary Shelley's *Frankenstein* and Karel Čapek's prophetic play *R.U.R.*, which introduced the word and the concept of the "robot" into our cultural imagination. In this case, non-sexual reproduction refers to the actual attempt to create new humans, or at least close facsimiles of them, by non-sexual, technical, and/or artificial, and thus cultural means.

Part III, "Our Two-Track Minds: A Dual Inheritance Perspective on Some Classic Psychoanalytic Issues," brings a dual inheritance perspective to bear on some classic aspects of psychoanalytic theory and practice. Chapter 7, "Incest Avoidance: Oedipal and Pre-Oedipal, Natural and Cultural," addresses the perennial question of the incest taboo in anthropology and psychoanalysis. I argue that there are actually two different kinds of incest avoidance, one that derives from Oedipal dynamics and is aligned with the genetic system and one that arises from pre-Oedipal sources, connected to the cultural system and the concerns of the wider society.

Chapter 8, "Sexuality: Biological Fact or Cultural Construction?," answers the question posed in the title with a qualified "both," describing the radical changes in the cultural construction of sexuality in very recent times while also recognizing underlying biological reality, and thus exemplifying the dual inheritance model. This chapter argues that psychoanalysis as a cultural practice itself has necessarily evolved in tandem with recent rapid cultural changes in sexual values, norms, and behaviors.

In Chapter 9, "Consciousness, Language, and Dual Inheritance" I address the question of how it is that making something that was unconscious conscious can actually change a person's psyche and experience for the better. Beginning with Freud's assertion that making a thought conscious depends on associating it with a linguistic presentation, I take as a premise that both language and consciousness are social, not only psychological, in nature. The ego, to which consciousness is attached, is thus a border entity connecting the organism and its genetically derived sexual, selfish, and aggressive impulses with the systems of symbols circulating in the wider "tribal" society. I show how doing this is in principle capable of relieving psychic suffering.

PART I

Dross into Gold: Recuperating Freud's Social Theory

1

Freud's Theory of Society

How is human society possible? The question arises because in nature, according to the theory of evolution, most organisms act in their own genetic self-interest, not on the basis of loyalty to any group beyond their immediate genetic kin. Therefore, any truly social animals, including humans, have to find some way to overcome this obstacle to the cooperation that collective life requires. One possible answer to the question I posed above, at least as far as humans are concerned, is that favored by those embracing a strong form of social constructionism. From this perspective, it would be argued that in the course of evolution humans have become so dependent on the influence of the cultural systems of the societies in which they live that genetic imperatives have faded into relative insignificance. The opposite view, espoused by many evolutionary thinkers, would be that genuine altruism, or prosociality, is indeed antithetical to the nature of life, and that therefore the veneer of sociality exhibited by humans is largely a mask for Machiavellian self-interest. The third solution, which seems to correspond better to the actual experience of living with others, is that there is a conflict inherent in human life between the urges promoting self-interest, both personal and genetic, and a genuine capacity for attachment to, care for, and identification with others beyond the family and thus to form a larger entity called society. Freud is perhaps the foremost advocate and theorist of this latter view.

Although he was primarily an investigator of the individual mind, Freud took a great interest in social and cultural matters, writing extensively about them throughout the latter half of his career. The works focusing on culture include *Totem and Taboo* (1913), *Group Psychology and the Analysis of the Ego* (1921),

Civilization and Its Discontents (1930), and several others (a comprehensive treatment of Freud's writings on culture can be found in Smadja [2019]). In these essays, Freud attempts to show how the inherently self-interested raw materials with which nature has provided humans, in common with other organisms, have been organized so as to transform humans into prosocial beings, who not only can but must live in relative harmony with others within large sociocultural systems. This is the problem of how "instincts" or "drives" representing our organismic genetic endowment undergo the "vicissitudes" that make society possible without, however, eradicating the continuing influence in our psychic lives of those same mostly inherently antisocial drives.

What are the organismic endowments that correspond to the self-interested imperatives that need to be transformed to produce cooperation and prosociality in human society? And by what miracle has this unlikely outcome been achieved, in the course either of human evolution or of individual ontogenetic development or both? The Buddhist "Wheel of Life" depicts the endless process of life in *samsara* as driven by the three poisons of lust, anger, and the ignorance that lead to egoism, represented in the iconography by a cock, a snake, and a pig respectively. Likewise, Freud's picture of the human psyche finds at its core the drives of sex and aggression, as well as the fantasy of omnipotent narcissism. From these not very promising ingredients—which are not at all inconsistent with the Darwinian picture of life in general—Freud will concoct a picture of a human being at least passably at home in society or "civilization" and capable of true fellow-feeling and regard for others. Let us see how, for Freud, the trick is done.

We must begin where Freud's own serious engagement with social theory begins, that is, with his book *Totem and Taboo* (1913). The ideas put forward in this work permeate and ground all his subsequent writings on the subject. In this work, he presents an evolutionary narrative according to which humans, before they became capable of civilization, lived in family units consisting of a senior male, his female consorts, and his biological offspring. The senior male of the group—the "Primal Father"—was characterized by supreme and unbridled selfishness, monopolizing sexual access to the females and enforcing his will by brute force; in other words, he lived by the untransformed imperatives of sex, aggression, and narcissism. His sons, by contrast, were driven by his absolute authority and by their enforced sexual deprivation into "group psychology." Forced to live in common subjection, they formed bonds of affection and comradeship with each other. Finally, having banded together, and emboldened perhaps by a new weapon, they killed the harsh tyrant who dominated them and established a new "civilized" form of society. Out of remorse, grief over the loss of a father who was loved as much as he was hated, and to prevent a recurrence of the war of each against all that would ensue if each enacted his own selfish wish to become the new "alpha male," they reached an agreement to forbid mating within the group as well as internecine violence. Instead of having a new human leader, they set up an imaginary substitute for the slain father, a divinity in the form of a totem animal who could enforce the new social arrangement with the borrowed authority of the slain father. This totem animal, in the course of the evolution of civilization, became the basis for all subsequent supernatural beings, culminating in the omnipotent lone God of monotheism who, like his human prototype, is experienced as the author and enforcer of the morality by which the group is able to sustain itself. In other words, out of self-interest, the sons each renounced the imperatives of sex and aggression, at least within the group, and reassigned his own fantasy of omnipotence to a new all-powerful but fantasized leader, whose authority, inherited from the primal father, enforced the new agreement.

What changes did this entail in the psyches of those humans who came into being under the new regime, and how were these maintained? The first point to make is that once the group as a collectivity of many individuals had been created by the sons, any single individual was no match for the collective will of the united others. If any man tried to put himself forward as the new all-powerful leader, the others would unite against him and prevent him from doing so. This dynamic, it might be mentioned, is indeed observed in the majority of those elementary foraging societies that have been ethnographically described: they share an ethos of rigorously enforced egalitarianism and unwillingness to infringe on another's autonomy among the adult males, and an antipathy toward anyone who shows signs of trying to elevate himself as a new dominant leader (Boehm 1999).

This power of the collective over each individual was the stick that enforced compliance within the new dispensation; the carrot was the (sublimated) homosexual love the brothers had developed for each other while they had lived in enforced celibacy under the conditions of the father's rule. But where did this capacity for brotherly love come from in the first place? Freud's answer is that humans, endowed with a powerful sexual libido that had developed as a feature serving the evolutionary purpose of reproduction, became able to inhibit the aim of this drive and redirect it to a different aim. This aim-inhibited libido, and in the present case specifically homoerotic libido, is much better suited to the creation of enduring social bonds among individuals than is uninhibited libido. Why this is so can be explained in the case of the two different circumstances of heterosexual versus homosexual bonding.

According to Freud, uninhibited libido when released in orgasm does not result in a bond with the sexual partner: once the organic urge has been satisfied, it leaves no residue of love, but is free to seek a new partner. This would of course serve the evolutionary purpose, at least for males, of maximizing potential reproductive fitness by impregnating many females without waiting for one to be ready to reproduce again (a process that among hunter-gatherers often requires a wait of three or four years). But if each individual pursued this course of action, it would lead to direct competition with all the others who were motivated by the same purpose. This was just the state of affairs that the killing of the primal father, who had lived by raw sexual imperatives and stayed in power by means of physical violence, was intended to overcome. Therefore the new social system required that each individual settle for only one mate (or, in polygyny, a small number of mates). Only this could ensure the harmony that society requires. The result of this modification of libido would be that the individual must embed sexual lust within a penumbra of aim-inhibited "love," which alone would enable an enduring bond to form between the mating couple. Our cousins among the higher primates by and large show no such lasting affectionate heterosexual bonds between mating couples.

This new arrangement, however, creates a new problem. As Freud argues in *Civilization and Its Discontents* (1930), no society has ever been simply composed of pairs of sexually united heterosexual couples working together for the common good. And indeed, he argues in *Group Psychology and the Analysis of the Ego* (1921) that the mating pair is actually intrinsically inimical to the formation of the larger group. As Freud puts it, once Eros has united two lovers in sexual love, he has completed his task and can go no further. But this would leave us back with the same self-enclosed familial units that the rebellion of the sons overthrew. How is this difficulty to be surmounted?

This is where the second factor, aim-inhibited homosexual libido, comes in. Originally this was caused by the father's sexual monopoly, which literally inhibited the sons' libido through the threat or reality of punitive violence, since he was the stronger party in any fight. Denied sexual access to the females of the group, the sons turned for partners to each other. But this "group psychology," built on aim-inhibited libido, remained in force under the condition of civilization, because it alone made it possible for the otherwise competitive males to tolerate living with each other. Two things had to happen to make collective living possible for the unruly males. One is that, thanks to homoerotic bonds of friendship and alliance, the sons could now maintain their love for their brothers (and by extension, for other unrelated group members, including ineligible women), by voluntarily submitting to the marriage rules and sexual norms of the group, enforced by their mutual submission to the will of the hypostasized father/god. The second is that each would have to forgo the impulse to press his own self-interests with force, that is, to control his potential for aggression. To do this, as Freud argues, it was necessary for each to withdraw some of his libido from his overtly sexual life and reinvest it in a powerful aim-inhibited form to act as a reaction-formation to hold his more aggressive lust-driven libido in check—whence the command, which struck Freud as absurd and impossible but powerful, to love one's neighbor as oneself.

But this does not yet get to the root of how originally competitive individuals, each seeking his own personal and genetic advantage, could turn into willing citizens of a rule-governed society. To understand Freud's view of this we must again turn to *Group Psychology*, in which he highlights the importance of the leader in making the group cohere. Already in his paper "On Narcissism" (1914) he had made the point that the primary narcissism that a child must abandon in the face of reality lives on as the basis for an idealized embodiment that is, through one means or another, externalized. In his theory of the leader put forward in *Group Psychology*, he posits that in the process of group formation each individual bestows his own disavowed omnipotent fantasy on the leader. This leader may be a real person, it may be a supernatural being, or even an idea or an ideal. The further step in the construction of a true social group is that, because each individual has taken the same leader as his own ego ideal, the repository of his own impossible narcissism, he sees in each fellow group member someone like himself with whom he can identify. Such identification is a fusion of his narcissism—the other resembles him in having the same ego ideal—and love, fueled by the libido but siphoned off and inhibited in its aim at the demand of the leader. The leader, as the shared collective ego ideal who is loved, identified with, and feared, authorizes those sacrifices of organismic imperatives that are required for the group to exist.

Because, as I have said, in actual existing foraging societies and probably in the prehistoric past no one might occupy the place of leader, that role is assumed instead by supernatural beings and/ or sacrosanct codes of conduct rather than human leaders. But as societies grew larger and more complex in the course of cultural evolution, the place of the leader was more and more occupied by actual individuals, supported by coteries of supporters.

In *Group Psychology*, Freud gives a further elucidation of how, in the course of ontogenetic development, an originally self-interested person becomes a willing member of a collectivity with others. We may start with two assertions Freud makes about the sources of love in humans. The first is that the biological foundation of love is the long-lasting bond that unites the helpless human infant and its mother, as he argues in *Inhibitions, Symptoms, and Anxiety* (1926). Precisely because the human infant is born prematurely and requires constant nurture and care for several years after birth, evolution has provided adult humans with the basis for a deep protective and affectionate relation to our offspring. This serves the function of connecting them closely with actual genetic kin and helps ensure their own reproductive success. This is a principle that also prevails in non-human nature in most mammalian species. Freud does not hesitate, in his *Three Essays on the Theory of Sexuality* (1905), to derive this love from sexual drives: the mother, he says, in caressing, kissing, and offering her breast to the infant uses elements of her own sexual life in bonding with her infant; and the infant responds by developing a lifelong need for such love. Indeed, Freud says that the epitome of perfect love is the infant falling asleep after nursing, an act in which its hunger and (oral and tactile) sexual drives have been simultaneously gratified. This is, for him, the original unity of the life drive that in the course of development separates into the life-preserving ones ("ego-libido") and the sexual ones ("object-libido").

Second, in "Instincts and Their Vicissitudes" (1915a), Freud argues that the infant's first response to an object outside itself is hostility: another being in the external world is at first felt as a threat to the infant's own fantasy of omnipotent self-sufficiency. The unambivalent love between the infant and the mother (or her breast) does not violate this rule, because in the infant's mind the mother, whose care and feeding give pleasure, is incorporated into the "pleasure ego," the forerunner of the mature ego. Before the more mature ego develops the reality principle, the pleasure ego operates on the principle that whatever brings pleasure is in fact part of the self, or of the as-yet undifferentiated symbiotic self-and-other dual unity.

Building on these two ideas, in *Group Psychology* Freud argues that the child, in its desire to have all the mother's love, and to be its sole object, responds with hostility to a new baby, who is its rival for the mother's affection. But the child learns from experience that the parents (ideally) love each sibling equally. Therefore just as the brothers in the primal family agreed to a renunciation of their own self-aggrandizing wishes for the sake of a viable communal life, which provides more stable and adaptive advantages for each member, the child turns from hostility to aim-inhibited love of its rivals. The *esprit de corps* of a group flows from this transvaluation. It can occur because the parent holds over the child the threat of the loss of her love, to which it has become so attached. At this point, the parent fulfills the role of the child's "leader" or ego ideal, and paves the way for the later process whereby love in the group beyond the immediate family is enabled. As Freud says, the group member agrees to unite with the others, first in the family nursery and then in the wider group, *"Ihnen zu Liebe"*— for love of them. Here again, aim-inhibited libido acts as the counter-force that restrains the aggression by which the individual might otherwise pursue his selfish aims.

But a group is held together not only by love; and the human inclination to aggression does not simply go away even when suppressed by a reaction-formation of brotherly love. How then is aggression prevented from erupting and destroying the group solidarity? (Admittedly, of course, sometimes it isn't, as history and experience so clearly show.) One obvious answer Freud offers is that the aggression that is forbidden within the group is encouraged against other groups; we are all too familiar with this dynamic. However, in *Civilization and Its Discontents*, Freud makes another extremely important point. By a process that he has elaborated most tellingly in his essay on "Mourning and Melancholia" (1917), individuals are able to use their own aggression against themselves. The superego, derived originally from the parent who can withhold love or deliver punishment, and then extended to society at large, can utilize the person's own aggression to keep him or her in check. By setting up such an agency in the psyche, embodying the superior power of the parent, the group, and/or the leader, a person becomes his own harsh taskmaster; the result of this turning of aggression back on the self is the state of guilt. And it is guilt, alongside the love for others that springs from an original hate, that transforms the group member into one who obeys authority and follows the rules even though they work against his own deep and fundamental biological impulses and wishes.

How is this guilt produced in the individual, then? Here again, the answer parallels on an individual level the process whereby society was created (according to Freud) in the course of evolution: after a period of "amorality" in earliest youth, a transformation sets in that results in latency and the compliance with social norms that go with it. The motor of this transformation is the Oedipus complex and its resolution. The diphasic onset of sexuality in human children means that there is an initial erotic phase that comes to a climax with a fixation on one or another of the parents leading to rivalry with the other one. This love is both affectionate and directly sexual—except that the child has only an incomplete and confused idea of what sex actually is and has to make do with fantasies. For Freud these fantasies are self-generated, but also derived from the ministrations of the first caretakers. This first passionate love comes to an end through a fear of the loss of love and the threat of punishment from the rival parent, who is then incorporated into the individual's psyche as the punitive superego. Society puts this dynamic to use, by using this psychological process to instill a sense of guilt and hence of obligation in the individual to the group, its leader, and its rules.

Thus just as alchemy turns dross to gold, so in Freud's view the vicissitudes that the raw organic drives—sex and aggression, along with narcissism—undergo in the course of both human evolution and individual development turn them into the very bases of the bonds that make society possible. Unfortunately, though, as we all know, alchemy doesn't actually work; and the fragile web of civilization can all too easily be resolved back into its raw materials, as Freud in his essay "Thoughts for the Times on War and Death" (1915c) saw clearly in the middle of world war and the unchecked mayhem it unleashed.

I will only add one critical observation here: it is evident that this theory focuses on men and the dynamics among them rather than on all society members, male and female. Although this bias certainly reflects the ideas about the sexes prevalent in Freud's day, to which he too subscribed, it may also be partly justified by the empirical fact that in the great majority of societies in the ethnographic record males do dominate and set the rules for the group. Furthermore, it is men who need rules and organization more than women to control their far greater capacity for dangerous aggressive rivalry. And while men may be united by identification with a leader, one might hypothesize in light of the idea of cooperative mothering in the evolution of human society (Hrdy 2009) that women's sociality could be grounded in their mutual identification through shared care for and nurturance of each other's children. The child would thus play the role for women that the alpha male leader plays for the men. This would account for why men, being more intrinsically antisocial, need stricter external rules to organize them, whereas women's sociality seems to spring more from intrinsic relationality arising from the nature of the maternal nurturing role.

Having briefly laid out the elements of Freud's theory of society, in the next chapter and the following one I will look in more detail into Freud's social theory as it is enunciated in two of his most important cultural texts, *Civilization and Its Discontents* and *Totem and Taboo*, to place them in a contemporary context and extract from them what still should hold interest for anthropologists, psychoanalysts, and all others concerned with the nature of human life in society.

2

Biology and Culture in
Civilization and Its Discontents

Introduction

Civilization and Its Discontents (1930), as its author readily admits, is a sprawling work with numerous side paths and detours that can easily tempt a commentator to explore them further. In this chapter, I will resist any such temptation and attempt instead to discern the central argument sometimes hidden in the thicket of rhetorical false starts and extended digressions. Once having laid out relatively briefly what I take to be the main argument, I examine it from the perspective of contemporary anthropology, including both evolutionary and cultural points of view, to determine its current validity and usefulness as a way to think about the relationship between nature and culture in human life. Having done that, I then present an alternative view that conserves many of Freud's insights but is not subject to some of the problems in his original analysis.

Before I begin, I need to clarify two important matters. Although Freud (1930) used the word "*Kultur*" throughout his essay, the English translators chose to use the word "civilization." Freud's definition of "*Kultur*," however, makes clear that he intends by it what anthropologists now mean by the word "culture" in the generic sense. He writes: "We shall ... content ourselves with saying that the word 'civilization' [*Kultur*] describes the whole sum of the achievements and the regulations which distinguish our lives from those of our animal ancestors and which serve two purposes—namely to protect men against nature and to adjust their mutual relations" (89). Any anthropologist would have to admit that this is about as good a succinct definition of "culture" as one could ask for. I therefore assume that in this essay Freud is indeed addressing the issue of nature versus culture, that is, the relative contributions of biology and socially transmitted knowledge in human life and society in general, not just in what we would call "civilization." And therefore, unless quoting from the English translation, I myself will use the word "culture" rather than "civilization" in this chapter.

The second issue has to do with the fact that Freud does explicitly state what he thought was the main argument of *Civilization and Its Discontents*, when he speaks of his intention "to represent the sense of guilt as the most important problem in the development of civilization and to show that the price we pay for our advance in civilization is a loss of happiness through the heightening of the sense of guilt" (134). The first part of this sentence does indeed correspond to what I present as the central argument of Freud's essay. But whether culture in general, or our particular modern Western culture, actually makes people more or less happy than they might otherwise be, or than they were in a putative "state of nature" (which has never existed), is not something about which I have any wisdom to offer, and I therefore say no more about it.

The Main Argument of *Civilization and Its Discontents*

Freud, following Darwin and other authorities of his day, begins from the assumption that early in their evolutionary history our ancestors were living as gorillas do, in relatively isolated polygynous family groups, most usually consisting of a single adult male, his female consorts, and their immature young. This family structure was itself, for Freud, the result of the loss of sexual periodicity in the form of the estrus cycle found in other primates, so that genital satisfaction "no longer made its appearance like a guest who drops in suddenly, and, after his departure, is heard of no more for a long time, but instead took up residence as a permanent lodger" (Freud 1930: 99). The men now felt a need to keep their sexual partners close at hand, and women were motivated to stay with the men for the care and protection of their young.

At a certain point it then occurred to people that there was an advantage to be gained by working cooperatively. Culture thus emerged from the twofold dynamics of the advantages of collective labor and of love, which knit families together. With both *Eros* and *Ananke* thus working side by side, Freud argues, it is hard to see how "this civilization could act upon its participants otherwise than to make them happy" (101).

The first disturber of what might thus appear to be an ideal state of social living is the conflict between the family and the larger group formed by cooperation. The family resists giving up its members to the society at large, making it hard for young people to break away. And in any event, the sexual bond that unites the family exists between two people only. Unmodified genitality, for Freud, is not easily generalized to any wider group and so, once having bound two people in sexual love, as we have seen, Eros can go no further. But even with this being so, Freud suggests that we could easily picture groups of families living side by side, each family bound together within by the sexual bond of the mating pair, and beyond the family each pair united with the others by the mutual advantage gained through cooperative work. "We can quite well imagine a cultural community consisting of double individuals like this, who, libidinally satisfied in themselves, are connected with one another through the bond of common work and common interests" (108). However, such a harmonious state of affairs has never actually existed, because culture is not content with only these ties to create a human group. Rather, culture, impelled by Eros—the life drive— following its own aims rather than those of the individuals who compose it, attempts to bind the members of a human community to each other in a libidinal way. Not stopping at mutual interest to keep sexually united couples socially linked to others like them, it tries to ensure that libidinal ties of both (aim-inhibited) object love and identification exist among all the members of the group.

How can culture accomplish this? Clearly it must withdraw some of the libido, or sexual interest, that would otherwise flow between husband and wife, and turn it from its genital aim to some other purpose, through the process Freud refers to as sublimation. This is accomplished through one of the vicissitudes to which the drives are subject, in this case, inhibition of the aim of the drive. As we know, Freud (1915a) analyzed a drive into four components, namely, its source, its quantum of energy, its object, and its aim. Although the organic source and the impetus of the drive are fixed, both the object and the aim can be modified and even replaced. Thus humans can use their sexual drive not only for its original biological aim, that is, genital intercourse biologically selected to lead to reproduction, but also for the aim-inhibited function of "affectionate" love of the kind that binds friends, relatives, and other consociates as opposed to lovers in the strict genital sense. Although aim-inhibited love retains some of the original features of purely sexual love—the wish to be near the other person(s), to act altruistically toward them, etc.—it modifies and tames the raw pleasure of pure genital sex for general use in binding the members of a human community together in mutual affection. It follows, therefore, that to create libidinal bonds within a community, because libido (being an energy) is in finite supply, culture has to restrict the unalloyed genital sexual life of lovers and divert some of that libido into aim-inhibited relations with others (not to mention into sublimated libidinal interest in the work everyone must perform together).

But this formulation only leads to the next puzzle—why does culture have to do this? Leaving aside the metaphysical proposition Freud endorses—that it is just Eros's job to do this (just as it is the aim of Thanatos to tear apart what Eros has united)—there is a more down-to-earth issue to be addressed: "There must be some disturbing factor which we have not yet discovered" (Freud 1930: 109). The clue as to what that disturbing factor might be is provided by the ideal demand our own culture makes of us that we love our neighbor (and indeed our enemy) as we love ourselves. This demand Freud finds so improbable, so far from what can actually be accomplished, that he can understand it only as a defense against something else. That something else in turn could only be the opposite of what the cultural demand is enjoining by means of reaction formation. If we are commanded to love one another, it can only be to hold in check our tendency to hate one another and our wish to bring harm and destruction to our fellow humans. The disturbing factor that makes culture have to establish love relations among consociates, therefore, is the human drive toward aggression, the eternal companion and antagonist of the erotic instincts of sexuality and love.

In short, then, culture, if it is to bind people together in society, cannot rely on people who are neutral about each other, but must counteract the aggressive tendencies that would otherwise tear the community apart by restricting sexual enjoyment and using some of its energy to create aim-inhibited relations of love among fellow-humans. The partial renunciation of sexuality in culture is thus an unhappy but necessary by-product of the need to control aggression within the group. But if sexuality can be diverted from its genital aim and refined into aim-inhibited neighborly love, what can be done with the quantities of unexpressed aggression that this love is supposed to hold in check? First, of course, they can be displaced and projected, that is, redirected against other groups, people who are not in the group, or scapegoats within the group.

More importantly, the conflicts of early childhood, especially the Oedipus complex, which for Freud is part of our evolved phylogenetic heritage, draw on this energy. Because as children we depended on the care of our parents, our fear of angering them, of losing their love, and of causing them to punish us for transgressions—real or imagined—of their norms and expectations, we have acquired the capacity to sign over some of our aggressive wishes, which would otherwise have put us at odds with our caretakers, to the agency of the superego. Acting as an independent agency within our minds, the superego, drawing originally on the internalized authority of the parents and through them of society at large, uses our renounced aggression to strengthen its own threats against us, making us feel "guilty," that is, in need of punishment. This anxiety is not necessarily caused by anything bad we have done, but rather arises from our wishes and impulses to do things that are forbidden in the realms of sex and aggression. The dread of losing the love of the superego, or of the group, forces us to renounce our hostile impulses and to use our own hostility to dominate ourselves in the ways culture demands of us. This leads to a vicious circle, for the more we renounce aggression, and alienate it from our own selves, becoming thus docile and "civilized," indeed better behaved, the more fuel we add to the arsenal of the superego, which then demands still further renunciations and penances to ward off the expected punishment. This of course leads to yet further fierce denunciations of us on the part of the superego, which has been strengthened precisely by our reassigning of our aggression to it—and so on. "Thus conscience doth make cowards of us all," as Freud says quoting Hamlet (Freud 1930: 134)—or, to put it more benignly, thus does guilt make usually well-behaved citizens out of beings potentially driven by intense disruptive antisocial sexual and aggressive impulses.

Thus, integrating his theories of the drives, their vicissitudes and the defenses against them, childhood sexuality, Oedipal fantasy, and other distinctively psychoanalytic ideas with the evolutionary and cultural thinking of his day, Freud proposes to have achieved his aim of "representing the sense of guilt as the most important problem in the development of civilization" (134).

Civilization and Its Discontents in Contemporary Evolutionary Perspective

Humans are social animals, like a great many others throughout nature. Freud is, however, clearly on the side of those who would argue that the social dimension of our existence, our web of relations with others, does not sit entirely comfortably on us, that it is in conflict with some other factor or factors in our constitution.

> It is a mark of our present condition that we know from our own feelings that we should not think ourselves happy in any of these animal States [those of bees, ants, and termites] or in any of the roles assigned in them to the individual. (123)

What are those other factors that make us resistant to being at one with the demands of our social life? For Freud, there are primarily these three: our narcissism, our sexuality, and our aggression. Our narcissism places our self-interest in conflict with our concern for the welfare of others and makes us see others as interferers with our wish for omnipotence; our sexuality puts us in competition with others for desired sexual objects and drives us toward aims that can't be reconciled with other friendlier dimensions of social life; and our aggression makes us bad neighbors when we are crossed or frustrated.

One doesn't have to subscribe to old-time drive theory to agree that this is a fair description of what it's like to be a person. Beyond subjective recognition of this picture of ourselves in the mirror, however, we can look to contemporary evolutionary theory, which is very consistent with Freud's view. The mainstream version of evolutionary theory, Darwinism as propounded by thinkers such as Dawkins (1986), Dennett (1995), and Pinker (1997), rests on the assumption that the form organisms take is the result of natural selection, which, acting on individual organisms developed and guided by the genome passed to them in the process of reproduction, favors those individuals who adapt the best strategies to compete successfully in reproducing their genome in future generations. In sexually reproducing organisms such as ourselves, this means that succeeding in sexual competition for mating opportunities is *the* paramount biological value. And this competition, in turn, may and often does involve aggression against rivals for reproductive advantage. Thus, just as in Freud's theory of the human organism, life throughout the animal kingdom is marked by the "self-interest" of genes and of individuals bearing them in achieving the paramount sexual aim of reproducing, and in doing so competing successfully against rivals through aggression. It is not, however, by that token, always nasty, brutish, and short, at least in social species. Why not?

The social animals, including humans, have figured out ways of allowing groups of individuals to live together without expending energy or excessively endangering themselves in constant competition. At a minimum, they put up with one another for some mutual benefit in which they all share, such as being in large herds for protection against predators. In other animals, including many species of primates, there are active prosocial behaviors and relationships, such as pair bonding, long-term consortships both heterosexual and homosexual, grooming partnerships, alliances, coalitions, and what one might call real friendships. In all these cases, the advantages of group living and of enduring relationships have an adaptive value of their own and lead toward positive and even altruistic behaviors—which, however, ultimately derive their existence from the fundamental principle of self-interest in sexual success that evolutionary theory requires. Thus, for example, coalitions among males lower in a chimpanzee dominance hierarchy may allow them strategically to advance in ways each could not accomplish on his own. Because advancement in the hierarchy brings with it enhanced mating opportunities, the relationship serves the "selfish" purposes of each one in the alliance.

Evolution has, then, provided a number of mechanisms whereby the Hobbesian situation that might be expected to prevail where self-interested sexual competition is in play is kept under control, and relative harmony usually prevails. Among those mechanisms that are common among the primates are dominance hierarchies, which establish relatively stable orders of precedence to determine which individuals have sexual mating opportunities without constant renegotiation; the estrus cycle, whereby females are only reproductively active for limited periods, so that in the interim there is no cause for male-male competition; and, especially among our closest ape relatives, ritualized aggression and rituals of reconciliation that avoid harmful overt aggression and bring hostilities to an end, as described by de Waal (1989, 1996).

Too close inbreeding, likewise, is avoided in all species by some mechanism or other. Among the primates, this is usually accomplished by what is called "transfer," whereby juveniles of one sex or the other leave their natal group on reaching reproductive age and end up breeding in a different group. Most commonly it is males who transfer—except in the great apes most closely related to humans, where it is female transfer that prevails.

One general evolutionary principle that rescued neo-Darwinian theory from the positing of stark individualism and, indeed, made possible the modern field of sociobiology was the recognition that it was the gene, not the individual bearing the gene, whose reproduction was the engine of natural selection. Therefore, if several individuals shared the same gene, they might well engage in altruistic behavior with each other, because they would still be promoting the dissemination of copies of their own genes. From this, it followed that individual organisms needn't be selfish at all, provided they were working for the good of a group of closely related kin, who had many genes in common. The social insects to which Freud alludes have this characteristic. For this reason, genuine altruism among these insect societies is accounted for by the hypothesis of inclusive fitness.

It should be clear that there never has been a period in human history, of the sort imagined by Freud to have existed in some primordial time, in which individuals lived unfettered by any restrictions on their sexuality, their narcissism, or their competitive aggression. All these have always been managed in social life. Nor is it likely that proto-humans lived in family units, and then joined together to form larger societies. On the contrary, the weight of contemporary primatological and anthropological opinion favors the view that from the start the hominid line that branched off from our common ancestor with the chimpanzees about 5 or 6 million years ago lived, like the chimpanzees, in multi-male, multi-female groups, and only gradually developed pair bonding within the group (Ingham and Spain 2005, Chapais 2008).

Chimpanzees, who give us our best insight into our own evolutionary pre-history, live in multi-individual groups, but without reproductive pair bonding. Breeding is, on the contrary, promiscuous, although competition is kept from getting out of hand by dominance hierarchies and by the estrus cycle. What the chimpanzees have that is quite unique in the animal world is multi-male groups, with cooperation in defense of the group shared among cooperating males, and with female transfer. In almost all other primates, transfer involves the ejection of maturing young males from their natal group and their eventual establishment of a breeding situation in an unrelated group. Among the chimpanzees and bonobos, however, it is females who transfer. The chimpanzees are thus what is called philopatric (when speaking of animals) or patrilocal (when speaking of humans)—meaning that the enduring members of the group are related males, whose daughters and sisters leave to breed elsewhere, and who themselves breed with in-migrating unrelated females.

It is extremely rare in the animal kingdom for there to exist philopatry as well as male coalitions and cooperation within a group, and this is for a simple evolutionary reason: the asymmetry between paternal and maternal investment in reproduction. Females must commit to one pregnancy at a time, and to the nurture of the resulting infant, with a great strain on their own physiological resources. There is a sharp upper limit on how many reproductive opportunities they can have altogether no matter what. The male investment is limited to an activity that can take no more than a few minutes or even seconds, so that in principle a male can father hundreds of offspring. This latter situation doesn't usually occur, however, because instead there is breeding competition among the males which is much more intense than the mating competition that occurs among females (Hrdy 1981). This in turn is the reason (or one of the main reasons) why males are so much more aggressive than females (Sanday 1981, Maccoby 1998).

Although there remains some dispute about the matter, it seems most likely that the common ancestor of humans and the other African apes, and therefore probably the first proto-humans in the hominid line, was philopatric or patrilocal as well. The best argument for this is that we are descended from a common ancestor all of whose other descendants—chimpanzees, bonobos, and gorillas—are also philopatric. At the same time, it appears likely that not only did human women lose the estrus cycle and evolve concealed ovulation, so that there was no temporal regulator on opportunities for reproductive sex, but dominance hierarchies were replaced by egalitarian social structures, at least among the adult males (Knauft 1991). There was thus selection pressure for something to replace these checks on sexual competition, while at the same time the advantages of group cooperation, and especially of male cooperation, for example in the area of group defense, exerted pressures in the direction of finding ways to offset intragroup male aggression. What was it that was selected for in humans that filled the gap? There can only be one satisfactory answer: culture, or more accurately, the evolution of the human capacity for creating and embodying culture, to which I will now turn.

Before doing so, however, I summarize by saying that although it appears that Freud was incorrect about the form of life from which human life in culture evolved, his picture of the necessity of finding solutions to the threats posed by narcissism, sexuality, and aggression to social life is accurate, and, as I will now argue, his finding of those solutions in culture, and in the psychological mechanisms on which culture depends, is likewise highly plausible.

Civilization and Its Discontents in Contemporary Cultural Anthropological Perspective

Culture is humankind's greatest adaptive advantage. It allows human groups to adapt to almost any ecological and social situation in the world, not by the slow process of biological evolution through natural selection, but by the rapid invention and dissemination through learning of extra-somatic adaptations. For example, in moving into the arctic regions, groups of humans did not have to evolve fur and other cold-resistant features but could figure out how to kill animals that had already done so and use their hides as clothing. Culture is a system of social, technological, and ideological skills and rules for living transmitted by means of symbolic forms, of which the most spectacular is language. These symbolic forms exist in a collective space that is created by the joint focus of individuals not only on each other but also on the objects of the other's attention, creating a collective arena in which shared ideas, norms, and practices can be enacted, negotiated, and disseminated (Tomasello 2019). Although it is essential for humans to have the brain capacity to create, understand, and transmit these symbolic forms, it is distinctively human that these forms exist out in perceptual space where many people can have access to them. Geertz (1973: 214–16) called this the "extrinsic theory of thought."

A good way to picture it in a concrete metaphor is to picture a poker table around which are distributed a number of people playing the variant of poker known as Texas Hold 'Em. There is a fixed and known deck of cards (the symbols), the cards in play are on the table and almost all face up and in full view, and the rules organizing the symbols into a game are public and known to all. Each player has his or her own hand, and plays his or her own strategy which he or she tries to keep to him or herself. But the game itself is not in their brains, as some have argued; it is on the table. This is what Durkheim ([1915] 1967) meant by "collective consciousness"—everybody knows the same rules and sees the same "up" cards and can participate in this shared perceptual space. As Tomasello (2019) persuasively argues, the distinctively human capacity that emerges both in evolution and in development is the ability to share a mutual gaze with someone (presumably mother in the first instance) at some third object and in this way begin to learn to help create and enter such a shared cultural arena.

The evolving pre-frontal cortex that enabled us to do all this, to have foresight and to be able to conceptualize, so that we could invent fur coats and play Texas Hold 'Em, also has the capacity to inhibit impulses that come from the more primitive parts of the brain. A poker game is a form of competition; and in trying to deceive and beat each other, the players are employing aggression; but it is a highly stylized, contained, well-regulated form of mutual aggression in which the losses are symbolic (money is symbolic) although nonetheless very real. True enough, now and again, an enraged loser might leap up from his chair, turn over the table, draw his .45 and shoot the winner—this happens. And, as mental illness does in relation to "normalcy," it shows us what lies beneath the veneer of a friendly game. But the essence of the game is that it is normally a well-regulated arena in which aggression can be put into play without any raw outbursts of violence because everyone agrees to play by the rules and to inhibit the aggression that is in play.

Robin Fox (1980) vividly portrays the evolutionary advantage of being able to inhibit impulses and develop long-term social strategies. Likewise, for Freud, the ego is a very large inhibiting apparatus that has the capacity to take the unformed motivational impetus of violent or transgressive sexual wishes and impulses and subject them to refinement through sublimation into the symbolic system, in the same way a Porsche takes the raw explosive power of gasoline and, running it through an elaborate engine that titrates it, coordinates the firing of tiny amounts of it in just the right way, uses it to power a beautifully calibrated smooth-running machine. (I will develop this point at greater length in Chapter 4.)

Following this line of thought, it is evident why Freud depicted the drives in humans not as instincts, which in animals have a fixed course of action, but as unformed energies that must be run through the ego, and through the symbolic system that it embodies, before they can turn into any form of socially constructive action. Our adaptive ability to "evolve" cultural instead of somatic forms of action depends on not having many fixed action patterns, but instead relying on the interplay between the motivations or "drives" that come with the territory of being a living, evolved organism with the symbolic forms provided by any particular cultural context or system.

The human revolution, then, involved the process whereby, through the evolution of brains that have the capacity for culture, humans were able to create a form of society in which positive feelings for others could prevail over aggressive, competitive tendencies, especially among the testosterone-besotted men. The key, as Freud (1913) saw, anticipating the insights of many subsequent anthropologists, was the institution of marriage rules. Like many others, he viewed these as resting first and foremost on the prohibition on incest. In reality close inbreeding had never existed, and so did not need to be prohibited. The importance of incest prohibitions, which are cultural norms and cross-culturally correspond only very imperfectly to actual genetic relatedness, is that they regulate mating, and for the most part people in society accept the rules of the game and play by them. (I discuss incest avoidance at greater length in Chapter 7.) In this way, cultural norms play the same role in human society that dominance hierarchies and estrus play in chimpanzee society. But how can mere symbolic systems exercise control over men in the grip of sexual and/or violent passions?

The Oedipus complex, in this view, is the evolved developmental process whereby compliance with the rules and entry into the adult social arena is initiated, because it is there that powerful impulses of desire and rage are countered and inhibited, sublimated, or neutralized, to usher in latency, during which period the individual can learn the skills of the social and cultural game that is in play without being overtly troubled with strong pressures from unmodified sexual and aggressive impulses. That this happens in relatively early childhood is important, because in that era, the individual really is at the mercy of those in authority over him, that is, most usually, his parents and through them the wider group. The motive for submitting to extraneous influence is easily discovered in the child's helplessness and dependence on other people, and it can be best designated as fear of loss of love. If the child loses the love of another person on whom he or she is dependent, he or she also ceases to be protected from a variety of dangers. Above all, he or she is exposed to the danger that these stronger person will show their superiority in the form of punishment (Freud 1930).

The renunciations thus enforced induce the developing individual to establish a superego, through identification with the loved and feared authority and caretaker, which then has access to the aggression the individual ego has renounced, and which it can use to coerce and control the ego. The sexual and hostile dimensions of the Oedipus complex are thus suppressed, repressed, or renounced, leaving in their wake a psychology ready to comply with the rules prevailing in the public social arena.

Recent work by Boehm (1999), Goldschmidt (2006), Rochat (2009), and others affirms from other academic perspectives that the collective judgment of the group and the wish to be loved by it, and by its representatives in the form of the parents, are one of the most powerful incentives, if not the most powerful one, to conform to and uphold the rules in play in society (which is why it is more plausible that our angry poker player who shot off the legs of his rival probably did so because he suspected the other had cheated, not because he had beaten him fair and square). The emotions of pride, shame, and the whole gamut of feelings concerning self-esteem, which are distinctively human and do not have analogues even among the chimpanzees, relate to one's sense of recognition by, and inclusion in, the public social arena in which culture is enacted. Where does the love that fuels these dynamics come from? For Freud (whose picture of humans in society is often erroneously depicted as one-sided and Hobbesian), love and strife are in equilibrium, just as narcissistic love and object love are both present and may be in balance or in conflict. His explanation of the power of guilt as a prerequisite for harmonious social functioning rests on the assumption that the love of parents and authority figures is as great as is the resentment of the limitations and frustrations of impulse that they enforce, and once the latter is expressed, even in wishful fantasy, the former comes forward to balance it. Far from being the Hobbesian cynic he is sometimes imagined to be, Freud clearly says in the essay on group psychology: "We will try our fortune, then, with the supposition that love relationships ... constitute the essence of the group mind" (1921: 91). The breeding ground for this uniquely human capacity and need for love is, in turn,

> the long period of time during which the young of the human species is in a condition of helplessness ... so that the value of the object that alone can protect it against them [the dangers of the external world] ... is enormously enhanced. The biological factor [premature birth] establishes the earliest situation of danger and creates the need to be loved which will accompany the child through the rest of its life. (1926: 154–5)

Recasting *Civilization and Its Discontents* for the Contemporary World

It should be clear from the foregoing that in my view the main argument of *Civilization and Its Discontents*, in spite of some inevitable errors and of attitudes that have changed with time, remains a powerful analysis that is consistent with much evolutionary and cultural thinking. One of its main values, as I have tried to show here, is indeed that it manages to be consistent with both evolutionary and cultural perspectives simultaneously, without giving short shrift to either—something that remains remarkably difficult to achieve in today's intellectual climate in which evolutionary thinkers frequently fail to appreciate the reality and autonomy of culture, while cultural thinkers are often highly allergic to even the mere mention of biological factors in social life. This pattern in anthropological circles is paralleled in psychoanalysis by the split between drive theorists and relational theorists (Greenberg and Mitchell 1983). Freud's capacious view of human life continues to stand as a model for the overcoming of these unproductive dichotomies, once one accounts for its now-outdated aspects.

Having said that, I will now go on to say that a main stumbling block for the appreciation of the claims of *Civilization and Its Discontents* has to do with Freud's use of drive theory. I think it is self-evident that love and conflict, altruism and self-interest, all characterize human life, and that in all societies transgressive wishes and fantasies (and acts) of sex and violent aggression are the "wild cards," in terms of both social harmony and individual experience. But Freud's understanding of the drives has not fared well in the light of subsequent understandings of psychology and physiology, if only because, although he wanted to treat them as quantities of energy in dynamic interplay with each other, the fact that they cannot be located and observed (other than by inference), much less measured, obviates any use they might have as concepts upon which to ground a viable theory of human behavior and of social life.

In rewriting the main argument of *Civilization and Its Discontents* for today's intellectual climate, I would therefore leave to one side the drive model as an inadequate physics of the mind, and recast the conflict that is basic to human society and to individual life in terms of dual inheritance model. This model is based on what I should think would be the uncontroversial observation that a human being comes into existence on the basis of information and instructions carried along two separate channels, one of which is the genetic channel and the other the cultural channel.

We can assume that the cultural system and its channel of inheritance evolved in the first place to serve the purposes of the genetic system, that is, to enhance the inclusive reproductive fitness of individuals bearing genes that better enabled them to create, use, and learn culture. Culture itself is after all, as I have said, humankind's greatest adaptive advantage. But whereas many who attempt to create biocultural co-evolution models (e.g., Durham 1991, Lumsden and Wilson 1981) only end up showing the impact of culture on genetic advantage, a true dual inheritance model recognizes the fact that a feature of human evolution is that the cultural symbolic systems have, over the course of time, emerged as autonomous reproductive systems, serving their own reproductive fitness which may or may not correspond with the genetic fitness of the individual(s) whom it helps to construct.

The dual inheritance model to which I subscribe therefore replaces "either/or" attitudes with that of "both/and," recognizing the genetic and cultural forms of reproduction as having different characteristics which can cause them to interact in a variety of ways which is the business of comparative ethnography to describe and analyze. One of the most important differences is that genetic evolution depends on the differential rates of birth and mortality of individual phenotypic organisms in a population working under particular selection pressures, thus requiring many generations to act; whereas cultural evolution is independent of the life and mortality of individuals, can be accomplished very rapidly, and operates with capacities of memory and foresight that are excluded from classical Darwinian evolutionary theory.

Two other key differences, as I discussed in Introduction to this book, are these: first, the sole "value" in the process of natural selection is reproduction, and in sexual species, therefore, in the successful performance of fertile sexual union. Certainly other factors in differential reproductive success are also crucial, such as a minimum of parental investment in young after birth, more or less favorable environmental conditions, etc., but in humans, all evolutionary success has to pass through the very narrow defile of the union of sperm and ovum achieved through heterosexual genital intercourse. (I am, of course, well aware that this statement, although valid for most of our evolutionary history, has recently been superseded by various reproductive technologies [Mann 2014].) Cultural evolution depends on no such thing. If I discover or invent a new technique for making a better bow and arrow, or a new vaccine, or if I formulate a new philosophy, and I disseminate this to others who may or may not be my immediate kin and who can then make it part of their own experience and derive adaptive benefit from it, heterosexual intercourse doesn't enter into the matter at all one way or the other.

Second, sexual reproduction in humans, through which genetic inheritance is achieved, can only produce one single new copy (except in the rare case of multiple births) at a time, and the newly formed phenotype is acted upon in its development as an embryo and infant from within by copies of the genes that were in the one original fertilized egg in interaction with RNA and proteins. Each individual is informed from within, as it were, by the particular genetic information contained in the innermost chamber of every cell comprising its body. Cultural reproduction, on the contrary, thanks to the nature of the shared public arena in perceptual space, can inform many people at once, whose number is limited only by the technology of communication available in any given place and time. If I invent a new dance step, I can show it to any number of observers who can then imitate it themselves. And as a very important corollary of this, if I compose a new melody, I can teach it to you and we can all sing it in perfect unison. Such unison is impossible in the genetic realm except in the exceptional cases of identical twins (and nowadays of clones). And just so, if I come up with a new religious teaching or political philosophy, I can at least hope that I can create a group of followers all informed by exactly the same message, whereas even with my closest biological kin there can be no such complete identity of genetic interest.

It follows, then, that there are two essential but different value systems at work in humans: one, the genetic, in which heterosexual intercourse is the highest ultimate priority and inclusive genetic fitness is the goal, and in which each individual is inherently to some degree a self-interested lone actor in competition for breeding opportunities and for long-term inclusive reproductive fitness; and a second, the cultural one, that is by its nature collective, social, and relational, in which heterosexual intercourse occupies no privileged place, or even necessarily any place at all—as long as someone is reproducing and creating new organisms, from the cultural point of view I can reproduce through them as well as through my own biological offspring. These two systems are both inherent and necessary in the creation of individual humans as well as of human society, and, I would propose, it is they that should be seen as the source of the inevitable conflict that Freud perceived to characterize human existence.

I would propose that over the course of human evolution and history, the cultural program—the "road" in Cooley's terms—has gradually separated itself from the genetic program—the "stream"—and not only established its autonomy from it, but taken on a more and more successful open competition with it (as in the reproductive technologies mentioned above). In the quite small hunting and gathering societies such as the ones in which our ancestors evolved, the two programs probably worked in relative harmony, the cultural system through marriage rules, religious rituals, and other norms and values helping establish a society relatively free of overt internal conflict over the fair distribution of mating partners, with individuals living lives marked by the alternation of autonomous self-direction and immersion, for example through ritual, in the larger collective. With the growth of towns and cities after the Neolithic revolution beginning about 10,000 years ago, the cultural program began to depart from its subservience to the genetic program, and, with the great leap forward in communication made possible by the invention of writing, could include larger and larger numbers of more and more genetically unrelated people into communities united by cultural identity and inheritance as opposed to genetic relatedness.

Very often in human history and throughout the ethnographic record, the antagonism of the cultural program toward the genetic program has resulted in a denigration of the whole process of sexual reproduction, which, from the point of view of the wider society and the cultural system, is, as Freud noted, a problem and a disruption. Frequently this has resulted in a value system in which "culture" is seen as higher than "nature," often enough, too, with men identified with the former, and women, because of their obvious role in pregnancy, lactation, and other aspects of child nurture and care, with the latter (Ortner 1974). Sex is then marginalized and thought of as somehow antisocial. We live in a key historical moment at which the genetic program, by means of the cultural inventions of reproductive technology, has actually been able to render sexual intercourse unnecessary for reproduction. The cultural ramifications of this are impossible to predict, but one could propose that the entire complex of sexual difference and heterosexuality in general is already less dominant than it once was (and still is in many societies), as an organizing principle, as a value, and as a metaphor. (I pursue this topic further in Chapter 8.)

If, then, I were to rewrite Freud's main argument as I have presented it here, I would replace the language of drives and their mutual forces and counter-forces to address the structure of human society, its necessarily conflictual character, and the critical role of guilt in converting aggression into compliance. I would instead use the idea of the construction of human life by two different inheritance programs, the genetic and the cultural, that work together at best with some awkwardness, and that often, especially as society has gotten more and more complex and technologically sophisticated, are fated to conflict, manifesting as such at both the social and the individual levels.

A full elaboration of the dual inheritance theory and its value in understanding the construction of human societies in their similarity to each other as well as in their vast cultural differences from each other is beyond the scope of this chapter; I have given just such an extended account in my book *Mixed Messages* (2015). Here I hope to have at least indicated how thinking with it allows us to retain many of the important insights of *Civilization and Its Discontents*, while also putting them in conceptual terms more in tune with the evolutionary and cultural thinking of the decades since it was written. Whatever its faults, Freud's late meditation on the nature of human life in society continues to serve as a model for the effort to integrate the biological and the cultural in human existence without minimizing the contributions of either.

In the next chapter, I turn to a discussion of another core foundational claim of Freud's social theory, namely, that human society began with a historical rebellion against the regime of a jealous and despotic father by his united sons, as he argues in *Totem and Taboo*.

3

Yes, the Primal Crime Did Take Place

Introduction

I am one among what must be at most a small handful of anthropologists and/or psychoanalysts who continue to take seriously the theories Freud proposed in his four essays collected under the title *Totem and Taboo*, first published in 1913. I have written a number of works dealing with this text, culminating in my book *Moses and Civilization: The Meaning behind Freud's Myth* (1996). In that work, I tried to show, through a detailed analysis of the text of the first five books of the Hebrew Bible, and of the legends, folktales, and commentaries that had accreted around them over the centuries, that the story told in that most foundational of all religious texts in the Western tradition parallels Freud's scenario of the "primal crime" with great precision. Using methods derived from both psychoanalytic theory and the structural study of myth, I argued that just as in Freud's proposed story of the originating deed transforming us from animals to humans living in organized society, the leader of a band of oppressed "brothers"—Moses—murders the jealous tyrant—Pharaoh—who had enslaved them, and then proceeds to receive from a vastly greater but now immaterial and immortalized "father"—God—a set of laws that order proper human relations with divinely sanctioned binding force. I further argued that the myth, as I called it, spelled out in the Torah narrative provides a model for the dynamic creation of a personality based on inhibition and renunciation of instinctual impulses, with a strict and punitive superego, that helps construct the "conscientious," that is, rule-abiding, person essential to the ongoing operation of social organization, especially in Western, Judeo-Christian society.

There is no point attempting to flesh out and trying to render persuasive here a case that it required an entire book to make. I direct the interested reader's attention to that work for further details. In the present chapter, I want to raise and address a question left hanging in the book, so let me take as granted my assertion that the two texts—Freud's myth of the Primal Horde and the Five Books of Moses—mirror each other with uncanny accuracy, and ask what that similarity might mean. In my book, I did not attempt an answer to that question, thinking it enough to have simply demonstrated that an identical structural schema underlay both narratives. Any of the following conclusions, or several combined, might be plausibly drawn from this fact:

1. Either consciously or unconsciously, Freud was guided by having read the Bible when generating a fantasy about prehistoric times.

2. Freud and the authors of the Bible, children of the same cultural tradition, although separated in time, resorted to the same stock of cultural themes when attempting to concoct an account of the origins of human civilization.

3. An Oedipal reading of prehistory reflects a feature about the unconscious life of its inventor, namely Oedipal dynamics, and these were likewise present in the unconscious fantasies of those who wrote the Bible—perhaps because the fantasy is universal, perhaps by virtue of their belonging to the same sociocultural tradition, or perhaps by coincidence.

4. Freud discovered a truth about human social organization, and the Bible derives its hold over vast numbers of people because it is structured by whatever it is Freud discovered.

Various other conclusions are also possible, of course, but I am going to pursue the last mentioned possibility: that Freud's theory contains an important truth about human social organization, one that indeed lends power to the Bible story that, I might mention, now holds sway in one or another transformation, Jewish, Christian, or Muslim, over a large percentage of humans on the planet. In my book, I did not consider Freud's myth, or the biblical one, as accounts of historical events that could be falsified or verified but, rather, as two comparable narratives that showed point-by-point correspondence. I now want to take up the substantially more controversial claim that Freud's formulation, with all its faults, does after all tell an important story about the evolution and history of human social organization, as well as about its present constitution.

I am well aware of the array of criticisms, each supposing itself to be the final nail in the coffin, that have been leveled at Freud's theory of the Primal Horde, and I have addressed myself to some of these elsewhere (1976). For now, I throw in my lot with Robin Fox who, in his underappreciated book *The Red Lamp of Incest: What the Taboo Can Tell Us about Who We Are and How We Got That Way*, wrote of *Totem and Taboo*: "When virtually to a man the whole tribe of social and behavioral scientists—and even the Freud-worshipping psychoanalysts—pronounce the theory to be mere fantasy, I can't help nursing a suspicion that it has more than a 50 percent chance of being right" (1980: 54).

The Argument of "Totem and Taboo"

Let me begin with a necessarily brief and overly hasty sketch of some intellectual history. The period during which Freud wrote *Totem and Taboo* was also a major turning point in the field of anthropology. The overarching theories of the evolution of civilization put forward by thinkers such as Morgan, Tylor, Frazer, Spencer, and many others gave way (in the American context) to the Boasian tradition of cultural particularism. Rejecting the implicit or explicit social Darwinism of its predecessors, this new cultural anthropology tended to reject any version of biological thought in favor of some form of cultural determinism. Although other aspects of psychoanalytic thought were quite influential among the Boasians of the first few generations (Groark 2019), *Totem and Taboo* could easily be rejected as belonging to the era of the Victorian anthropologists and social Darwinists whose work had been superseded.

When evolutionary theorizing in reinvigorated guises entered mainstream anthropological discourse in the 1970s in the wake of sociobiology and then of evolutionary psychology, the situation was no more favorable to Freud's evolutionary theories—this time, however, because they weren't Darwinian enough. By assuming that a traumatic event, such as the proposed primal crime, could become part of the phylogenetic inheritance of subsequent humans, Freud seemed to have been making the "Lamarckian" error of assuming that a mental impression experienced by individuals— an "acquired characteristic"—could be assimilated into the genotype. That would violate the so-called central dogma of then-contemporary neo-Darwinism, according to which the arrow of causation can only run from the genome to the phenotype, never the reverse.

At the current historical moment, that central dogma itself has come under scrutiny, along with the "selfish gene" theory that it entails (Dawkins 1976). A number of theorists have sought to diminish the absolute hegemony of the genes in relation to the environment from various perspectives, and to challenge the doctrine that the unit of selection for fitness must be the individual organism and its closely related kin, not the species or group. Among the thinkers one might mention in this regard would be Ingold (2016), Maturana and Varela (1980), Oyama (1985), Richerson and Boyd (2005), and Sober and Wilson (1998). Although none of these thinkers propose an outright return to Lamarckism, they would collectively seem to question an overly strict genetic determinism and so perhaps pave the way for a more charitable reception of Freud's theory. In this chapter, however, much as I sympathize with these developments, I have opted not to rely on this revisionist thinking. Instead I have chosen the more rigorous path of showing, through a reading of Freud's texts, that even assuming the neo-Darwinian theory to be entirely correct, the theory of the primal crime Freud envisioned can be accommodated well within the boundaries of mainstream evolutionary thinking. Given the likelihood that the central dogma will actually need to be modified in the future, my argument will then still hold good.

What I want to argue here is that Freud's idea of the "primal father" can without much difficulty be assimilated to the concept of the "alpha male" at the apex of a status hierarchy such as that found among our closest relatives, the chimpanzees, and that probably characterized the last common ancestor of the three

African great apes and the hominid and hominin [proto-human] line. At some moment in human evolution—I would hesitate to specify at exactly what moment—it makes sense (as I will argue) to suppose that there was a definitive "rebellion" that not only killed or ousted the alpha male, but also overthrew the hierarchical social organization in which he flourished, replacing it with an egalitarian ethos that characterizes most contemporary foraging peoples, and presumably did so when our ancestors were all foragers. I do not assume, as did Freud (and Darwin), that our pre-human ancestors lived in gorilla-like units of polygynous families but rather that our early social organization developed out of a system rooted in a larger group with multiple individuals of both sexes. I follow Chapais (2008) and Ingham and Spain (2005), among others, in assuming that a major direction of the evolution of human society was a trend in a direction that culminated in pair-bonding, or monogamy, rather than starting there.

From this it follows that I do not, as Freud did, imagine that the primal crime was literally the murder of their own father by a band of his sons, to seize the former's harem of incestuously related females. Instead, I assume that a multi-male, multi-female system in which mating success, feeding opportunities, and social power were determined by a dominance hierarchy headed by a senior alpha male was transformed into one in which dominance itself was effectively eliminated or at least suppressed and replaced with an egalitarian social system. It might be argued that to make my argument I have actually thrown out the most characteristically "Freudian" part of the scenario—the "Oedipal" features of patricide and incest—but I will argue later in this chapter that this is not so.

The Problem of the U-Shaped Curve of Human Evolution

Research on our closest primate relatives in the wild—the chimpanzees—has revealed that an earlier idyllic picture of them as peaceable, vegetarian, and playfully friendly was one-sided at best. Chimpanzees have a form of social organization typified by intense competition among males over access to food sources as well as to mating opportunities with females, and by hunting and intergroup violence (Wrangham and Peterson 1996, Stanford 1999). Competition is managed by a number of factors that not only keep outright hostility within the group under control but also even enable cooperation, such as in hunting parties and border patrols, among related males and non-estrous females. Among these factors are a relatively stable but always implicitly contested dominance hierarchy with a single alpha male at its head, the phenomenon of estrous cycles that reduce male-male competition when females are not sexually receptive, and many elaborate peacemaking and reconciling mechanisms and behaviors extensively charted by de Waal (1989).

As with early perceptions of chimpanzee social life, there also has prevailed an idealized view of humans living in hunting and gathering bands. Although this was once, until quite recently, human social organization *tout court*, foraging band societies surviving into the twentieth century have largely been marginalized, living in reservations or inhospitable environments. These include such people as the !Kung San of Botswana in southern Africa, the Pygmies of central Africa, the aboriginal Australian peoples, the Inuit of the Arctic, some American Indian groups of the northern forests and the far western part of North America, and a few scattered communities in south, southeast, and northern Asia. Observation of such groups has found them to be in the main comparatively peaceable, respectful of the rights of each individual, and, among the adult men, egalitarian. By and large, ethnographic observation has suggested that members of such communities tend to have an explicit ethos of cooperation and to value good fellowship to an extraordinary degree. No leaders or chiefs exert their will over others; people do not (normatively) interfere with others or tell them what to do; and the major resource outside of gathered vegetable foods (mainly collected by women of individual households), that is to say killed game of any size, is shared according to agreed on formulas in which the successful hunter himself typically receives no more than anyone else.

This picture, like that of the happy-go-lucky chimpanzees, seems too good to withstand closer scrutiny. Yet although further ethnographic investigation has found competition, subtle hierarchical differences, age and gender asymmetries, and evidence of not infrequent homicide and raiding, the general picture has held. If this is indeed what human social organization in band level societies has been since the beginning of our species up until the horticultural and agricultural food producing revolution, it certainly appears at first blush to be the very opposite of Freud's primal horde, or indeed of the picture of selfish, non-altruistic social actors implicit in the sociobiological viewpoint of evolution.

In an influential article entitled "Violence and Sociality in Human Evolution," Bruce Knauft (1991) pointed out an apparently paradoxical situation. Knauft noticed that in anthropology's contemporary view of things, there was a marked discontinuity between what is known of primate social organization, especially that of the chimpanzees, and what supposedly was the original social life of humans. Whereas the former had strong, even fierce competition held in check by pronounced dominance hierarchies under a single preeminent alpha individual, the latter, if they were anything like the contemporary foragers, would seem to have been without chiefs or leaders and to abhor competition among themselves in any overt form. But as one looks higher up in the range of social complexity, beginning with some tribal societies and then increasing in so-called big man societies and of course in agricultural and then urbanized states, hierarchy once again emerges as the norm, and the concentration of power in the hands of individual chiefs, rulers, and military leaders, supported by priesthoods, or small cliques of such rulers, seems to be a general trend.

Knauft thus proposed what he called a U-shaped trajectory in human evolution, whereby a social primate—our common ancestor shared with the chimps, gorillas, and bonobos—exhibited strong hierarchical and "despotic" tendencies, which then led to a protracted period of relative egalitarianism among our hunting and gathering first human ancestors. Shortly after the domestication of plants and animals, however, the trend toward hierarchy and despotism reappeared. The riddle is this: How could a species—our common ancestor—exhibiting pronounced sexual and aggressive competition resulting in strong dominance hierarchies and despotic alpha male social organization apparently lose this characteristic for millions of years, only to regain despotic hierarchy again once the production of surplus value through cultivation, herding, and the establishment of more or less long-term settlements became the norm in comparatively recent prehistory?

In Defense of Freud's Evolutionary Theory

We know what Freud's answer, proposed before the mystery was even formulated, would have been: according to him, the transition from pre-human to human social life occurred in the wake of the rebellion of subjugated males who overthrew the dominant primal father, or the "alpha male" in contemporary terms. (I am certainly aware that there is not a complete correspondence between the two.) Because Freud, following Darwin in this, assumed that ancestral human society more nearly resembled gorilla than chimpanzee social organization, he assumed that the dominant male was the lone keeper of a harem which may well have included related females, who drove out rival junior males, his own sons, as they matured. Freud could therefore easily assimilate the supposed pre-human state of society to the familial paradigm of the Oedipus complex. My defense of Freud's position involves understanding the "alpha male" as being like the "primal father" in that, as in chimpanzee and many other forms of hierarchical or "despotic" mammalian societies, the dominant male has if not a total monopoly on, then at least a predominant proportion of, mating and feeding opportunities. He can, furthermore, enforce submission from other group members without himself being subordinate to anyone in a hierarchy by virtue of success in real or potential tests of physical force.

In Freud's account, following on their rebellious deed, with their aggressive impulses now sated, the junior males, who all along had harbored profoundly ambivalent views about their despotic alpha overlord, loving him and hating him equally at the same time, now fell back on their loving tendencies, and in their remorse, imposed inhibitions on themselves that led to exogamy in marriage, that is, the giving away of the women of the group who had been the original prize they were seeking, in exchange for the women of other groups. They also prohibited intergroup aggression, and to enforce these new rules they invented the totemic religion that established a ritual relationship to the remembered ghost of the slain patriarch in the form of an ancestral animal.

Through a mechanism directly analogous to the repression of an infantile trauma in an individual, Freud proposed in *Moses and Monotheism* (1939) that human civilization at first repressed the memory of the trauma of the primal murder, which expressed itself in indirect symbolic ways such as in the rituals and myths of the constellation of beliefs and practices that anthropologists of Freud's day called totemism. There was then a period of "latency," just as there is after the Oedipal upheavals of individual childhood, and this might be understood to correspond to the "latency" during which the sexual aggression that had led to the primal crime was successfully defended against by repression. In a gradual process parallel to the "return of the repressed" in individual lives, however, the memory of the primal deed reasserted itself, as the evolution of religious forms passed through stages of hero worship, polytheism, and henotheism, culminating in monotheism and the reinstatement through "deferred obedience" of the alpha male despot in the form of God the Father. The whole process would recapitulate the development of the mature restrictive superego of the well-socialized, rule-obeying, conscientious citizen of human society.

This scenario, once one filters out the antiquated theoretical framework and translates it into the more contemporary terms I have suggested above, has just enough uncanny resonance that one is tempted—or at least I am tempted—to exclaim along with Robin Fox: *"something like it must have taken place"* (1980: 61). But there is a least one huge problem here: the scenario makes no sense in terms of contemporary evolutionary theory. I myself have argued elsewhere (1996: 3–4) that the analogy, suggestive as it is, breaks down because a civilization, or indeed the whole of human civilization, cannot really be compared to an organism that has a birth, a childhood, a latency, and a maturational and developmental trajectory culminating in death.

The stumbling block that has tripped up most critics of *Totem and Taboo* and prevented them from (or as I would be actually be more inclined to say "allowed them to resist") seriously considering Freud's theory is the accusation of Lamarckianism, that is, the belief in the inheritance of acquired characteristics. Because the story of a memory disappearing from conscious awareness over the course of many generations of individuals only to reappear at a later date requires that the memory somehow be stored somewhere other than in the brains of mortal individuals so that it can sustain itself through generations without being lost, Freud's theory has seemed to many, including Freud himself, to necessitate positing that a searing traumatic memory like that of the primal crime can so affect the mind that a memory trace of it enters the genome where it can be dormant until such time as the repression barrier begins to fail.

As illustration of my contention that the Lamarckian fallacy has indeed been responsible for a quick and easy refutation of Freud, let me quote, at random, from an article in a recent issue of *American Imago*, by Charles Hanly, a highly respected analyst and theorist, and past president of the International Psychoanalytic Association. In a discussion of the scientific status of psychoanalytic theory, he writes: "Psychoanalysis has abandoned Freud's hypothesis of an archaic heritage because it implied the inheritance of acquired characteristics, which, biochemistry has shown, cannot occur" (2006: 263). This statement seems clearly to say: end of story, case closed. Because science is right, Freud's theory, or at least the phylogenetic part of it, must be wrong, and nothing further need be said. This, I think it may fairly be stated, is probably the generally accepted view among psychoanalysts and most other scholars to this day.

However, I have myself shown on several occasions (1976, 1996) that as stated in *Totem and Taboo*, Freud's theory does not imply or even suggest any Lamarckian process. On the contrary, he writes, in answer to his own question, "what are the ways and means employed by one generation in order to hand on its mental states to the next one?": "An unconscious understanding ... of all the customs, ceremonies and dogmas left behind by the original relation to the father may have made it possible for later generations to take over their heritage of emotion" (Freud 1913: 158–9). That is, he explicitly puts forward a cultural, not a genetic, channel of the inheritance of archaic memories. And culture, unlike genetics, is not subject to the prohibition on transgenerational transmission of acquired characteristics, because it is precisely the nature of culture to be capable of being learned, modified, and passed along to others across generations without involving the genes at all. The road of culture is parallel to, not directly connected to, the stream of the genes.

It is, of course, also true that in later writings Freud did ascribe the retention over the millennia of the memory of the primal crime to a phylogenetic, that is, inherited, memory. And one must admit that even in *Totem and Taboo*, Freud hinted at a biological underpinning to this process, suggesting that "a part of the problem [of the continuity of mental life across generations] seems to be met by the inheritance of psychic dispositions which, however, need to be given some sort of impetus in the life of the individual before they can be roused into actual operation" (1913: 158). But even with current revisions of neo-Darwinian and gene-centric theories, it remains implausible if not impossible that a single occurrence in human history, no matter how dramatic, could enter the gene pool once and for all.

It is important to note, therefore, that even in *Totem and Taboo* (his first work on the phylogenetic basis of human social organization), Freud begins to qualify his apparent derivation of these "dispositions" from a single momentous event in history. He writes in a footnote:

> The lack of precision in what I have written in the text above, its abbreviation of the time factor and its compression of the whole subject-matter, may be attributed to the reserve necessitated by the nature of the topic. It would be foolish to aim at exactitude in such questions as it would be unfair to insist upon certainty. (1913: 142–3)

Ten years later, in *The Ego and the Id* (1923a), Freud clarifies his view of how primal memories might survive the death of successive generations of individuals in terms of his newly emerging structural theory of the mind:

> The experiences of the ego seem at first to be lost for inheritance; but, when they have been repeated often enough and with sufficient strength in many individuals in successive generations, they transform themselves, so to say, into experiences of the id, the impressions of which are preserved by heredity. Thus in the id, which is capable of being inherited, are harboured residues of the existences of countless egos. (28)

As was hinted at in the previous quotation, Freud now suggests that the primal crime did not take place just once, but was a repeated process going on in many proto-human groups over many generations, until finally it became engraved in the collective unconscious or id and so became part of the inheritance of every subsequent individual.

But the quotation raises more issues than it resolves; for it remains unclear whether we should think of the id as a biological entity or as a mental one, albeit collective and unconscious. And if we try to translate from the language of id and ego to that of genotype and phenotype, respectively, then Freud does seem to be saying that the experiences of the phenotype, if forceful enough and repeated with sufficient frequency, transfer themselves to the genotype—a transfer considered impossible according to the "central dogma" of modern genetics.

Finally, with the end near and nothing to lose, in his last major work, *Moses and Monotheism* (1939), Freud lays all his cards on the table. He first states plainly that the primal crime was not a single historical event, but a widespread and protracted phase in human evolution:

> An essential part of the construction is the hypothesis that the events I am about to describe [the rebellion against the primal father and its aftermath] occurred to all primitive men—that is, to all our ancestors. The story is told in enormously condensed form, as though it had happened on a single occasion, while in fact it covered thousands of years and was repeated countless times during that long period. (80)

Then he discusses his conviction that numerous phenomena encountered in analysis "only become intelligible phylogenetically— by their connection with the experience of earlier generations" (99). And next follows a passage that I will quote at some length because of its centrality to my topic:

> On further reflection I must admit that I have behaved for a long time as though the inheritance of memory-traces of the experience of our ancestors, independently of direct communication, and of the influence of education by setting of an example, were beyond question. When I spoke of the survival of a tradition among a people or of the formation of a people's character, I had in mind an inherited tradition of this kind and not one transmitted by communication ... My position, no doubt, is made more difficult by the present attitude of biological science, which refuses to hear of the inheritance of acquired character by

succeeding generations. I must, however, in all modesty confess that nevertheless I cannot do without this factor in biological evolution ... If it is not so, we shall not advance a step further along the path we entered on, either in analysis or in group psychology. The audacity cannot be avoided. (99–100)

There it is, so it would seem: the smoking gun. Freud was indeed self-consciously making "Lamarckian" assumptions in his theory of the primal rebellion and its future effects. So shall we just say "case closed" and write off the whole thesis? Perhaps; but I suggest we hold our fire for the moment.

Let me point out, to begin with, that Darwin himself also made Lamarckian assumptions, because in that era no one, including that great visionary Darwin himself, understood how genetic inheritance works. Did everyone abandon the theory of evolution by natural selection on that account? Far from it. Instead, building on Darwin's insights, subsequent thinkers augmented and rectified his theory with more recent methods and discoveries, including Mendelian principles of inheritance, the statistical study of population genetics, and the understanding of DNA and now of epigenetics. What we now think of as Darwinian theory is thus not unadulterated Darwin, but rather what is called the modern Darwinian synthesis; and that too is in the process of being enhanced by what is called the "extended synthesis."

I propose that, for the sake of argument, we grant Freud the same privilege of being right about a lot of things and wrong about some things (like every other major contributor to world thought) and see how his insight can be squared with what we think today about how evolution happens. We are given our direction in the paragraph following the one I just quoted from *Moses and Monotheism*:

If any explanation is to be found of what are called the instincts of animals, which allow them to behave from the first in a new situation in life as though it were an old and familiar one ... it can only be that they bring the experiences of their species with them into their own existence—that is, that they have preserved memories of what was experienced by their ancestors. The position of the human animal would not at bottom be different. (100)

Now it is certainly undeniable that animals other than humans behave in ways that they do not learn but that must be derived from evolved aspects of their genome. How else would a spider know how to build a web, a caterpillar know how to turn into a butterfly, a migrating bird know how to read the pattern of stars in the night sky, a lion know the behavior patterns of a herd of wildebeest? Freud is not here talking about "instinct" as in the more usual term "*Trieb*" (more correctly translated as "drive") but about "*Instinkt*," a relatively fixed pattern of behavior of any degree of complexity that is not learned by the individual organism, but is derived either entirely or in part from information transmitted through the genome.

How do these fixed action patterns—call them inherited memories of the experiences of earlier generations if you will—come about, then, if not by the inheritance of acquired characteristics? This is precisely the conundrum that the theory of evolution by natural selection is designed to address: if the lion, in its phenotypic lifetime, successfully tracked and killed a wildebeest yet could not pass on this knowledge to its offspring via biological reproduction, how does adaptation occur? The only answer that can be given that is consistent with contemporary biological thinking is that it happens through the interaction of random mutation and external selection pressures operating differentially among individuals in a population. That is, the lion that happens, by a favorable but unintended mutation, to be able to track the running patterns of wildebeest better than its rivals will flourish, find a mate, and leave more offspring who inherit the gene (or allele) for this behavior, until the ability becomes spread throughout the population of surviving lions. Just so, and by the same mechanism, it is no less possible to imagine that the same thing occurred among humans with respect to the psychology of the primal crime; and indeed contemporary evolutionary psychology proposes a whole array of inherited modules in the human mind that facilitate the performance of mental tasks from making tools to classifying animals, plants, and kinspeople to learning language and making music to going into altered states of consciousness. Humans, like other organisms, create their own niche by altering their phenotypic environment to create situations to which the genetic system then adapts itself.

Thus, Freud's theory is rescued for contemporary science by his insistence that the primal crime was not a unique event but happened countless times in countless social groups over eons of evolutionary time. Such a context constitutes precisely the condition under which a trait such as the supposed mental *sequelae* of the primal crime can be propagated by natural selection, rather than by the (highly improbable) memory of a single traumatic event. Hence, even though Freud himself may have subscribed to Lamarckian ideas, his theory does not necessitate them, and the phenomena he was describing can be explained as effectively, and more plausibly, by ordinary acceptable evolutionary mechanisms. If having a memory of the rebellion against dominance hierarchy served individual fitness—as it would have if it enhanced social cooperation—then it would have been selected for regardless of whether the event itself ever happened. In this case, I make the stronger argument that the psychological dispositions supporting dominance hierarchy and its overthrow were not based on fanciful memories, however, but rather on long-lasting evolved psychological propensities that arose under the conditions of the new social life of our ancestors. The knowledge that was first passed down the road of culture was incorporated into the stream of the genes.

A Solution to the Problem of the U-Shaped Curve

I make the assumption that when humans assumed their modern biological form, they acquired the capacity for culture and symbolic communication including language, and that this transformed them in dramatic ways. This transformation did not replace genetically transmitted information, but rather built on it, interacted with it, and enhanced and augmented it in the myriad forms we know from the ethnographic record. With that in mind, let me return to the U-shaped evolutionary curve, whereby in the course of our descent from the so-called common ancestor of humans and the three great African apes, a species probably characterized by alpha male despotism and competitively determined hierarchical rankings turned into one marked by a high degree of egalitarianism and a lack of any centralized authority; and then after a long period in this condition turned back into a hierarchically organized social being with a tendency for strong central leadership and despotism to emerge.

Two years after Knauft posed his riddle, Christopher Boehm, who possesses the rare credential of having gained professional expertise as both a cultural anthropologist with ethnographic field experience and a student of chimpanzees in the wild, published an article entitled "Egalitarian Society and Reverse Dominance Hierarchy" (1993). A few years later he published a book, based in part on the findings reported in that article, entitled *Hierarchy in the Forest: The Evolution of Egalitarian Behavior* (1999). Boehm noticed that data on those band-level foraging societies that have survived into the twentieth century, as well as on many tribes practicing fairly rudimentary levels of cultivation or herding, showed that although there is always some degree of social hierarchy, and indeed the power differential among the genders, generations, and within nuclear family households may in fact be quite great, there is considerable equality otherwise among those of the same generation and sex, and an absence of central authority. Furthermore, an ideology is in effect that places the highest value on the personal qualities of generosity and composure, and that strongly censures any tendency toward overt expressions of hostility, competition, selfishness, or self-aggrandizement.

Boehm argues that in these societies, along with a powerful moral code of conduct, there are effective methods of enforcing the code. These include spoken disapprobation, such as in gossip, ridicule, and insults, increasing through mild ostracism to banishment and, in some cases, collectively agreed-on killing of the offending individual, as Wrangham (2019) has recently argued. Among non-human primates, the social emotions that would be necessary for such a system to operate, including shame, pride, envy, and admiration, are absent, and as Goodall (1986) has argued, chimpanzees do not use these sorts of disapproval or approval as a form of social control as human groups do. All of the techniques Boehm cites represent the superior power of the group over any particular individual who seeks to deviate from the norm of cooperative non-interference and peaceable, rule-governed sharing of food resources as well as of spouses in systems of marriage exchange.

Freud expressed much the same view when he wrote, in *Civilization and Its Discontents*:

Human life in common is only possible when a majority comes together which is stronger than any separate individual and which remains unified against all separate individuals. The power of this community is then set up as "right" in opposition to the power of the individual, which is condemned as "brute force." This replacement of the power of the individual by the power of the community constitutes the decisive step of civilization. (1930: 95)

Boehm argues, as does Freud, that the egalitarianism of hunting and gathering societies, and, insofar as we can use them as a model, of what early human band society looked like, was not the result simply of a peaceable and friendly disposition, but a compromise agreement that, in Boehm's formulation, was a literal and dramatic reversal of the dominance hierarchy. Instead of there being a single alpha who dominates a group of subordinates who show deference all the while they are cautiously biding their time and waiting for an opportunity to climb up in the hierarchy, there is in a human band society a community of horizontally equivalent members (among the males) who collectively, under the banner of a moral ideology opposed to self-assertion, are able to dominate any would-be alpha who puts himself forward.

Boehm phrases the reasoning underlying this moral imperative as follows:

There are individually variable human tendencies to outstrip or control one's fellows, which can lead to domination by the strong ... Rather than countenance modes of competition that will permit us to dominate the others, we all agree to give up our statistically small chance of becoming ascendant—in order to avoid the very high probability that we will be subordinated. (1999: 123–4)

Many will I am sure recognize this strategy as a discovery in game theory that won the Nobel Prize for the mad genius John Forbes Nash, as depicted in the popular film version of his life *A Beautiful Mind* (2001). Boehm borrows from the ethnographer Harold Schneider the following pithy formulation based on the latter's fieldwork among fiercely egalitarian cattle herders in East Africa: "All men seek to rule, but if they cannot rule they prefer to remain equal" (Boehm 1999: 124).

The parallel in Freud's thought could not be clearer. Freud writes in *Group Psychology and the Analysis of the Ego* (1921): "The first demand made by this reaction-formation [against jealousy of sibling rivals] is the demand for justice, for equal treatment for all ... If one cannot be the favourite oneself, at all events nobody else shall be the favourite" (1921: 52). He goes on to spell it out even more baldly:

> What appears later on in society in the shape of ... *esprit de corps*, "group spirit", etc. does not belie its derivation from what was originally envy. No one must want to put himself forward, every one must be the same. Social justice means that we deny ourselves many things so that others may have to do without them as well, or, what is the same thing, may not be able to ask for them. (1921: 52–3)

If we think about primordial human foraging band social organization in this light, then it becomes clear that the solution to Knauft's paradox lies neither in Freud's analogy to the latency period in individual development nor in the implausible supposition that our early ancestors suddenly changed their most basic inner nature and stopped being competitive and prone to dominance and submission and, as my daughter used to say, "turned nice"; nor in the equally unlikely position that when culture and symbolic thought and communication entered the picture, our inherited patterns of social behavior and the psychological correlates that went with them were suddenly erased. Rather I believe it is far more plausible to hold that the human revolution involved the transformation, by reversal, of a psychology suited to a society dominated by alphas at the pinnacle of a hierarchy to one in which the alpha role was still recognized and often covertly sought, but given an explicit negative value in the regnant moral system. This, I submit, is the evolutionarily acceptable analogue of Freud's primal crime, or rebellion; and, as Boehm argues, it left us with a psychology marked by a profound ambivalence, in which both the struggle for dominance and the opposition to it found a place.

Compare Freud's story as I have presented it, and his indecision about whether it happened all at once or over long evolutionary time, evident in the passages cited above, with Boehm's account:

> Did egalitarianism arrive very quickly, on a revolutionary basis, or was it an instance of very gradual evolution? With the degree of political tension I have documented ... and with the high

predictability of upstarts arising, the origin of such societies might not have been at all gradual. Indeed, to eliminate the alpha role decisively, the rank and file may have needed to use force to displace a specific alpha, and further force would keep his would be replacements sufficiently cowed to allow an egalitarian situation to stabilize ... One can also imagine large, stable coalitions ... moving gradually in the direction of increasing their power over the alpha types, until they were finally in a position to eliminate the alpha role entirely. With either scenario, the political tool used by the subordinates would have been the ability to operate in large coalitions that had specific and sophisticated political objectives. (1999: 173)

But what natural or social conditions, what selection pressures, would have prompted and enabled such a scenario to take place? Why would humans be able to do what even the relatively sophisticated chimpanzees could not do, that is, form effective coalitions to eliminate and then for countless millennia prevent the reemergence of dominating alpha-type individuals?

The outlines of a plausible evolutionary scenario might run like this. At some point, humans became capable of group cooperation beyond the level of anything available to chimpanzees or other higher primates. Various theories about how this came about have put forth, but for the present argument I will propose that at least one factor could well have been hunting. I do not mean to resurrect the theories associated with "man the hunter" wholesale; but it remains the case that for a long period of human prehistory, hunting large game formed a crucial part of the human economy. Killing large animals is often best accomplished through cooperative hunting parties, usually of men, although sometimes of mixed genders. Large animals cannot be eaten by one person, and in the absence of effective food preservation techniques, the most reasonable approach is to share the meat from any given kill among members of the band equally or according to a fixed formula. All this is made possible by the development of tool-making, and particularly of effective weapon-making, ability, as well as by the cognitive skills of language and symbolic communication more generally. Group hunting, which presupposes a coalition of men (usually), able to plan an attack and armed with lethal weapons, could only sustain itself if these men did not pose a constant danger to each other. Therefore the ability to suppress aggression and to cooperate rather than compete would have been highly fitness-enhancing traits insofar as they made possible hunting and other collective tasks. The aggression of each member of the hunting party would be redirected from other men to the hunted animal. This process could well explain how it might have occurred to them to turn the alpha male into the hunted quarry as well.

It is also empirically the case that the evolution of human society entailed greatly enhanced brain capacity, and that with this came not only planning and forethought but also the ability to equilibrate, or inhibit, affectively charged, drive-propelled, or instinctually programmed impulses and, with the capacities of the ego that psychoanalysis has so richly described, to transform id drives into adaptive ego actions. These developments can well be imagined to have reached what these days we call a "tipping point," when subordinate individuals, instead of cowering alone after being dominated in a fight or in a display competition by a more senior individual or the alpha male, might conspire among themselves and agree to form a rebellious coalition.

But let us recall that chimpanzees are also capable of this. So the crucial next step is to consider the impact of the skills and weapons that made it possible to kill a large animal such as a mammoth or even a large antelope or giraffe. Let me quote Boehm again on this point:

> After weapons arrived, the camp bully became more vulnerable. Such political equalization could have had meaning as a preadaptation for an egalitarian cultural revolution, particularly if one considers the *combined* weapons of a group of rebellious subordinates being directed at a *single* too-aggressive alpha. The latter could be readily dispatched at a relatively safe distance or driven from the group, with little immediate physical risk to the rebels. (1999, 177; emphasis in original)

Now compare Freud's exposition of his reconstruction of the primal rebellion in *Totem and Taboo*:

> One day, the brothers who had been driven out came together, killed and devoured their father and so made an end of the patriarchal horde. United, they had the courage to do and

succeeded in doing what would have been impossible for them individually. (*Some cultural advance, perhaps, command over some new weapon*, had given them a sense of superior strength). (1913: 141–2; emphasis added)

You will agree, I think, that the parallel is more than a little striking.

In order to show that in thus defending Freud's proposed evolutionary scenario I am not relying overmuch on the views of a single modern theorist, albeit one as persuasive as Boehm, I now add further support to the view I have just described by referring to the important book by Bernard Chapais, *Primeval Kinship* (2008), probably the most authoritative contemporary account of the evolutionary emergence of human society out of its primate precursors. Chapais writes:

A phenomenon whose evolution was progressive, irregular, and largely cultural did equalize the competitive abilities of hominid males, namely the rise of technology. Any tool, whether made of wood, bone, or stone, and whatever its initial function, from digging up roots to killing animals, could be used as a weapon in the context of intraspecific conflicts, provided it could inflict injuries. Armed with a deadly weapon, especially one that could be thrown some distance, any individual, even a physically weaker one, was in a position to seriously hurt stronger individuals. In such a context it would have become extremely costly for a male to monopolize several females. Only males able to monopolize tools or males forming coalitions could do so. But because all males *can* make tools and form coalitions, generalized polygyny was bound to give way eventually to generalized monogamy. (2008: 177)

The parallel between this formulation and those of both Freud and Boehm is unmistakable, and certainly not the result of any intention on Chapais's part of supporting Freud's hypothesis, but rather the result of a careful and well-informed analysis of the context and probable dynamics of early hominid social evolution. Yet what he has done, like Boehm, is to state in contemporary terms the argument that Freud had already made a hundred years ago— one that has long been ignored or dismissed for largely spurious reasons.

If, then, it was the collective power of the armed group that ultimately enforced the rule of a leaderless and harmonious company of equals such as that which prevails in band society, what brought an end to this egalitarian state of affairs? It is generally assumed that it was the development of the skills of cultivation and the domestication of animals, occurring in various parts of the world beginning about 10,000 years ago that transformed human society. Key points are that cultivation requires such innovations as the ownership and inheritance of land; the requirement of longer-term settled villages than existed in largely nomadic band societies; and the production of surplus values in the form of food resources that were not immediately consumed but could, in the form of grain or tubers for example, be stored and thus accumulated. In other words, there was now something to be unequal about, namely wealth that could be transmogrified from its original form as food into trading goods and prestige markers. Furthermore, in small nomadic bands, when and if conflicts arose, one faction could just hive off and set out on its own. In contrast, in horticultural communities, and even more so in agricultural societies, people are required to live together even if they have reason not to get along any more, and these pressures, along with the possibility of competing for resources, would have encouraged the development of hierarchy and long-term leadership roles to resolve conflict just as similar and other pressures had done among the chimpanzees. Greater population growth also exerted pressure that exacerbated the situation and called for more sophisticated systems of exchange, political integration, and conflict resolution. Although foraging bands did engage in homicide, and some small-scale raiding, organized warfare only emerged as a systematic practice under the new conditions brought about by cultivation and settlement and provided the environment for the emergence of individuals who could offer military leadership and hence protection, which took on greater and greater value as competition between warlike groups increased.

The solution to the puzzle of the U-shaped curve, then, seems to be that modern humans, as social beings, are neither inherently despotic nor egalitarian, but rather, as Boehm proposes, and as Freud insisted, that they are profoundly ambivalent: there is a tendency to dominate and a tendency to submit, but also a resentment of submission and a wish to climb in a hierarchy; and opposed to the whole dominance/submission schema there is also a capacity and a preference for egalitarian good fellowship. Under the right circumstances that I have briefly outlined here, ones that prevailed for most of human history, the operable solution is an egalitarian one. But under other circumstances, the descent of humans from a hierarchical primate with an alpha at the top means that this stratified social structure is always ready to reemerge, as it has done so often since the Neolithic revolution changed everything.

What the Primal Rebellion Made Possible

The picture painted by Freud, and to a certain extent by Boehm, resembles what is sometimes referred to as a Mexican stand-off, in which peace is maintained only by the threat of mutually assured destruction if it is violated. But surely human society rests on something more than controlled conflict. Does not empirical observation reveal not only that people in groups are envious of each other and afraid of each other but also that real ties of affection, friendship, love, attachment, and loyalty unite members of human groups? The ideas are not as mutually contradictory as they may at first appear: for if egalitarianism enforced at the point of a spear in the hand of each member first enabled group success that in turn enhanced the fitness of individual group members, then psychological dispositions of altruism, affection, and cooperation would be favored by selection, enhancing the fitness of any individual. These traits would predispose that individual to better control his aggression and modulate disruptive impulses so as to retain the goodwill of the group and not see it turn to enmity. Likewise the evolution of those social emotions that distinguish humans from other primates, such as shame, pride, envy, gratitude, admiration, and disapproval, would likewise have been possible only in a context in which there is a public arena in which the actions of each can be observed and evaluated by all the others according to the scale of values operative in the society.

Erdal and Whiten, agreeing with Boehm's analysis of the evolution of egalitarianism, make an equivalent point: "The psychological predispositions which underlie counter-dominance—for example, resentment at aggressive behaviour, discomfort or anger at being dominated, satisfaction when consensus is reached, respect for others' feelings—form part of our psychology because they were more effective functionally than the dominance/submission psychology out of which they must have evolved" (1996: 146). It seems furthermore very likely that the "raw material" from which human prosocial abilities evolved must be the primary loving attachment formed during the long period of infantile dependence on maternal care, as well as on the more extended cooperative caretaking that characterizes many foraging societies (Hrdy 2009). The evolution of the prefrontal lobes of the brain—the very ones that enabled both forethought and the control and inhibition of affects and impulses—may also be called on to account for the premature birth of human infants, because the birth canal can only accommodate the greater cranial size required for bigger brains up to a certain point. This in turn leads to the need for prolonged maternal care and the deep dependence of the human infant on the mother's protection. Goldschmidt (2006) proposes, to my mind quite convincingly, that the wish to elicit loving kindness from the mother and other caretakers—what he calls "affect hunger"—is what formed the "bridge to humanity" that enabled our ancestors to escape from the domination of biological factors and to enter the domain of true social relations within a culturally constituted surround.

Here, too, Freud long ago anticipated such contemporary thinking. Already in 1926, he wrote of

> the long period of time during which the young of the human species is in a condition of helplessness and dependence. Its intra-uterine existence seems to be short in comparison with that of most animals, and it is sent into the world in a less finished state ... Moreover, the dangers of the external world have a greater importance for it, so that the value of the object which can alone protect it against them and take the place of the former intra-uterine life is enormously enhanced. The biological factor, then, establishes the earliest situations of danger and creates the need to be loved which will accompany the child through the rest of its life. (1926: 154–5)

What about Oedipus?

But where in all this are those central Freudian ideas about patricide and incest? I argue that they are still there, but in a new role. If the proto-human society was not, as Freud supposed, a polygynous family but, rather, a larger group comprising both sexes, then the family unit was *brought into existence* by the primal rebellion, rather than being the prior structure in which it occurred. In the larger group setting, regulated by a dominance hierarchy, it would make more sense to speak of the conflict in the terms proposed by Robin Fox (1980), that is, the struggle between the senior males in the hierarchy and the peripheral males for mating access to the females, without necessarily specifying whether the individuals involved are close blood relatives or not.

In my analysis of the biblical narrative (1996), I deliberately avoided the terms "father," "son," and "mother," employing instead as a basic analytic tool a generic structure composed of the three statuses of "senior male," "junior male," and "female." The structure is still "Oedipal," but in a more generalizable way than the specific family story of Oedipus Rex or anyone else. I showed how the various different narratives about Moses could be understood as elaborations, or transformations, of the basic structure of those three "blocs" that, as Fox argues, are intrinsic to many primate societies: mature males, mature females, and peripheral or junior but already sexually mature males trying to make their way up the hierarchy.

Once the trend toward pair bonding is well established, after the primal rebellion, what was once a generalized social structure is necessarily reduced in each family to the three individuals of the Oedipal triangle. The first woman whom the young male child encounters and loves is in fact likely to be his mother, and the senior male who owns her love and whom he wishes to displace if not kill is most usually his father.

In the pre-human group, there was neither "incest" nor "appropriate mating," because both of these concepts are the products of culturally constructed marriage relations, which by definition did not yet exist in pre-human times (although there were no doubt in place mechanisms for the avoidance of inbreeding with immediate relatives). "Incest" as a category was therefore a *product* of the emergence of monogamous families governed by a system of marriage rules after the primal rebellion, not the other way around. I discuss incest avoidance further in Chapter 7.

Dual Inheritance and the Primal Horde

Freud's story of the primal crime presents an image of the opposition between genetic reproduction and the genetic program on the one hand, and cultural reproduction and the cultural program on the other, as a relation of temporal succession: the primal father/alpha male is the winner in an all-out competition for mating advantage, as per the genetic program. But the cultural program succeeds in displacing that regime and putting in its place a system of cultural reproduction whereby cultures form themselves from symbols and pass these along over generations to sustain the societies that bear them.

We may translate this historical picture into a social structural and psychological one, in which we can see human societies, and the individuals who form them, containing within themselves both the genetic and the cultural tendencies in some degree of either conflict or equilibrium. In his recent book *Genesis*, E. O. Wilson (2019) offers a theory of how the very rare phenomenon of "eusociality" arose is the course of biological evolution. By that term he refers to the situation in which the group itself is coherent enough to be treated as a unit on which selection acts; such cases, which include some insects such as bees and termites, as well as a few others including humans, contradict the general evolutionary rule that selection favors individual reproductive success. In eusociality, according to Wilson, "the colony is divided into a 'royal' caste specialized for reproduction, and a non-reproductive 'worker' caste that performs the labor of the colony" (2019: 60). One has only to think of a fertile queen bee and her army of sterile drones to grasp Wilson's point. But how would this apply to humans?

For Wilson, the case for true eusociality in humans, that is, for genuinely cooperative society to have evolved, is evidenced by the postmenopausal "caste" of grandmother helpers, the readiness of individuals to join professions useful to society but counter to their own reproductive success, monasticism, and the fact that homosexuality appears to be in part genetically determined and is often culturally valorized by institutions such as the *berdache* role in some Native American groups. All these instances are meant to show that among humans, as among bees and termites, there have emerged the equivalents of non-reproductive worker "castes." This list does not seem to me to be anywhere near the equivalent of the sterile members of bee and termite societies and not robust enough to have resulted in generalized eusociality in human groups.

What Wilson misses is that it is not in cases such as those he mentions that the preconditions for human eusociality are to be found, instructive though they are, but rather in the essential condition of human life and society, which is that it is always and at the same time driven both by the genetic imperatives of inclusive reproductive success and also by the opposite trend, the non-genetic, symbolic reproductive program deriving from the unique human institution of highly developed and externally realized culture. As Richerson and Boyd (2005) have shown, humans have both kin-based and tribal social instincts (or if one prefers, "capacities"). Humans have within themselves as fundamental givens the ability to seek individual reproductive success and also to override that interest to join wider groups through cultural identification through the suppression, surmounting, and sublimation of the strictly genetically reproductive program. This is exactly what Freud meant when he proposed as the core human dynamic the psychological conflict between libidinal urges and the forces that oppose them, and when he argued that the same conflict is repeated at the social level as well. In Wilson's terms, we might conclude that humans are intrinsically both members of a reproductive "caste" and of a non-reproductive "caste" simultaneously. The road is parallel to the stream. And human societies have built institutions that represent the interests of both, in some degree of serviceable balance.

In Freud's story of the primal crime, then, one can read a plausible scenario of the movement from nature to culture on the part of *Homo sapiens*, as I have done in this chapter; but one can also see in it a broader argument for the fact that the struggle between nature and culture, understood as the broad genetic program versus the tribal, symbolic program, is ongoing and inherent in the human condition thanks to the fact of dual inheritance. In the next chapter of the book, I explore how the dialectic of sexual versus non-sexual reproduction has played out as illustrated by some important and interesting aspects of our own Western culture.

PART II

Like Rabbits or Like Robots? Sexual versus Non-Sexual Reproduction in the Western Tradition

4

The Genealogy of Civilization

According to the traditional Jewish understanding, the very first of the 613 commandments contained in the five books of the Torah is the blessing God gives to Adam and Eve as soon as he has created them: "Be fertile, and increase, fill the earth and master it" (Genesis 1:28). We learn soon enough that God is ambivalent about just how good a thing he has done, and that he decides to extinguish human and animal life once and for all in a flood. But after the second "creation," when human and animal life begins again after the deluge, each species from a single ancestral couple, God reiterates still more forcefully his insistence on the requirement to procreate:

> God spoke to Noah, saying "Come out of the ark, together with your wife, your sons, and your sons' wives. Bring out with you every living thing of all flesh that is with you: birds, animals, everything that creeps on the earth; and let them swarm on the earth and be fertile and increase on earth." (8:15-17)

And again:

> God blessed Noah and his sons, and said to them: "Be fertile and increase, and fill the earth." (9:1)

And yet again:

> For in His image did God make man. Be fertile, then, and increase; abound on the earth, and increase on it. (9:6-7)

Genesis, being as it is an elaborate genealogical chronicle, is dominated by a single overriding value, that of reproductive success. This is clearly illustrated in the exchange between God and Abraham initiating the great covenant between them. God says to Abraham (who is still "Abram" at this point):

> "Fear not, Abram, I am a shield to you. Your reward shall be very great." But Abram said "O Lord God, what can you give me, seeing that I shall die childless ... Since you have granted me no offspring, my steward will be my heir." (15:1-3)

There is, to underline the obvious, absolutely nothing God can offer Abram to compensate for the fact that he has no biological heir.

It is then that God tells Abram to look to the heavens to count the stars, for even so numerous as they will his progeny be. The dramatic tension of the story of Abraham arises from the question of how he is to become the forefather of a great nation if his favored wife (and sister) Sarah is barren, and if, when she miraculously gives birth to Isaac in her old age, Abraham obeys God's command to sacrifice the son destined to sire the father of the twelve tribes: a question, in other words, of reproductive success. In that era chronicled in Genesis, before the Law is given at Mount Sinai, anything goes as long as it leads to the continuation of the proto-Israelite line. Mating proceeds unregulated and the clear preference among the patriarchs is for wives from within their own close patriline. Although no one, it is true, marries his mother, there are in this lineage marriages with sisters, nieces, and aunts (as in the case of Moses's own parents). Among the sons of Jacob (later renamed Israel), for example, Reuben sleeps with his father's wife Bilhah, the mother of two of his brothers; and Judah sleeps with his daughter-in-law Tamar. These are just the sorts of goings on one expects to find in the primal horde.

In this social world, political strength is dependent upon, indeed consists in, reproductive success: "sons are guns" as the saying has it. It was precisely the anxiety of the bad pharaoh that the subject Israelites would become too powerful by virtue of their increasing numbers that led him to oppress and then attempt to exterminate them.

The God of Genesis, of Abraham, Isaac, and Jacob—the "Patriarchs" as they are fittingly called—is thus a god of reproductive success: he commands it, he requires it and expects it, and he bestows it upon his favorites. No other moral code or competing value interferes; anything that leads to the continuing descent and propagation of the family patriline is good, and anything that interferes with it is bad. This principle is nicely exemplified in the story of Jacob, whose wiles and deceit in his relations with his father, his brother, and his father-in-law, from all of whom he wrests reproductive advantage by cunning stratagems, are rewarded by his success in the production of sons as in the increase of his flocks. Despite having pulled almost every deceptive trick in the book, Jacob lives under God's benevolent protection, with no hint of sin, guilt, punishment, dishonor, or fear off damnation. His sole narrative mission is to father a nation, and he succeeds admirably.

The major distinction between the era of the patriarchs, on the one hand, and Freud's primal horde, on the other, is that in the patrilineal descent system portrayed in the Hebrew Bible, the father's jealousy of and rivalry with his sons must, in the end, be overmatched by his willingness to let them live and reproduce, to strengthen the collective might of the patriline and thus of his own genetic line of descent. The story of the Akedah, the "binding of Isaac," thus represents the principle that the father's infanticidal impulse toward his son gives way before his desire for genetic continuity. Even as he cedes to his son's preeminence in physical might and reproductive advantage, he thereby fulfills his own political and genetic self-interest. The latter two are linked, not only because sons are guns, but because Abraham's own reproductive, genetic self-interest coincides with the long-term success of his offspring, not his individual dominance of his juniors.

Freud's primal patriarch, by contrast, is motivated only by narcissistic self-regard at the expense of a commitment to genetic reproductive success. The patriarchs of Genesis, truer to the rank order of values under conditions of natural selection, accept personal decline and death with equanimity and a sense of fulfillment, provided only that they are assured of the continuity of their descent line. It is just this that distinguishes the benign Jacob, who lets his sons live and reproduce, from the wicked pharaoh, who is the enemy of all Israelite genetic success and thus, unwittingly, as it turns out, of his own: his intransigence leads to the slaying of the Egyptian first-born in the course of the Israelites exodus from Egypt.

If the pre-Sinaitic social conditions described in Genesis are under the unchallenged rule of the value of inclusive reproductive fitness, what occurs to change the system? When the sons of Jacob/Israel enter Egypt to escape a famine, they are a single patriline, nothing more. In Egypt, they are at first favored guests, because of the political success of one of the twelve Israelite brothers, Joseph. It is only after the death of Joseph, and of the pharaoh who elevated him, that the situation of the Israelites turns into that of the sons in Freud's mythic scenario of the "bad" primal horde. In Egypt, the Israelites are no longer a single family of wandering pastoralists living in uneasy reciprocity with their settled hosts. They have become subjects of a centralized, stratified, urban empire: they have become part of the life of the state.

In a social situation in which kinship and descent are the predominating principles, and in which reproductive success *is* political success, the fate of the son is difficult but not hopeless. While he is under the dominion of his father and of the senior males generally, he has only to be patient and wait for the life cycle to take its course. In a matter of time, he too will, if all goes well, gain the reproductive prerogatives and political sway he envied in his father when he was young.

The relation between lord and bondsman is different. The lord has no motivation ever to relinquish his power over the bondsman, nor does the bondsman have any hope of leaving his subordinate position except by an act of violent rebellion. The master and his personal servant are in a relationship of stable asymmetry. Hereditary classes of masters and servants constitute a permanent stratification of society.

In the state, by definition, a ruling elite stands in relation to the ordinary citizens as lord to bondsman, insofar as the ruling stratum has an institutionalized power advantage over the rest of the population, whom they tax, press into military and labor service, and otherwise organize, control, and dominate, if necessary by force. The sources of power in a state society no longer rest on personal reproductive success, but rather on the ability to command, organize, administer, and exploit a citizenry to whom one has no necessary relation of kinship at all. While membership in the ruling class may well be hereditary along genetic lines, and while there certainly are hereditary castes, guilds, professions, and ranks in the state in its various forms, yet the project of the state as an institution is quite decidedly inimical to the supremacy of biological reproduction—that is, kinship—as a value, goal, guiding principle, and source of political power. Robin Fox has put the matter very well:

> The state, despite its persecution of the individual from time to time, is much happier with individuals as units than with kinship groups, for the simple reason that they are easier to control ... Thus it comes easily to the nation-state to promote the values of individualism while remaining totally suspicious of the claims of kinship. (1993: 184)

It is far from irrelevant that Fox makes this claim in the context of a discussion of Sophocles's *Antigone,* which is precisely about the conflict between the demands of the state and those of biological kinship.

The ruling elite may, of course, begin as a particularly successful lineage or descent group. But the enduring aim of the state is to override kin relations among the governed, and to redirect people's energies into loyalty toward and service to the state, regardless of other, kin-based loyalties. The state succeeds by turning societies organized around kin-based loyalties and kindreds into populations of individual citizens responsible to and ruled by an impersonal central authority, which promulgates "universal" laws and codes of conduct for this purpose. The enforcement of these laws is made possible by the delegitimation of the rights of kin-groups to exact justice in the form of revenge and compensation, and the monopolization of justice and policing by bureaucratized agencies of the state. Aeschylus's *Oresteia* is precisely about the supersession of the kinship-based demand of blood vengeance by the legal authority of the state.

Summing up, we may conclude that in the patriarchal era, dominated by reproductive success, the "lord and bondsman" asymmetry between senior and junior males is overridden by fathers' genetic interest in allowing their sons to succeed them. But in a stratified state society such as Egypt, the "lord and bondsman" aspect of the senior male/junior male relationship is ascendant, and the two opponents are then doomed to see themselves as if they were implacable enemies, for whom a struggle to the death is the only resolution.

The Israelites under the wicked pharaoh can wait as long as they like but they will never be granted senior status. The balance has shifted from the predominance of the principle of reproductive success to its subordination under the paradigm of the perpetual domination of the bondsman by the master. But the Israelites are not subjects of the state even in the same way as the ordinary Egyptian citizens are subjects. They are a bonded nation, that is, a self-contained, endogamously reproducing ethnic population occupying an inferior status within the overall state hierarchy. Whatever rights the Egyptians may enjoy under Egyptian law, the Israelites are denied freedom from persecution by the simple fact of their birth. Israelite status in Egypt thus combines determination by biological reproduction with permanent subordination in the asymmetric relation of lord and bondsman.

After the liberation from Egyptian bondage and the granting of the covenant of Sinai, the status of Israelite combines being a member of the Israelite descent group by virtue of biological birth—that is, being a lineal descendant of one of the twelve sons of Jacob/Israel—with the requirement to observe and transmit to the next generation of offspring the set of rules encoded in the Torah. The code of conduct is incumbent on all those born of Israelite parents, so that Israelite ethnicity is ideally constituted by a combination of both biological and symbolic, cultural descent. To be a Jew one must have inherited the genes for it (so to speak), but one must also have learned the culturally transmitted regulations of the Law. Jewish tradition has maintained throughout its history that those born to biologically Jewish parents also have a natural propensity and/or obligation to be ruled by the Mosaic covenant in the conduct of life.

Moses's own story is illustrative of the co-equality of the principles of genetic descent and of cultural tradition. He is a man of dual nationality, having been born to Israelite parents, but raised socially and culturally as an Egyptian. But Moses's great life achievement, unlike Jacob's, is based not on reproductive success, but on the success and replicability of the symbolically encoded legal, mythic, and ritual system he introduces, namely the Torah itself. While he does have two biological sons, their importance in the biblical story is negligible. What makes Moses great is the written law, which, as I demonstrate in my book *Moses and Civilization* (Paul 1996), has a power of self-replication equal and comparable to, but different from, genetic self-replication. Until Sinai, genetic success is the sole preeminent value in the biblical text. After Sinai, learning, transcribing, observing, and teaching the Torah itself become as constitutive of being an Israelite as is Israelite birth. The stream and the road run along a parallel course.

At the same time, the two modes of ethnic replication become the separate province of the two sexes. In traditional rabbinic terms, it is only birth from an Israelite mother that constitutes biological Judaism. But the transmission of the written code becomes exclusively a matter between senior males and junior males—only men are traditionally supposed to learn and teach Torah.

When all is said and done, however, despite the apparent co-equality of the two parallel tracks of transgenerational inheritance (genetic and cultural), the ultimate goal of religious practice in biblical Judaism, including the transmission of nongenetic, symbolic replicators, is still the genetic success of the House of Israel as a biologically defined descent group. Observance of the law is to be undertaken not out of any desire for personal immortality or "salvation," or even solely for its own sake (although that is certainly adequate reason for the individual actor). Rather, there is the clear promise that if Israel keeps up its side of the covenant with God by obeying and transmitting his commandments, God will ensure the success of the people as a whole across generations. Thus, to take one example, God proclaims that

> if you follow my Laws and faithfully observe My commandments, I will grant you rains in their season, so that the earth shall yield its produce. I will look with favor on you, and make you fertile and multiply you; and I will maintain my covenant with you. (Leviticus 26:3-9)

We may thus conclude that despite the introduction of a cultural, symbolic system comparable in many ways to the genetic one, distinguishing the society of the post-Sinaitic Israelites from that of the proto-Israelite patriarchs, cultural reproduction remains a practice in the service of, and yoked to, the still higher aim of reproductive success for the Israelite nation as a biological descent group.

Christianity emerged after the fragmented successors of the Davidic Israelite nation-state had succumbed to foreign conquest and domination. It was under the Greeks, and their own successors, the Romans, that serious efforts were made by the dominating imperial power not simply to rule, but to replace local cultural and religious traditions with their own. The Jews were, once again, as in Egypt, a subject ethnic population, only this time in what had once been, and still remained to some extent a caricature of, their own national state.

The founding and ultimately tremendously successful move of the originators of Christianity was to liberate the universal law of Moses from its linkage to Israelite descent, and to establish it as the basis for a free-standing code of conduct applicable to anyone, regardless of biological birth. With this stroke, it became possible for the symbolic replicators—the "customs, ceremonies and dogmas" (to allude to Freud) of the Judeo-Christian religion—to propagate through populations unrelated by kinship or ethnicity, "fictive" or otherwise, to the Israelite lineage. And in the context of a universal empire, such as Rome proclaimed itself to be, the capacity of a free-standing symbol system to replicate itself represented a significant strategic advance beyond replication rooted in, or tied, to, genetic reproduction. One could transform whole new populations into Christians by simply teaching them a set of texts and practices, without waiting around for them to breed new generations of heirs in the relatively clumsy and inefficient way provided by nature. Christianity also rendered void most of the laws enunciated in the Torah.

It would be hard to improve upon the unique combination of stately eloquence and blunt candor of Edward Gibbon's classical account of the remarkable victory of the Christian religion:

> The Jewish religion was admirably fitted for defense, but it was never designed for conquest ... Their particular distinctions of days, of meats, and a variety of trivial though burdensome observances, were objects of aversion for other nations. The painful and even dangerous rite of circumcision was alone capable of repelling a willing proselyte from the door of the synagogue. Under these circumstances, Christianity offered itself to the world armed with the strength of the Mosaic law and delivered from the weight of its fetter. ([1776–89] 1962: 131–2)

Chief among those fetters, Gibbon neglected to add, was the requirement of Israelite birth, something that could not be transferred.

With Christianity, we witness the crucial transition from a system in which biological reproduction is still paramount to one in which it is not only not paramount but viewed with suspicion, contempt, and derogation by a cultural system of reproduction that has outstripped it, having found a way to bypass it. Jesus, as portrayed by the founders of Christianity, disdained to marry and reproduce sexually; but he and they succeeded in producing "spiritual" descendants in numbers vastly beyond the capacity of a Jacob/Israel to produce genetic descendants. Christianity could become the unifying cultural ideology of societies replicating along non-genetic lines, as in priesthoods, monastic communities, religious brotherhoods and sisterhoods, and the like, on the one hand, and by conquest and/or conversion of unrelated ethnic groups on the other. Sexual reproduction could be safely left to the laity, and their biological children could then be inducted through purely symbolic means into the family of Christ.

Since the denigration of this-worldly reproductive success leaves the individual without a transcendent goal under which to subsume, redeploy, or counteract possible anxiety over individual mortality, death takes on a dire and central place in the cultural hierarchy of concerns. Quite foreign to the Christian gospels is anything like Abraham's despair about his childlessness. By the same token, the concern to avert or overcome individual death as if it were an unacceptable and intolerable punishment is equally foreign to the Israelite system of values expressed in the Torah. Biological success in future generations is, after all, of little moment in a system that relies on the expectation of the end of the world in one's own lifetime. Under the latter conditions, the only thing worth worrying about is how one is personally going to fare in the upcoming judgment.

The salvation of one's own soul is ideologically transformed through reaction formation from an egotistical concern to an altruistic zeal for bringing the news of salvation to everyone else, with whom one is supposed to identify. This transformation is made possible by the mutation of hostility to others, again by means of reaction formation, into aggressive universal love for others. This universal altruism of Christianity has little in common with the "nepotistic" altruism that follows from a prioritization of maximal inclusive genetic fitness, such as Abraham exemplifies. In the latter, selflessness toward close kin is based on the priority of the success of future generations replicating one's own genome. This latter variety of altruism remains operative not only among the patriarchs, but even, as I have said, among the Israelites under the terms of the Mosaic covenant at Sinai.

Jesus himself, as he is portrayed in the Christian Bible, saw clearly the fundamental antipathy between his message and the values of kinship. An exemplary expression of this view of his is to be found in a passage in which he is instructing his apostles about the rules of preaching to the Israelites. He warns them that

> brother will deliver up brother to death, and the father his child, and children will rise up against parents and have them put to death; and you will be hated by all for my name's sake. (Matthew 10:21-2)

And he continues:

> For I have come to set a man against his father, and a daughter against her mother, and a daughter-in-law against her mother-in-law and a man's foes will be those of his own household. He who loves father or mother more than me is not worthy of me; and he who loves son or daughter more than me is not worthy of me. (Matthew 10:35-7)

He could hardly have been plainer about his intention to supersede the supreme value of kinship and genealogical relation, and to supplant it with a doctrine unrelated and indeed antithetical to biological reproduction.

Liberated from any biological grounding for membership in the group or for receipt of the teachings, Christianity is able to conceptualize a far stricter dichotomy than did Judaism between spirit and flesh, assigning guilt, sin, and corruption to the flesh and finding a possibility for purity only in a spirit that would be better off freed from its carnal vehicle. The gendering of this dichotomy between flesh and spirit, following on the gendering of the Judaic one I discussed earlier, is by now widely recognized.

It is as if the brother horde in Freud's myth, forced into sexual abstinence, and thus into "group psychology" by the persecuting jealous sire (identified by the Jewish tradition as the wicked pharaoh, but by the Christian tradition to a large extent as Moses and "the Jews" generally), takes revenge not by simply overthrowing the father, but by a more radical transvaluation of all values: an overthrowing of biological fatherhood itself as the paradigm of male success. The junior males win a victory not by becoming senior males in the old style, but by forcefully establishing the principle that the nonsexual, cultural reproduction to which they had been relegated actually supersedes, outranks, and ultimately should eliminate sexual reproduction altogether and replace the flawed, embodied, mortal life with a disembodied, spiritual, immortal life.

In my book on Moses (1996), I show how the Mosaic covenant appears as a defense against the expected retribution of the slain father, while Christianity may be understood as a defense against the first defense, which has now itself taken on the terrible aspects of that it was designed to ward off; it is here that we may find a basis for the totalizing zeal of Christianity. Having suppressed a regime governed by the value of sexual reproduction, and hence genital sexuality, and its form of senior authority, Christianity as an ideological system must henceforward search out and eliminate anything that threatens the return of the repressed. At the same time, Christianity has reconstituted just this terrifying return of the vengeful slain father through its expectation of an imminent Judgment Day, on which the deified slain father/God will consign to eternal and unspeakable punishment all those guilty of having rebelled against or disobeyed him, that is, everybody. On that day of reckoning, the only hope lies precisely in the glimmer of a recollection that, while a spurned tyrant has no pity in the persecution of rebels against him, a father allows compassion— and genetic self-interest—to stay his hand, and lets at least some of his insubordinate sons survive and have their day. The hope to be among those saved by God's gracious, not to say whimsical, mercy toward a chosen few on the last day finds expression in some very influential Christian eschatologies.

We may ask ourselves, though, what makes this doctrine, which seems to demand the sacrifice of much that is pleasant in life and requires faith in something unseen and on the face of it hard to believe, as successful as it empirically has been in world history. Transposing the question into the terms of my earlier discussion, we may answer that in the Western mythic system, that aspect of Oedipal fantasy presupposing insuperable conflict of interests between senior and junior males, imagined as lord and bondsman, has been stressed at the expense of that aspect rooted in the community of reproductive interests between father and genetic sons. And this has been so, we can further postulate, because it has occurred in the context of a relatively new sociocultural system—the state—which, on the one hand, really is characterized by unbridgeable status differences and, on the other, is actively engaged in the process of denying and suppressing the importance of biological reproduction as a value, opposing to it values that favor other forms of production and reproduction that benefit either the individual as a free-standing citizen or the state as an entity, or both, rather than the descent group, the kindred, the lineage, or the gene pool.

From the perspective just sketched, then, there may perhaps be no more fateful line in the entire Bible than this well-known one from the Gospel of Luke:

> In those days a decree went out from Caesar Augustus that all the world should be enrolled. (Luke 2:1)

Rome under the Caesars intended to be a universal empire, and this represented a step beyond the nation-state as great as that which the nation-state represented beyond kin-based societies. The Roman Empire, a multinational, multi-ethnic, cosmopolitan polity, offered full citizenship regardless of nationality, having put in place of ethnicity or descent a universal legal code. Christianity made the same universalizing move at the level of religion; and the two came together in the ambition that "all the world should be enrolled." This project continued, and continues, even after the fall of the empire in its distinctly Roman phase, in the idea of making Christendom a global reality.

It is no coincidence at all that the origins of Christianity correspond, in history as in the text itself, with the inception of the Roman Empire, within whose capacious boundaries it spread and flourished until it became the official, and soon enough the only, religion of that empire and its successors. In the cited passage, Luke draws a direct connection between the birth of Christ and his contemporary Caesar Augustus. A more apposite connection could hardly be found. It was under Caesar Augustus that Rome ceased to be an expanding military power governed (at least in theory) by republican principles, and became a stable "universal" empire commanded by a single leader. It was for Caesar Augustus that the very word "emperor" was coined, and his own name became a synonym for the office of emperor up through the reigns of the German kaiser and the Russian tsar. He was the first Roman ruler to allow himself to be worshipped as a divine king, and it was he who set in place the fundamental institutions of empire that dominated much of the world for centuries to come (into our own time, so might one argue). It was he, too, who initiated the policy of the "Pax Romana," the Roman Peace, seeing the Roman mission no longer as the continuing subjugation of more and more of the world's territory and peoples, but rather as the guarding of harmony and stability within its already existing limits.

If the rise of Christianity was an aspect of the establishment of the Roman Empire, then, it is to the distinctive features of this empire that we must look for an understanding of how the Judeo-Christian message changed from a local phenomenon into a universal, imperial one. The key is to be found, I believe, in the Pax Romana itself. The Romans had known very well how to be masters of war, but they had less of an idea about how to be princes of peace. For that they needed to recruit, from the farther reaches of their empire, the Prince of Peace himself.

Peter Rudnytsky (personal communication) has pointed out that Virgil's fourth Eclogue can be viewed as documenting the link between Augustan Rome and the coming of Jesus and the era of Christianity. Subsequent interpreters commonly read the poem as foretelling the birth of the messiah; it is often referred to as the "Messianic Eclogue" because of its foretelling the heavenly blessing of a boy "Whose birth will end the iron race at last and raise/A golden through the world" (Virgil, 57) and who will nullify remaining traces of sin.

Norbert Elias, that great student of the "civilizing" process whereby Europe developed its distinctive social, cultural, and political system, identified as the hallmark of the "civilized" citizen of the modern state an internal capacity for self-regulation, self-restraint, and the refined calculation of costs and benefits, and causes and effects. As for how this frame of mind came to be an automatic "self-compulsion" as he calls it ([1939] 1982: 233), Elias ascribes the process to the effects of pacification, whereby a strong central state has established such firm and total control that both the right to and the need for physical violence and armed protection can be wrested from individuals, or from local or kin-based groups, and absorbed entirely into the domain of the central ruling stratum of the state: "The peculiar stability of the apparatus of mental self-restraint which emerges as a decisive trait built into the habits of every 'civilized' human being stands in the closest relationship to the monopolization of physical force and the growing stability of the central organs of society" (235).

Freud too, in his considerations of the nature of "civilization," recognized the central role of the monopolization of physical force by the state. Thus he writes: "The power of [the] community is ... set up as 'right' in opposition to the power of the individual, which is condemned as 'brute force.' This replacement of the power of the individual by the power of a community constitutes the decisive step of civilization" (1930: 42). Freud is more explicit still in this passage from his essay written in direct response to the carnage of the First World War:

> The individual citizen can with horror convince himself in this war of what would occasionally cross his mind in peace-time— that the state has forbidden to the individual the practice of wrong-doing, not because it desires to abolish it, but because it desires to monopolize it, like salt and tobacco. (1915c: 279)

Although both Elias and Freud were writing about the modern European nation-states that arose out of medieval feudalism, the Roman Empire in the time of Caesar Augustus and his successors also fits the description very well. Its armies were preeminent both internally and to a great extent externally, but it was essentially a time of stability and even peace, with the legions relegated to a defensive posture intended to maintain the status quo. For Elias, in such a sociopolitical situation, as the functions within the state become more complex and differentiated, people become enmeshed in webs of dependency on others within which ever-more refined forms of strategizing, advantage-seeking, and position-jockeying favor far-sighted calculation at the expense of force, which has in turn been banished from the pacified interior to the boundaries of the empire.

The psychological result is a life not only less passionate but also less dangerous:

> The moderation of spontaneous emotions, the tempering of affects, the extension of mental space beyond the moment into the

past and future, the habit of connecting events in terms of chains
of cause and effect, all these are different aspects of the same
transformation of conduct which necessarily takes place with the
monopolization of physical violence, and the lengthening of the
chains of social action and interdependence. It is a "civilizing"
change of behavior. (Elias [1939] 1982: 236)

And, as Nietzsche ([1872 and 1887] 1956) had observed in *The
Genealogy of Morals,* the success of such a civilizing process is
assured because "a race of such men will, in the end, inevitably be
cleverer than a race of aristocrats, and will honor sharp-wittedness
to a much greater degree" (172). For Nietzsche, the essential story
line of Western civilization revolves around the question of how
the Romans—"the strongest and most noble people who ever
lived" (186)—allowed themselves to be seduced by the "narcotic
power" of the "bait of the crucified God" dangled before them.
Why did a state whose conscience barely seemed to trouble it at
all during its era of ruthless world conquest transform itself into
the seat of a religion based on "bad conscience," a universal sense
of guilt? Nietzsche's answer anticipates Freud's and provides a
dynamic key to understanding the psychological transformation
that accompanied the Pax Romana. "Bad conscience" results, for
Nietzsche, from that "progressive sublimation and apotheosis of
cruelty which not only characterizes the whole of higher culture,
but in a sense constitutes it" (198).

With no new worlds to conquer, the Roman passion for cruelty
and domination which had fueled the expansion had to go
somewhere. A society organized for war found itself "forced to
think, to deduce, calculate, weigh cause and effect—unhappy people
reduced to their weakest, most fallible organ, their consciousness!"
(217). Turning inward, they developed an interior empire of the
"soul" to be conquered and dominated in the same way they had
grown used to doing with the outer world:

> The formidable bulwark by means of which the polity protected
> itself from the ancient instincts of freedom ... caused those wild,
> extravagant instincts to turn in upon man. Hostility, cruelty,
> delight in persecution, raids, excitement, destruction all turned
> against the begetter. Lacking external enemies and resistances,
> and confined within an oppressive narrowness and regularity,

man began rending, persecuting, terrifying himself, like a wild
beast hurling itself against the bars of its cage. This languisher,
devoured by nostalgia for the desert, who had to turn *himself*
into an adventure, a torture chamber, an insecure and dangerous
wilderness—this fool, this pining and desperate prisoner, became
the inventor of "bad conscience." (218; emphasis in original)

There is a striking parallel between this astonishing passage
(truly written with hammer blows!) and that in which Freud, in
Civilization and Its Discontents (1930), answers for himself the
question of how civilization inhibits and renders harmless the
aggression that constitutes part of the instinctive endowment of
humanity. What happens, for Freud, is

something very remarkable, which we should never have guessed
and which is nonetheless quite obvious. His aggressiveness is
introjected, internalized; it is, in point of fact, sent back to where
it came from—that is, it is directed toward his own ego. There
it is taken over by a portion of the ego, which sets itself over
against the rest of the ego as super-ego, and which now in the
form of "conscience" is ready to put into action against the ego
the same harsh aggressiveness that the ego would have liked to
satisfy on other, extraneous individuals. (1930: 123)

The superego is thus, for Freud, in a very "Roman" metaphor, an
internal agency set up to keep watch over the disarmed self "like a
garrison in a conquered city" (124).

Freud's text would actually amount to little more than a
restatement of the work of his great predecessor Nietzsche, were it
not for the additional leap to the insight that "bad conscience"—a
sense of guilt—is not at all related to actually having done something
reprehensible, but is itself rather the result of the inhibition of
aggressive impulses, that is, of *not* doing anything bad. As I just
noted, the Romans felt nary a twinge of guilt as long as they were
actually conquering and subjugating people, and only started
feeling guilty, under the sway of Christianity, after they had left off
attacking their neighbors.

A transformation similar to that which Elias, Nietzsche, and
Freud describe as characteristic of "civilization" occurs in the
psychic life of the ideal or prototypical individual member of

"civilized society," namely the "good obsessional" or "conscientious personality." The (male) child, in the heat of the Oedipal drama, experiences powerful and passionate longings as well as death wishes toward the parent who interferes with these wishes. But under the threat of drastic punishment, of which castration is the paradigmatic case, he retreats from the Oedipal position, renounces the volcanic emotions that had stirred him, and hands over his own aggressive wishes to the superego, that internal "garrison" set up to guard against any future dangerous outbreak of the feelings that had led him to humiliation and disappointments. This garrison, it must be mentioned, is not composed of foreign invaders somehow representing "society," but rather of elements of the individual's own psyche that have switched loyalties to the external regime— that have identified with the aggressor, as we say.

But a boy does not resolve his Oedipal conflict in a cultural vacuum, but rather does so under the influence of important adults and through them the cultural myths and idea systems they exemplify, enact, and inculcate. The boy's own fantasies, in which he attempts to reorganize and synthesize the humiliations and defeats of the Oedipal complex, take shape in a cultural milieu already saturated with collective fantasies in the form of tales, legends, and myths encoded in various public media. (In our day, these include television, movies, recorded music, video games, and the like.) As Sarnoff writes in his authoritative study of the structure of latency, the defensive mechanisms of that crucial era of psychological development

> actively produce fantasies and symbols to be used for discharge, in which the hero can be covertly identified with the child's own self. Myths characteristic of the culture provide ready-made heroes for fantasies. Through such myths, the mechanisms of the structure of latency are adapted to passive identification with tales and legends characteristic of the child's social group. Ethical patterns conveyed by the myths are incorporated into superego contents. (Sarnoff 1976: 154)

In the case of a typical Western individual exemplifying the conscientious personality, the myth of Moses, and/or its Christian transformation, its underlying Oedipal meaning "deciphered" in unconscious thought, would link up with the individual's own fantasies and be elaborated to organize and master his persisting Oedipal conflicts. The myth's hero is a man who really did wreak upon his father the pharaoh all the massive destructiveness one could imagine; who remained nonetheless the favorite of the now-idealized and deified father who survives his own death; and who imposed upon himself (and on his people) a set of rituals, sacrifices, prohibitions, and rules that, if obediently observed, could stave off the destructive wrath that, having now denied to himself, he experienced as threatened against him (and his people) by an external offended authority of unimaginable power.

Such a person would, under the weight of his own personal burden of Oedipal guilt, be inclined, if relatively healthy in other respects, to identify with the culturally provided myths and so to devote himself to the observance of rules, to great care in all his undertakings, and to a life of hard work undergone unconsciously as penance. People like this are the backbone of "civilized" social life under the bureaucratized, stratified, professionalized regime of the state, occupying those various positions in the "interdependent webs" of which Elias spoke.

The word "civilization" which I have been using uncritically so far is a highly tendentious and problematic one. It may variously connote all that is worthwhile in life, or the source of all our misery, or almost anything in between. I mean by it, in the present chapter, something specific, descriptive, and without any necessary value judgment, namely life in cities. I refer, that is, to those particular social, cultural, economic, and political arrangements that prevail in regions under the influence of a pacified, centralized, urbanized national state or cosmopolitan empire. There have been many such on the face of the earth over time, beginning with the original states of Mesopotamia over 8,000 years ago, from which our own civilization emerged.

On the basis of my analysis here it is possible to specify precisely what is distinctive about the regime of our civilization as opposed to whatever came before it. In the condition of society without civilization, at least of our sort, the arts and techniques of culture finally exist to promote, enhance, and sustain life, whose continuation across generations represents the paramount value served by all others. Under the regime of our civilization, the situation is reversed: life is reproduced to serve, sustain, and further the (non-genetic) goals of the civilization, whether these be the building of pyramids, the augmentation of the gross national product, or the pursuit of happiness.

Formulated thus, my conclusion points to a consideration I introduced in my book concerning the historical sources of the paradigm of the primal horde that itself underlies the myth of Moses and hence today's global civilization. I argued that the schema of the primal horde described by Freud might well be drawn from the actual practice of pastoral stock breeding, where the females are devoted to sexual reproduction while the males are divided into "senior" reproducing studs and non-reproducing "junior" animals who are, like the unfortunate sons in Freud's tale, castrated, enslaved, and/or eaten. In pastoral situations, I showed, there is a further split in the role of senior male: the pastoralist does not participate in the reproductive life of his herd himself, but delegates that role to his chosen stud animals. He himself acts in relation to his herd as supreme authority, choosing who is to live and who is to die, exploiting the life and labor of the herd, and managing its reproductive fate not according to the value of reproduction and continued life for its own sake, but rather for his own economic advantage. This is all borne out in the well-known words of the Psalmist "The Lord Is My Shepherd."

While state society has come into being a number of times according to a number of different conceptual models, both history and the analysis of our core myth suggest that our own civilization derives at least in part from a situation dominated by a pastoral ideology. This would happen if a pastoral society conquered, pacified, and dominated one or more agricultural regions, exploiting the surplus produce of the farmers and providing in return a form of "protection" from enemies, of course, but also from themselves. Under such circumstances, it would not be hard to imagine the ruling stratum picturing their relation to the producing population on the model of the relation between the herdsman and his flock.

If this were so, it is still less difficult to imagine how the primacy of sexual reproduction could be relegated to the ordinary citizenry, while the ruling elite would see themselves as the "masters," exempt from the primacy of sexual reproduction while exploiting and managing that of others for their own benefit. To replenish their own ranks, they would not have to reproduce biologically, but could instead "cull" from the general population recruits to be made members of the elite by training and education, rather than through genetic inheritance. Here would be a basis for the enmity between the elite and the whole domain of life pertaining to sexuality, reproduction, and ultimately the carnal, mortal, "female," and profane as opposed to the spiritual, immortal, "male," and sacred.

The schema I have just outlined is a complete inversion of the formula E. O. Wilson (2019) ascribed to "eusocial" species including humans, as I discussed in the previous chapter. In Wilson's account, as I have said, a typical eusocial society such as that of bees consists of a royal reproductive caste and a caste of non-reproductive workers. But what I have just described for the Judeo-Christian tradition, and have elsewhere (Paul 2015) showed is far more widely distributed ethnographically, is the opposite of Wilson's model: the dominant "caste" is the non-reproductive authoritarian or bureaucratic elite, while mere biological reproduction is conceptually relegated to the masses and to women in particular. The higher rates of reproduction in the lower classes in many contemporary "civilized" societies, compared with that of the ruling elites, could be taken as a manifestation of this culturally dominant schema.

The situation I have just described provides a plausible context within which the transition to state society would be accompanied by the normative transformation I have posited, whereby economic production ceases to be subordinated to the ultimate goal of reproduction, and instead reproduction is subordinated to economic production on behalf of a desexualized, impersonal bureaucratic elite.

The ideological and psychodynamic underpinnings of this reversal of values can be traced in the various progressive moments of the narrative of the myth of Moses and its Christian variants. It is, at least in part, through the continuing life of the myth itself that compliance and/or identification with the project of civilization is achieved among individual actors. The myth helps direct the individual to inhibit and redirect the sexual and aggressive energies that might otherwise go into the pursuit of goals serving a program conducive to enhancing genetic reproductive success, and galvanizes people in the direction of the pursuit of the work of civilization for its own sake. That all this is changing in our own time is partly explained by the process I discuss in Chapter 8.

Such a reorientation is accomplished by maintaining in the individual a sufficient degree of guilt and fear of a harsh internal authority—the superego—so that the typical preferred character structure grounds itself in a deflection of reproductive genital sexual aims toward the position characteristic of latency, that is, pre-genital anal sadomasochism. The impulses stemming from this position, in turn, are transformed by the successful defenses and adaptive strategies of reaction formation, isolation, intellectualization, and doing and undoing, reinforced by the educational system, into a fear and renunciation of violence, a love of order, beauty, law, and abstract thought, and commitment to a life of "penance" expressed both through work as a duty and through the practice of religious rituals and ceremonials organized around the central myth and its institutions.

Sadism, or "cruelty," as Nietzsche saw, being forbidden direct unauthorized expression in the pacified state characterized by the monopoly on violence, becomes a vital source of strivings that, through sublimation, reaction formation, and inhibition, lead to the mastery of self, nature, and society, and to the refinements of the arts and sciences that enhance the quality of life in the civilized condition. Nor should we be surprised that on a regular basis the defenses are shifted enough so that more direct and legitimized expression of the cruel impulses, in the form of violence and war, occurs in a culture- and ego-syntonic way.

Meanwhile, the very fact that the work of civilization does indeed, at base, draw upon aggressive and sadistic energies is perceived by the harsh superego, which cannot be fooled. This perception constantly renews the experiential basis for the self-inflicted guilt that keeps the whole system going.

To conclude, then, in a somewhat overly formulaic way: the condition of civilization produces guilt, in virtue of its monopolization of violence and enforcement of the renunciation of sadistic and aggressive impulses. Guilt, in turn, produces the conscientious personality structure. And the conscientious personality, in its turn, is what makes people voluntarily, sometimes even cheerfully, produce and reproduce the work of civilization. To translate into the terms of dual inheritance, at both a collective and a psychological level, the cultural program comes to supersede, transform, and dominate the genetic program.

5

Sons or Sonnets?

Having illustrated the conflict between the differing values placed upon sexual versus non-sexual reproduction on a macroscopic scale in the historical context of the transition from the world of the Hebrew Bible to that of Christendom, I turn in the present chapter to a microscopic illustration of the same process as it is made manifest in one of the great monuments of the Western literary tradition, Shakespeare's *Sonnets*. I will show how within the span of the first nineteen sonnets the poet's stance turns from one favoring genetic reproduction to one favoring symbolic reproduction. In this case, the medium in which symbolic reproduction is accomplished is poetry itself, which in Shakespeare's case is quite literally "immortal."

My choice of topic is determined by the circumstance that these first sonnets concern themselves almost exclusively with a debate about the relative merits of sexual reproduction and poetry—a form of symbolic, cultural production—as avenues to immortality. An analysis of this Shakespearean expression of the "nature/culture" dichotomy is situated in the context of the intertwined destinies of people, genes, and signs, as I have presented them in the form of dual inheritance theory; this in turn is congruent with Freud's understanding that a core of human conflict lies in the competing agendas of the libido, or the "id," and the forces opposed to them— the defenses, the resistance, the "ego," and the "superego." The former are the representatives of imperatives originating from the genetic mode of inheritance; the latter are in the service of the external, cultural symbol system.

The original edition of Shakespeare's *Sonnets* announces my own theme even before the first line of the first poem, in the famous dedication from the publisher that serves as an epigraph to the volume. This brief inscription, printed all in capital letters with full period stops between each word, has occasioned as much speculation and debate as any passage in Shakespeare or indeed in literature itself. It reads:

TO. THE. ONLIE. BEGETTER. OF. THESE. INSUING. SONNETS. Mr. W.H. ALL. HAPPINESS. AND. THAT. ETERNITIE. PROMISED. BY. OVR EVERLIVING. POET. WISHETH. THE. WELL-WISHING. ADVENTURER. IN. SETTING. FORTH.
T.T.

We feel reasonably sure that "T. T." must be the publisher, Thomas Thorpe, and there seems every reason to suppose that it is to himself that he refers as the "well-wishing adventurer in setting forth." Here "setting forth" implies both beginning a journey but also "bringing out," that is, publishing a work of literature.

But what is meant by the phrase "onlie begetter" of the sonnets? Who is "Mr. W.H."? And who is "our ever-living poet"? For the last named status, the main candidates to have been proposed are first Shakespeare himself, a poet who gains immortality by the publication of his verses; or else God, the "poet" of all Creation, whom the well-wishing publisher hopes will bestow eternal Christian salvation on the otherwise mortal Mr. W.H., whoever he might be.

Many commentators have guessed that this Mr. W.H., as the only begetter of the poems, must be a person who inspired or perhaps commissioned them, and a number of candidates for this honor have been put forward, the leading favorites including William Herbert and Henry Wriothesley (with his initials for some reason reversed). Another line of argument supposes that the mysterious Mr. W.H. is not the poetic inspirer or addressee, but rather the procurer of the poems, that is, the go-between who somehow or other got these very personal verses out of the hands of the poet, or the addressee, or the intimate circle among whom they circulated, and turned them over to Thomas Thorpe for dissemination to the great world.

For my purposes in the present chapter, I will venture to go along with what I believe to be the mainstream of modern scholarship, which inclines to the view that the apparent "Mr. W.H." is a compositor's error for what should have read either "Mr. W. S." or "Mr. W. SH.," a straightforward dedication to William Shakespeare, the author, who, after all, seems better suited to the role of "onlie begetter" of the sonnets than anyone else.

The word "to beget" means, first and foremost, to conceive a child, and, more specifically, it has the distinct connotation of "fathering" a child. We are all quite familiar with the metaphorical extension of this prototypical meaning of "beget" as it seems to be employed here, whereby the author of a poem or creator of any cultural product is likened to the father of a child. Both the writing of a poem and the fathering of children are ways for a man to achieve something of "that eternitie" we are denied as mortal beings. Both are extensions into the future of the products of one's mortal being, one in the form of a descendant who is a living replication of oneself in a strict, though partial, genetic sense and the other as a symbolic, cultural form that enters the arena of objective, materialized things that circulate independent of individual lives and can survive across unlimited generations, as have indeed Shakespeare's sonnets, as "alive" today as when he wrote them.

It may be a happy coincidence, or it may have been Thomas Thorpe's intention, that the theme of the two channels of immortality whereby humans can attempt to transcend themselves in space and time, by putting out objective embodiments of some aspect of themselves, be it biological or cultural, shows up not only as the metaphor employed in the dedication I have just discussed, but also as the main theme of the first 19 of the 154 individual poems that comprise the complete set of Shakespeare's *Sonnets*.

These first poems are addressed by the poet to another person who emerges from them as a handsome young man so enamored of his own beauty, and so beguiled by the universal admiration it arouses, that he shows no interest in responding to opportunities, temptations, promptings, or exhortations from importuning others to marry and become a father. Among those admonishing the youth to mend his ways, either on his own or perhaps on behalf of someone who has commissioned him, is the poet himself. In arguments that seem designed to play upon the youth's high opinion of himself and his good looks, the poet reminds him that it is selfish to refuse to bestow upon the wondering world more copies of himself; and, somewhat more pointedly, that this beauty of his is destined to fade, at which time the young man, now grown older, will regret not having produced one or more junior versions of himself in a son or sons. Knowing, it seems, that only flattery will get him anywhere with the object of his versifying, the poet writes:

> From fairest creatures we desire increase,
> That thereby beauty's rose may never die,
> But as the riper should by time decrease,
> His tender heir might bear his memory ... (Sonnet 1)

and:

> Look in the glass, and tell the face thou viewest,
> Now is the time that face should form another ...

Drawing a parallel between the young man and a hypothetical future child of his own in relation to a parent, the poet continues:

> Thou art thy mother's glass, and she in thee
> Calls back the lovely April of her prime;
> So thou through windows of thine age shalt see,
> Despite of wrinkles, this thy golden time ... (Sonnet 3)

The reference in these lines to the youth's resemblance to his mother draws attention to the sexual and procreative meaning of "begetting." What the poet seems to be urging is for the young man to find beauty and sexual attraction in a potential wife and mother of his own children rather than admiring the image of his own mother he sees in the mirror. This intimation of heterosexuality will contrast with the later sonnets in which cultural reproduction is to be effected by non-sexual means, in which the woman's role is unnecessary. The youth and the poet, both men, can accomplish it themselves via the homoerotic love that will bind them sublimated as verse.

Shakespeare uses a variety of metaphors to state his case that the youth should marry and father sons: in Sonnet 4, the youth is told that his beauty is a loan from nature from which he fails to profit by "having traffic with thyself alone," and in Sonnet 6 he is assured that it is not usury to loan out his abundant beauty's treasure to a woman, since his favor "happies those that pay the willing loan."

In Sonnet 3, the young man is likened to a farmer who disdains to fertilize with his "husbandry" some "unear'd womb." In Sonnet 7, the youth is likened to the sun, whom all look upon amazed at noon, but from whom eyes are turned when "with weary car/Like feeble age, he reeleth from the day"; the message is clear: "So thou, thyself out-going in thy noon/Unlook'd on diest, unless thou get a son." In Sonnet 9, the poet speculates that perhaps it is "fear to wet the widow's eye" that keeps our hero from marrying. He counters this possible scruple by remarking that the whole world is now the young man's widow, weeping "that thou no form of thee hast left behind."

Thus far the poet has delivered his not-very-subtle advice from a relatively neutral standpoint, without alluding to his own possible interest in the case. Self-references by the poet to himself first emerge in Sonnet 10, in which the author asks the youth to change his thought (i.e., the thought that makes him conspire against himself by not "repairing his beauteous roof") "that *I* may change *my* mind! (my italics)" And he concludes with this plea:

> Make thee another self *for love of me*,
> That beauty still may live in thine or thee. [my emphasis]

Here we see the first overt hints of the poet's own love for the youth, destined to emerge full-blown in Sonnet 20, as if the poet had been asked or hired to persuade the young man to marry by some concerned relative, perhaps, or prospective father-in-law; but found he had to speak on his own behalf.

If I may summarize the message of the sonnets thus far, it could be paraphrased thus:

> You are so handsome I can see that looking in the mirror and being admired is the only thing that matters to you. However, if the world, and I in particular, get such great pleasure in looking at your face, imagine what a favor you'd be doing us by making a whole bunch of copies so we can be all the more in love with you. And if you won't do it for the world, or for me, then wouldn't you yourself take some pleasure in seeing your likeness reflected in the faces of those you had fathered— especially when your own mirror doesn't show such a pretty picture any more?

What starts to emerge in Sonnet 10 is the new thought "you are so attractive I'm falling in love with you myself."

Sonnet 11 is another unadorned exhortation, again using the theme of passing time and its inevitable ravages, ending with the thought that while it may be all right for the "Harsh, featureless and rude" products of Nature to die barren, "She [Nature] carved for thee her seal, and meant thereby/Thou shouldst print more, not let that copy die." With these lines, the metaphor of printing emerges, foreshadowing a new idea that will begin to take shape a few sonnets later. The importance of this metaphor is that it refers to an inorganic, cultural, mechanical means of reproduction in writing rather than to the biological one the poet has so far been recommending. In Sonnet 12, the poet again speaks in the first person, with proliferating self-references:

When *I* do count the clock that tells the time,
And see the brave day sunk in hideous night,
When *I* behold the violet past prime,
...
When lofty trees *I* see barren of leaves,
...
Then of thy beauty do *I* question make. [my emphasis]

Now the poet is speaking of his own thoughts about the youth, rather than concentrating on the young man himself and the lesson he has started out to impart to him. The passing of the youth's beauty has become a matter of direct personal concern for the poet, and the poetry expresses his inner contemplation, though the sonnet ends with another direct lesson: "And nothing 'gainst Time's scythe can make defense/Save breed to brave him when he takes thee hence." In Sonnet 13, the poet does not use the first-person pronoun, but lets slip his feelings even more plainly in the first lines: "O that you were yourself! But, love, you are/No longer yours than you yourself here live."

Perhaps sensing that with his use of the term of endearment "love" he has given himself away, the poet now begins to undergo a radical metamorphosis. He realizes that not only is he himself the youth's lover, but he has power over him as well, not in his role as a would-be mentor, but as one who, taking inspiration from his beloved's beauty, can transform it into art, and with that art himself

give the youth the immortality he wishes for him. Sonnet 14 depicts
the poet finding his own powers:

Not from the stars do I my judgement pluck,
And yet methinks I have astronomy,
...
Nor can I fortune to brief minutes tell,
Pointing to each his thunder, rain, and wind,
Or say with princes if it shall go well
By oft predict that I in heaven find:
But from thine eyes my knowledge I derive,
And, constant stars, in them I read such art
As truth and beauty shall together thrive
If from thyself to store thou wouldst convert:
Or else of thee this I prognosticate,
Thy end is truth and beauty's doom and date.

In Sonnet 14, the poet has limited his powers merely to those
of prognostication. In Sonnet 15, a decisive one for the argument I
want to develop here, the poet shows himself prepared to do battle
over the beauty of the beloved young man with the adversary who
threatens to destroy it, Time. His weapon against the all-powerful
adversary is Poetry itself:

When I consider everything that grows
Holds in perfection but a little moment,
...
Then the conceit of this inconstant stay
Sets you most rich in youth before my sight,
Where wasteful Time debateth with Decay
To change your day of youth to sullied night,
And all in war with Time for love of you,
As he takes from you, I *engraft you new*. [my emphasis]

In the final couplet, the poet no longer sits on the sidelines despairing
for the waste of the young man's flower of youth, but offers to do
something about it, "for love of you." Emboldened by his love, and
quite against the spirit of the earlier sonnets, he himself is going to
give back to the young man, or at least to his handsome face, that
which the ravages of Time take away.

The poet responds with surprise at his own audacity in this expression of confidence in his ability to defeat Time, and hastens to undo it with a return to his original theme in Sonnet 16:

> But wherefore do not you a mightier way
> Make war upon this bloody tyrant Time,
> And fortify yourself in your decay
> *With means more blessed than my barren rhyme?* [my emphasis]

It is as if, shocked by his claim to make the youth immortal by his poetic might, he retreats, denigrating that might in favor of a "more blessed means" than "barren rhyme," that is, breeding sons. He likens his own pen now to the one with which Time will draw lines on the as yet unflawed face, placing both in opposition to the "lines" of the other, natural means of achieving eternity, the one that only the young man can accomplish for himself by becoming a father.

> So should the lines of life that life repair
> Which this, Time's pencil, or my pupil pen
> Neither in inward worth nor outward fair
> Can make you live yourself in eyes of men:
> To give away yourself keeps yourself still,
> And you must live, drawn by your own sweet skill.

In Sonnet 17, the poet's self-doubt wrestles with the heady excitement that attends the realization that he can resolve the entire situation by relying on his own poetic genius. First, the doubts: "Who will believe my verse in time to come./The age to come would say 'This poet lies ... '"; "And your true rights be term'd a poet's rage/And stretched metre of an antique song." Then, the affirmation:

> But were some child of yours alive that time,
> *You should live twice, in it and in my rhyme.* [my emphasis]

The poet allows himself to believe that he can indeed render the youth immortal with his verse, provided the young man also begets sons so that people can see for themselves that what the poet says is true. Here nature and art are held in parallel regard.

But then one almost senses the poet saying to himself "Wait a minute! What am I talking about? I'm William Shakespeare, the greatest poet who ever lived. I can do whatever I want with my verse, including making this worthless charmer into a thing of eternal beauty, no thanks to his pretty face, or to Mother Nature, but thanks to me and my incomparable and limitless talent." Throwing off all humble pretensions and inhibitions and standing unmasked in his own sublime self-confidence, he writes:

Shall I compare thee to a summer's day?
Thou are more lovely and more temperate.

In other words, he himself creates a poem of the profoundest beauty, one that has become so familiar and yet remains so unhackneyed, so seemingly artless, that it seems always to have existed, one of the most sublime poetic achievements of our vast literary tradition. Here at last the poet has become fully aware of the fact that the youth, whose beauty is indeed fading, will remain beautiful not just as the poet sees him, but as the poet writes him. In the writing of him, the poet's own verse has usurped the beauty he sought originally to preserve through advising sexual reproduction, and gone it one better by making it, if not literally immortal, than certainly very long-lasting. For indeed we have no idea who the descendants of beautiful youth among us today might be, if he did have any; nor do we even have much of a firm idea of who William Shakespeare might have been; but we all know, or can learn to know, these sonnets that remain for us unchanged 400 years and more after their composition. Indeed, as we learn here, when it comes to producing "copies," it is the printing press that wins against the organic mode of reproduction. Even if the youth had sired children, and his descendants are alive today, we would see no fair copy of his face, but rather one at best radically transformed by its intermixture with the other genes that have entered the line of descent since then. But anyone can see a fair copy of the original printing of Shakespeare's sonnet, for example, by looking at the reproduction of them in any recent edition.

The gist of Sonnet 18, then, is that every natural thing to which the poet tries to compare his theme—the beautiful youth—is subject to change, decay, or finitude. But "thy eternal summer shall not fade": why not?

But thy eternal summer shall not fade,
Nor lose possession of that fair thou ow'st,
Nor shall Death brag thou wand'rest in his shade,
When in eternal lines to time thou grow'st.
So long as men can breathe or eyes can see,
So long lives this, and this gives life to thee.

The poet, in other words, now directly contradicts the diffident and self-deprecating observations he made in Sonnet 16, to the effect that his own "barren rhyme" was an unworthy competitor of life itself, that is, biological procreation, which alone could repair the "lines of life." In Sonnet 16, the "lines" refer to those that would compose a "painted counterfeit" of the fair youth's face. Time's pencil, and, in imitation of it, the poet's "pupil pen," could only draw lines of age, that is, wrinkles or disfigurements, on the beloved brow. But in Sonnet 18, it will be the lines written by the poet's pen that defeat Time and render the youth's beauty eternal, that beauty having been transferred from the face to its apotheosis in a sonnet that will be, and has been, admired for its beauty ever since. Indeed, in the very act of composing these words, I am aware that I myself am participating in the chain of reproduction whereby the sonnets continue to propagate themselves through— and against—time.

Time itself is addressed in Sonnet 19, and told it can do what it likes with lion's paws and tiger's jaws (i.e., blunt and defang them with age), but it must not "carve with thy hours my love's fair brow,/ Nor draw no lines there with thine antique pen." But instead of urging the youth to beget heirs, as he did through the first seventeen sonnets, the poet rests in the final couplet on his newfound confidence in his own power to bestow immortality:

Yet do thy worst, old Time: despite thy wrong,
My love shall in my verse ever live young.

Thus does the poet resolve his conflict among his different wishes or motives: he abandons his exhortations to the young man to marry and breed children, and combines his own wish to immortalize the youth with his urge to express his overwhelming infatuation with the young man's beauty by writing the sonnets, chronicling the ups and downs of their "affair," whatever it may have been. Whatever it was, though, it could and did produce poems, but not children.

The crux of the evolution of the poet's ideas can be captured by concentrating on the three consecutive sonnets: Sonnets 16, 17, and 18. In schematized programmatic form, what they say is this:

1. I could try to save you from Time's ravages by portraying you in verse with my pen, but that would be a barren counterfeit. Only you, with your own living sexual substance, bestowed on some "maiden garden," can create a new version of yourself that is truly alive. (Sonnet 16)

2. If I write poetry that is as good as I think it is, and in it describe your beauty, nobody will believe me. But if you will breed and create a child to bear witness, then together, that child and my verses will keep you alive. (Sonnet 17)

3. You can do what you like about having children; if you are going to be remembered at all in the future, it is only because of my poetry. (Sonnet 18)

The progression encapsulated in these three sonnets concerns the relations between sexual reproduction, on the one hand, and reproduction by symbolic means (in this case, linguistic signs), on the other. In the first moment, sexual reproduction is represented as being the real thing, capable of producing new life, while poetry—a thing fabricated of words, ink markings on paper, or patterns of sound waves spoken into the air—can only be a counterfeit, a barren imitation of life. In the second moment, sexual and symbolic reproduction are represented as coequal, the product of the first—a child—serving as the redeemable value of the symbols of it in the second: because the child of the beautiful youth is also beautiful, those in the next generation who read the poem will be guaranteed that the symbols are worth what they claim to be worth by checking up on the reality the poem claims to represent. The specie of a symbolic form, in this moment, is as good as the gold backing it up in the Fort Knox of living reality. Finally, in the third moment, the symbol declares its independence from the product of sexual procreation, and asserts its right to stand on its own, with or without the compliance of "living reality." In other words, we find a movement that can be summarized thus:

1. Signs depend on people.
2. Signs and people can stand for each other.
3. People depend on signs.

Or, otherwise said,

1. Symbolic reproduction (as poetry) is secondary to, and depends upon, sexual reproduction;
2. Sexual and symbolic reproduction refer to each other in a relation of equality or mutual adequacy.
3. Sexual reproduction is secondary to, or even irrelevant to, symbolic reproduction.

In the previous chapter, I identified a similar structural progression in the relations between the three central mythic figures of the Judeo-Christian religious tradition, namely, Abraham, Moses, and Jesus. Abraham and the other patriarchs Isaac and Jacob ("Israel") are portrayed as the biological fathers of the nation that is to become the Israelites, while their involvement with any sort of symbolic system is of lesser narrative importance. It is only with Moses that a set of laws, and commentaries on them, all in linguistic form, achieve equal status with that of biological ancestry: after the revelation of the Law at Sinai, Israelites must be *both* genetic descendants of the patriarchs *and* schooled in the legal code the Torah and the commentaries on it inscribed in symbolic, specifically linguistic, form. Finally, with the message of Jesus, the symbolic code is detached from any requirement regarding genetic ancestry in the biological line, and anyone, Israelite or not, can become a Christian simply by subscribing to and internalizing the symbolic system itself.

In neither the first moment nor in the third moment is one or the other of the two modes of reproduction—sexual and symbolic— eliminated entirely; but the priority rankings between them do indeed seem to trade places. Neither sexual procreation nor symbolic reproduction can completely rid the field of the other. But the relations between them can vary in a tripartite schema: first, either equal or unequal; and then, if unequal, with one or another in the dominant and the other in the subordinate position.

In the present chapter and in the previous one, I have depicted a transition from the predominance of the values inherent in the genetic program to the supersession of these by the values of cultural program. However as I have also argued here, neither of the two competing and intertwined channels can utterly vanquish the other. In the following chapter, I illustrate ways in which the values of sexual versus cultural reproduction in the Western tradition actually seem to oscillate back and forth with regard to which one appears the better way to create new human beings.

6

The Pygmalion Complex

Introduction

Freud's theory of mental life, especially as it is revealed in neurosis, posits a conflict between drives, more specifically sexual drives, and forces opposing these drives. Why this conflict should exist at all is a problem that Freud wrestled with throughout his career. In accord with dual inheritance theory, I have been suggesting that this problem is an aspect of a more fundamental conflict in human society, resulting from the fact that we are formed in the course of our development from fertilized eggs to mature adults by two parallel channels of information: a genetic track, contained in the DNA and transmitted to a new human by an act of heterosexual genital intercourse; and a cultural track, transmitted to a new organism by external systems of symbols perceived through the senses. As I said in the Introduction to this book, and at greater length in my book *Mixed Messages* (2015), as a result of the role of the cultural system in regulating and containing the sexual imperatives of the genetic program, there is a widespread (though not universal) tendency to denigrate and devalue sexual reproduction at the expense of cultural reproduction. Sex itself, and with some regularity women, whose bodies are the primary sites of biological reproduction, are likewise devalued and regarded as animal-like, unclean, sinful, and so on. Sexuality, therefore, unless sanctioned by the prevailing cultural rules of normative behavior in society, for example by marriage legitimized by law and God, is thus seen as disruptive and to some degree set apart from social life in the public arena.

One striking dimension of the conflict I have just described is the occurrence in various parts of the world of fantasies and rituals in which humans are somehow created by some means other than by sexual procreation. I have described several of these cases in *Mixed Messages*. Lest these beliefs and practices be seen as bizarre and irrational exotica, however, in the present chapter I offer a sketch of the conflict between the sexual and asexual reproduction of humans in our own Western historical and cultural context. The wish to find a way to populate the next generation without having to engage in sexual intercourse, which at first blush may seem implausible, has in fact animated our own cultural world no less than it has that of many other societies, with this key difference: we have made significant technological advances in actually being able to achieve this goal, and are pursuing it with undiminished enthusiasm. New reproductive technologies, on the one hand, and the production by non-sexual means of human-like beings in the fields of robotics and artificial intelligence on the other, are only the latest manifestations of a quest that goes back to the origins of our civilization in the world of the ancient Greeks. I discuss this phenomenon at greater length in Chapter 8. Here I offer a picture of some of the salient moments in the enduring struggle between sexual and non-sexual reproduction in the Western imagination, from long before we were actually able to do anything about it.

Deucalion and Pyrrha

In Greek mythology, as Ovid recounts the tales for his Roman readers in his *Metamorphoses*, the first humans to create new human life without resorting to copulation are Deucalion and his wife Pyrrha. (They in turn were made out of earth by Prometheus, but he was a titan, not a human.) When Jove, outraged on a visit to earth in human form where he is made the object of an assassination plot by the wicked King Lycaon, decides to wipe out debauched humanity by means of a universal flood, Deucalion and Pyrrha alone manage to survive in a rowboat. Wondering what to do next, now that they are the sole humans left on earth when the waters recede, they petition the oracle of Themis to tell them how to proceed. One might have thought the answer would be obvious, given that they are husband and wife: that they should get busy and multiply in the usual way as the sons of Noah did after surviving the biblical flood as recounted in Genesis 9; but they do not do so. Perhaps the difference is that while Noah had three sons, whose offspring could intermarry in the next generation without committing egregious incest, this would not have been so for the children of Deucalion and Pyrrha, who would have been full siblings rather than first cousins.

Instead, Themis advises them to "throw their mother's bones" behind them. At first bewildered, the distraught pair come to realize that the oracle must mean by this that they are to throw behind them stones, which are the bones of Mother Earth. They do so, and then

> The stones—who would believe it, had we not
> The unimpeachable witness of Tradition?—
> Began to lose their hardness, to soften, slowly,
> To take on form, to grow in size, a little,
> Become less rough, to look like human beings,
> Or anyway as much like human beings
> As statues do, when the sculptor is only starting,
> Images half blocked out. (1964: 15)

With these people newly made from stone, Deucalion and Pyrrha repopulate the world.

Comparing this story with that of the biblical flood, a key distinction emerges between Greek and Hebraic cultural values. Whereas the former favors the cultural over the genetic means of reproduction, the latter requires the sexual method. This ancestral divide has had lasting implications for the West: as I showed in Chapter 4, the Hebraic emphasis on biological descent was turned on its head by the transformations wrought by Christianity, a product of the evolution of Israelite religion within a Hellenic cultural milieu.

Pygmalion

Ovid's image of the creation of humans out of stones, as a sculptor might do, leads us to two more of his closely associated tales of

metamorphosis. In the first, we learn that because the daughters of
the town of Amathus, in Cyprus, would not acknowledge Venus,
she, in her wrath,

> Made whores of them, the first such women ever
> To sell their bodies, and in shamelessness,
> They hardened, even their blood was hard, they could not
> Blush any more; it was no transition, really
> From what they were to actual rock and stone. (1964: 241)

We may infer that it was the practice of unregulated sexuality, and
its separation from the socially acceptable aim of reproduction in
marriage, that undid the humanity of these women, who should
have been well-behaved wives and mothers instead of sexual
objects. Or perhaps their crime against Venus was that they
pursued sex for money, rather than for love or for its own sake. In
any event, their metamorphosis in effect reverted them back to the
stone from which they had once come (like everyone else) in the
earlier tale of Deucalion and Pyrrha.

But in the very next story, the direction of the metamorphosis
from stone to human (Deucalion and Pyrrha) back to stone (the
women of Amathus) is reversed once again:

> One man, Pygmalion, who had seen these women [the whores of
>   Amathus]
> Leading their shameful lives, shocked at the vices
> Nature had given the female disposition
> Only too often, chose to live alone,
> To have no woman in his bed. (1964: 241–2)

Rejecting real women as the means of sexual reproduction,
Pygmalion carves a beautiful statue of ivory (admittedly not actually
stone, but, like stone, a hard and inanimate material, as opposed to
living flesh) and becomes entranced by its charm. When the holiday
in honor of Venus comes around, Pygmalion prays for the goddess to
send him a wife just like his virginal ivory woman. Venus responds
by making the statue come to life as Galatea. Pygmalion marries her,
with Venus's blessing; and, after nine months, a daughter Paphos is
born, from whom a Greek city in Cyprus takes its name.

Pygmalion, like Deucalion the lone worthy man living in degenerate times, is horrified by the outrageous sexual behavior of the women of Amathus, and so finds favor with Venus, who has dominion over all things having to do with love and sex. But she clearly does not approve of (heterosexual) sex for unsanctioned purposes and its attendant potential to lead to procreation, as the story of the daughters of Amathus reveals. It is thus with her approval and divine intervention that the miraculous metamorphosis of ivory statue to living human form is accomplished. Pygmalion thereby becomes the mythic prototype of the human who, through cultural artifice, could create a living human being—though of course it was really the goddess who did it, not Pygmalion all by himself.

However, it is important to note that although Pygmalion is widely regarded as the man who successfully created a living person from non-living matter, he did so with the intent, and with the result, of going on to procreate sexually with the woman he had created. His problem was that he was repulsed by the unmoored sexuality of the real women around him, and wanted an ideal real wife, as chaste and pure as ivory, with whom to start a biological family. Since none were available in the flesh in his vice-ridden community, he had to make one; Venus understood his motives, approved of his plan, and made it happen.

In this story, unlike that of Deucalion and Pyrrha, artificial, non-sexual reproduction (carving an ivory statue) is depicted as being undertaken not for its own sake but rather in the service of the ultimate aim of sexual reproduction, which Pygmalion accomplishes with his newly formed wife of flesh and blood. Pygmalion's story is one in which artificial and biological reproduction co-exist, with biological reproduction retaining the upper hand.

Plato and Aristotle

Plato, as is well known, had no use for making artificial likenesses of living things. His denunciation of mimesis in the *Republic* (2000) rests on his belief in the primacy of an immaterial virtual ideal world, of which the world we experience through perception is a mere copy. Art, which copies nature, is thus merely a copy of a copy, and hence without merit. Worse even than visual artists are poets and actors who make up and impersonate fictional people and make them seem to come alive through their art, thus leading people away from the search for truth.

Plato himself, however, was not completely above employing a "noble lie," or myth, when it suited his purpose. In his ideal republic, there would be a class of guardians who would execute the will of the philosopher king, and, since they were to have sole loyalty to the state, and not to family and kin, they were to be raised in the belief that they were born of the earth and not of biological parents. They were to live in common and not marry but rather reproduce with various different women (they themselves were of course men) rather than in ordinary families. As Fukuyama observes, it was not that Plato believed such sexual and reproductive communism was actually possible; rather,

> the purpose of the discussion was to highlight the permanent tensions that exist between people's private kinship ties and their obligations to a broader political order. The implication is that any successful order needs to suppress the power of kinship through some mechanism that makes the guardians value ties to the state over their love for their families. (2011: 199–200)

This dynamic which Fukuyama identifies between the kin group and the wider society is exactly that between the genetic program and the cultural program that Richerson and Boyd proposed in creating dual inheritance theory, and which I have discussed in previous chapters. The fiction that the guardians are born autochthonously from the earth rather than from sexual reproduction is a way of asserting the primacy of the wider society established by cultural means over the social ties of family operating in the genetic sphere.

This theme of being born from the earth echoes the creation by Deucalion and Pyrrha after the flood, and recurs in the Theban myth according to which the autochthonous clans of Thebes originated from the survivors among the armed men who had sprung from the ground when Cadmus, the founder of Thebes, sowed the teeth of the serpent he had slain. The armed men fought among themselves until only five were left, and these became the ancestors of the lineages of Thebes.

It is on the basis of these ideas that Lévi-Strauss (1967), in his famous analysis of the myth of Oedipus, proposed as the key set of oppositions in Greek mythic thought that between "overrating blood relations" (such as Oedipus marrying his mother) and "underrating blood relations" (as in his killing of his father), on the one hand; and that between the "denial of the autochthonous origin of man" (Cadmus killing the serpent) and the "assertion of autochthony" (as in the name "Oedipus," meaning "swollen foot," because autochthonous beings often limp as a result of their detachment, like plants, from the earth out of which they have grown), on the other hand. For Lévi-Strauss, the key question requiring mythic resolution in the Greek tradition is whether humans are born from one, that is, asexually, or born from two, that is sexually. Needless to say, this idea is clearly equivalent to the conflict I have identified as being the result of our dual inheritance as both sexual and non-sexual reproducers.

Aristotle, unlike Plato a keen and appreciative observer of the phenomenal world of nature, wrote a treatise on the generation of animals that contains many accurate statements about reproduction in the animal kingdom. Among his less valid ideas, however, from the standpoint of today's science, were those regarding spontaneous generation, such as seems to occur in the appearance of insects out of putrefying organic matter; and the belief that semen is a spiritual substance that contributes the "pattern" that gives form to the "matter" of menstrual blood, the maternal sexual substance. (I hardly need to point out that our words "pattern" and "matter"—"pater" and "mater"—themselves reflect and derive from this sexual theory.) To phrase the issue in Aristotelian terms, the female contribution to reproduction is the material cause, while the paternal contribution is the formal cause. These ideas, in the hands of later thinkers in the Islamic world and in the medieval West, for whom Aristotle became the ultimate scientific authority, made possible the speculation that human semen, allowed to gestate not in the womb of a human female but in some other warm organic putrefying material (the preferred substance usually being horse dung), could produce a living being without any female contribution. Since there would be no "material cause," such a being would be of a purely spiritual nature.

This set of beliefs set the stage for the project of the alchemists to try to create a "homunculus." Aristotle himself, by contrast, had no belief that any mere work of human hands could surpass the work of nature. As Kara Reilly writes, "For Aristotle, the essential difference between nature and art could be understood through biological reproduction. It was solely within the province of nature for organic things to regenerate their species and reproduce; therefore, this made reproductive nature superior to art" (2011: 17). As Aristotle himself put it in his pithy way, "Men propagate men, bedsteads do not propagate bedsteads" (Aristotle, *The Physics*, cited in Newman 2004: 16).

In the famous contrast between Plato and Aristotle, so eloquently depicted in Raphael's painting *The School of Athens,* with Plato pointing up toward to the ethereal realm and Aristotle pointing down to earth, we see epitomized the contrast between the relative valuation of the two modes of reproduction in these two great thinkers.

An Example from Islamic Alchemy

One of the earliest examples of a tale concerning the creation of an artificial man along Aristotelian lines is found in an Arabic story that was commented upon by Avicenna in 1037 (Newman 2004: 140), but is probably much older. It concerns an ancient king named Harmanus. He ruled a great empire but "he was childless and intercourse with women was repugnant to him" (Pines 1996, cited in Newman 2004: 140–1). His wise councilor, Qaliqulas, a great ascetic,

> advised the king to beget a male child by artificial means. He told him that all that was needed was some sperm of the king; this would be kept in a vessel, shaped like a mandragora [mandrake root] ... and Qaliqulas would apply to it a technique he knew, which would result in the production of a male son. After some demur the king agreed. Qaliqulas applied his technique, and the material compound that resulted received a rational soul and became a perfect human being. This male child was named Salaman. (Newman 2004: 141)

As Newman comments, this story illustrates the fact that the author, building on Aristotle's ideas, has assumed that sperm could create a living human by means of spontaneous generation in a mandrake root, because sperm is a pneumatic substance that contains the complete preformed pattern of a viable human.

In this story, we see that the purpose of creating a child artificially is so that the king can reproduce himself biologically but without the sexual intercourse he has foresworn, presumably in the interest of the higher ascetic strivings consistent with the anti-sexual bias of the cultural reproductive system, and without the participation of anything remotely female. The human organism is thought of as composed of material substance and Aristotle's immaterial "rational soul," consisting of form rather than matter. The rational soul is associated with maleness and granted a higher standing than the material, which is associated with the female and with menstrual blood, and hence regarded as putrescent. The goal then is to create a "pure" human from the spiritual essence without the necessity of contaminating it with supposed female impurity.

The Golem

In medieval European Jewish tradition, it was also considered possible to construct an artificial man, called a *golem*, by performing *gematria*, the mystical manipulation of the letters of the alphabet that would turn a human form made of clay into a living being. Such a figure was thought of as large and strong, but without the power of speech, the defining human characteristic. In many instances of the lore, the golem is created to play the role of a servant, doing menial labor for its maker. The magical introduction of life into the man of dust is achieved by writing the Hebrew word *emeth*, "truth," on its forehead. The way to destroy the golem once it has outlived its usefulness therefore is to erase the letter *aleph* at the beginning of the word *emeth* to produce the word *meth*, which means death. One legendary rabbi attempted this but was killed when the huge dying creature collapsed on him (Scholem [1965] 1996: 200–1).

In the case of the golem, it is not spiritual substance, equated with breath, that animates the inanimate clay, but rather symbolic units in concrete literal form—written letters of the alphabet. By manipulating these cultural equivalents of genes, the rabbis supposedly produce a being who is not actually a human in the full sense, but behaves like one in most respects. His animating spirit, however, is the rabbi who has conjured him and then gives him orders, like a slave or (to anticipate) like a robot or android. Robots and androids are not themselves alive, but rather simulate living humans in being able to do what humans can do. But they still lack some ineffable essence—the *élan vital* perhaps?—that would make them truly human, presumably some version of whatever it was that animated the stones of Deucalion and Pyrrha, or the statue of Pygmalion.

In this tradition, which appears to be quite distinct from the Aristotelian one, the artificial man, far from being a more spiritual being than a human, is less spiritual, since it can only hear and obey but not speak or initiate intelligent action itself. It is not produced with an erotic motive, as with Pygmalion, or with a wish to reproduce biologically but asexually, as in the case of King Harmanus and his miraculous son Salaman, but rather to provide its master with a mindless servant, who will do his bidding and take care of the labor of the household.

A very different picture of the golem is to be found, however, with a very different moral evaluation, in its most famous incarnation, the golem of Prague created by the sixteenth-century Rabbi Yehuda Loew, known as the Maharal (Wiesel 1983). This may or may not be a legend from that era, or it may actually be a nineteenth-century literary invention referred back. However, it seems possible that even if it is the latter, it is based on older oral traditions. In any event, Rabbi Loew creates his golem not to be his household servant, but rather to defend the Jewish community of Prague from anti-Semitism. Whenever the Christians would plan to kidnap a child and blame the Jews for killing it, thus inciting a pogrom with the notorious myth of the "blood libel," Rabbi Loew would send his golem out to find the child. The rediscovery of the child, who had been not killed but merely hidden away by the conspirators, would prove that the Jews were innocent of murder, thus saving the community. In this case, the golem, while still behaving as a servant, is not a mere drudge but rather a defender of the Jews, capable of superhuman feats, such as the ability to make himself invisible, to swiftly scour the neighborhood, and to locate missing persons.

The Alchemical Homunculus

The high point of European alchemical concern with the creation of a homunculus was reached in the person of Theodosius von Hohenheim, known as Paracelsus, the famous (or infamous) sixteenth-century Swiss writer on medical and religious subjects. A firm believer in the alchemical principle that things can be transformed into other things, in the animal kingdom as well as in the realm of chemical substances, Paracelsus asserted that "men too may be born without natural fathers and mothers" (cited in Newman 2004: 201–2). This feat could be accomplished by a skilled alchemist, using either sperm or menstrual blood. The former, Paracelsus held, being itself spiritual, was capable of producing a purified quasi-immaterial homunculus, or "little man," while the latter, being impure in the extreme, could, if gestated in a container of horse dung, be used to produce the creature called the basilisk, a monster above all monsters that can kill by its gaze alone. The comparative valuation of the male as spiritual and pure and the female as impure here reaches one of its most extreme formulations.

The method Paracelsus describes for producing an artificial man from sperm alone, without any admixture of impure femaleness, is as follows:

> That the sperm of a man be putrefied by itself in a cucurbit for forty days with the highest degree of putrefaction in a horse's womb [the usual alchemical euphemism for a container of horse dung], or at least so long as it comes to life and moves itself, and stirs, which is easily observed. After this time, it will look somewhat like a man, but transparent, without a body. If, after this, it be fed wisely with the arcanum of human blood and be nourished for up to forty weeks, and be kept in the even heat of the horse's womb, a living human child grows therefrom, with all its members like another child, which is born of a woman, but much smaller. (Cited in Newman 2004: 203–4)

Such artificially created homunculi possess great gifts, such as the knowledge of all hidden and secret things, because they themselves are the product of art and therefore are "born" with art innate in them. Homunculi could then serve as guides, or spirit familiars, of the alchemist, giving him the benefit of their superhuman qualities.

Here it is plain that a produced being made of pure "cultural" substance, conceptualized as male and inherent in semen, possesses qualities above those of mere humans, because the latter reproduce by mingling the superior male (cultural) essence with the defiling female matter that symbolically represents the mode of transmission of the genetic instructions.

Descartes and Automata

Sometime in Europe in the early to mid-1600s, the Renaissance episteme that could entertain the ideas of a Paracelsus morphed, as Foucault (1971) shows, into the Classical episteme, in which many alchemical beliefs and practices suddenly became obsolete and were replaced by a new spirit of empirical and rational scientific inquiry that took hold with remarkable speed and efficiency. Not only did many "magical" aspects of alchemical thought fade from the scene, but the Protestant Reformation effected a sea change in thinking about creating artificial people. The Protestant reformers, in their iconoclastic zeal, condemned the making of images of any kind, especially ones that might seem to move, or were moved by artificial means, on the theory that only God could imbue a being with a soul and that therefore the imitation of living things was blasphemy. This was a return to the Platonic low evaluation of the arts. This ideological construction of things in turn made possible the development of Deism, the theology that holds that God at the creation set the universe in its course, but that after that it could operate on its own on the basis of the laws that God had established in the beginning. This and related beliefs made it possible for the thinkers who developed modern scientific ideas to give purely mechanical, mathematically based explanations of God's creation without eliminating God altogether—though that was an obvious next step that would soon be taken.

For our purposes, the paradigmatic figure in the epistemic shift I have described was Descartes. It was Descartes's view that everything that is extended in space could be understood in purely materialistic terms based on mathematical reasoning about matter in motion. The only exception is the human being, who in addition possesses a purely immaterial soul. All other things in the world, including animals, could be explained in purely mechanical terms.

As for humans, they would, in a thought experiment he carries out in his book *Traité de l'Homme*, also be mechanical: the body of these men would be "nothing other than a statue or machine of earth, which God has formed expressly to render it as similar as possible to us" (Cited in Des Chene 2001: 7). As Des Chene writes of an alternate world imagined by Descartes:

> Their world will be like ours, their light, their bodies, even their sensations. But we know full well, from Descartes' other works, that the screen of resemblance erected between the world of the *homme-machine* and our own is a kind of feint. Our world is not just *like* the world of *Le Monde*, it *is* that world, and the people in our world *are* the people there. (7–8, emphasis in original)

In this Cartesian conception of the human being, the nutritive and vegetative souls of Aristotle's system have disappeared, and the human body is an automaton, not a "self-mover" at all really, but a machine obeying the laws of physics, as animals are supposed by Descartes to be. The animals, indeed, are identical with machines, and humans would be too but for the fact that they do have rational souls. These, however, have no direct connection whatsoever with the body, being of an entirely different substance. Human bodies, like all other natural phenomena, obey the laws of physics, that is, of particles of matter interacting on the basis of their velocity and their direction of motion. Descartes's resulting speculative physiology, as Des Chene expounds it, appears as bizarre a flight of imagination to modern minds as are any of the speculations of the alchemists.

Descartes was apparently very much influenced in his thinking by the perfection of artificially created automata that mimicked human action that were just then being constructed. According to Kara Reilly,

> Descartes' *The Treatise of Man* (1632) drew directly on his observations of the royal pleasure gardens at Saint-Germain-en-Laye. These gardens were full of theatrical hydraulic automata in the grottoes. At some time between the summer of 1614 and the autumn of 1615 Descartes lived in the Saint-Germain-en-Laye area just outside Paris .... [He] took long walks in these gardens, which began his life-long fascination with automata. (2011: 55)

Descartes reasoned that just as the gardener controls the whole hydraulic spectacle composed of these intriguing self-moving automata made by the hand of humans, so the rational soul sits at the control panel of the human brain, adjusting the flow in the various tubes and pipes that constitute the nervous system in his fantastic system of physiology. Thus Descartes conceives of the human being as a composite dual unity, an automaton animated by a spiritual master, quite like the relationship between a rabbi and his golem—only now the rabbi is internalized as the rational soul, which gives direction to the robot-like physical body to which it is somehow connected. (As is well known, the pineal gland was identified by Descartes as the necessary connector between his two supposed substances.)

After Descartes, the question of what was animate and what was not, what was alive and what was not became an important question as the skill of automaton-makers continued to improve. Their efforts reached their apogee in the form of the famous mechanical duck produced by Jacques Vaucanson in 1742. This duck apparently could do anything a real duck could do, including eating some corn, digesting it and finally defecating onto a silver platter that was passed around to the astonishment of the audiences to whom the duck was displayed. It was only in the next epistemic shift, ushering in the modern period at the turn of the nineteenth century, that the eighteenth-century optimism about and enthusiasm for automata turned, as Reilly argues, to a sense of uncanniness, and a realization that with the advent of such advances in human artifice, a deeply problematic genie had been let out of the bottle.

Faust

In Act II, Scene II of the second part of Goethe's *Faust,* set in the laboratory of that ambiguous medieval figure whose quest for knowledge involves him in a pact with the Devil, Goethe reflects back from the Enlightenment era on the world of alchemy in which Faust flourished. In this scene, Faust's famulus—or lab assistant—Wagner is engaged in his arcane labor when Mephistopheles enters and greets him. Wagner warns him to be silent:

WAGNER: Don't speak or even breathe, though, I implore!
    Achieved is soon a glorious undertaking.
MEPHISTOPHELES: [more softly] What is it then?
WAGNER: [more softly]. A man is in the making!
MEPHISTOPHELES: A man? And, pray, what lovesick pair
    Have you shut in the chimney-flue?
WAGNER: May God forbid! Begetting, as men used to do,
    Both vain and senseless we declare.
    The tender point whence life used to begin,
    The gracious outward urgence from within,
    To take and give, to have its likeness known,
    Near and remote alike to make its own-
    All that has lost its former dignity.
    Whereas delighted with it still the beast may be,
    A man with his great gifts must henceforth win
    A higher, even higher origin. (1932, 205–6)

With that, the experiment reaches its climax:

WAGNER: It rises, flashes, gathers on;
    A moment, and the deed is done
    A great design at first seems mad; but we
    Henceforth will laugh at chance in procreation,
    And such a brain this is to think transcendently
    Will be a thinker's own creation. (206)

Here Wagner clearly enunciates the belief that of the two possible modes of creation, the non-sexual far surpasses the sexual one, which is the one Mephistopheles at first imagines when Wagner talks of "making a man." While sexual procreation may involve tender impulses of give and take, it is subject to chance, and not rational human intention, which only artificial reproduction can accomplish.

The newly formed ethereal homunculus, inside the vial in which he has been conjured, now greets Wagner as his father, and goes on to attend the Walpurgis Night and ends his short life by breaking his glass vial and merging with the waters of the sea. It is evident from the conversation surrounding Wagner's experiment that Goethe is struggling with the relationship between sexual begetting and the "higher" aims of humans as rational beings. A poet like Goethe does not literally create a homunculus, but he does produce a work, such as *Faust* itself, that, as a symbolic, cultural creation will achieve immortality by being transmitted across generations. Most of us neither know nor care about Goethe's actual biological descendants (in fact his grandson died childless, so Goethe left no continuing biological lineage). But his Faust has an immortal existence across generations. It is this quite real immortality that symbolic creations can achieve that is one of the sources of their perceived superiority to biological beings, who die and decay. The drawback is that, unlike human beings, they are not alive. An actor playing Faust on stage can make that fictional character "come alive," but in the end it is still only a simulacrum, not the real thing as both Plato and Aristotle would aver.

Erasmus Darwin

Erasmus Darwin, Charles Darwin's grandfather, took the diametrically opposite view from that expressed by Goethe's Wagner. In his paean to sexual love in Canto II of his poem *The Temple of Nature* (1804), Darwin is dismissive of both Cartesian automata and alchemical fantasies about homunculi. Himself a great naturalist (who fathered at least fourteen children, thus practicing what he preached), in this work he is unstinting in his praise of sexual reproduction and in his deprecation of other methods of making "life":

> Self-moving Engines by unbending springs
> May walk on earth, or flap their mimic wings;
> In tubes of glass mercurial columns rise,
> Or sink, obedient to the incumbent skies;
> Or, as they touch the figured scale, repeat
> The nice gradations of circumfluent heat.
> But REPRODUCTION, when the perfect Elf
> Forms from fine glands another like itself,
> Gives the true character of life and sense
> And parts the organic from the chemic Ens.

For Erasmus Darwin, then, the organic world and its gift to us of sexual reproduction transcend mere chemistry (and alchemy) as well as the simulated procreation embodied in the automaton. This valuation of sexually produced organic life over mechanically or chemically conjured simulacra thereof might well be understood to coincide with the rise of Romanticism, as a movement linked with apprehension about the rapid advance of industrialization, mechanization, and the dehumanization of work that the new modes of production seemed to threaten. In this new age, workers either themselves became no better than automata or were actually replaced by automata, which are generally cheaper and thus preferable for factory owners. Thus was born the trope of human sexual, romantic, and familial love as the one antidote to the attack on humanity that, to many minds, the industrial and technological revolutions represented. This new frame of mind, in which optimism regarding technological "progress" is replaced with misgivings, is most aptly expressed in the immortal literary masterpiece penned by Mary Shelley.

Frankenstein

Contemporaneously with Goethe and his relatively favorable depiction of the homunculus, in 1816, Dr. Victor Frankenstein arrives on the cultural scene to inaugurate, or at least epitomize, the modern dread of the artificial man who, far from resembling Goethe's ethereal homunculus, or the Maharal's heroic protector golem, turns out to be a homicidal maniac. It is perhaps worth noting that Erasmus Darwin, that champion of erotic love and sexual reproduction, whom Mary Shelley knew through her father William Godwin, is actually mentioned in the very first sentence of the preface of her novel *Frankenstein, or the Modern Prometheus*: "The event on which this fiction is founded has been supposed by Dr. Darwin and some of the physiological writings of Germany, as not of possible occurrence" (Shelley [1818] 2012).

Presumably she is referring to Erasmus Darwin in his capacity as an authority on the question of the mutability of species in the course of the process of evolution—the theory he played a critical role in enunciating long before his famous descendant (along both cultural and genetic channels), Charles, provided the key to understanding its operation by means of natural selection. But perhaps she meant to remind us of the elder Darwin's appreciation of sexual reproduction and devaluation of any attempt to circumvent or outdo it by artificial means. Certainly her novel illustrates the folly of attempting to do so.

Victor Frankenstein begins his own narrative (as told to Captain Robert Walton, who relays it in letters to his sister Margaret Saville) with a statement indicating his pride in his biological genealogy: "I am by birth a Genevese [native of Geneva] and my family is one of the most distinguished of that republic. My ancestors had been for many years counsellors and syndics; and my father had filled several public situations with honour and reputation" (86). To a large degree self-educated in the library of his free-thinking parents, he becomes fascinated with the writings of the alchemists whose books he finds there: Agrippa, Albertus Magnus, and of course his fellow Swiss Paracelsus. Only upon going to Ingolstadt University does he learn that alchemy has been rendered obsolete and replaced by natural philosophy, embodying the new scientific spirit of his age. He masters the latter, but we must assume that he does so in the service of the project of the former to create life, only now with the possibility of actually doing so, thanks to the great advances science has made. He undertakes to create a living human, and succeeds in doing so, using body parts taken from charnel houses which he shapes into a being eight feet tall and animates by a process he refuses to reveal, for the excellent reason that it has unleashed on him, and potentially on the world, unmitigated misfortune and disaster. His reaction to the creature he has brought to life is horror and revulsion at the creature's monstrous appearance—a rejection by his maker/"parent" that eventually turns the creature into Frankenstein's mortal enemy. As Peter Rudnytsky (personal communication) points out, it is surely not immaterial in understanding Mary Shelley's motives, in creating this being turned rageful by parental rejection, that her own mother, Mary Wollstonecraft, died in agony of septicemia after giving birth to her.

What are Frankenstein's motives in creating an artificial man? When he realizes that he has actually done it, he tells us that life and death appeared to me as ideal bounds, which I should first break through and pour a torrent of light into our dark world. A new species would bless me as its creator and source; many happy and excellent natures would owe their being to me. No father could claim the gratitude of his child as I should deserve their's [sic]. Pursuing these reflections, I thought that if I could bestow animation upon lifeless matter, I might in process of time (although I now found it impossible) renew life where death had apparently devoted the body to corruption. (110)

In this passage, two different motives are intermingled: the humanitarian aim of freeing people from the curse of death, thus bringing light into the dark world; and the more self-centered aim of "fathering" a line of descendants in a "new species," artificially produced and presumably reproduced, who would be forever grateful to him as the ancestor and founder of their kind. In this way, he puts himself in direct competition with his own father, who merely produced him in the ordinary genetic manner; and with the genetic genealogy of which both he and his father were so proud, but which he now aims to outdo by technological means.

His creature, meanwhile, who has fled and roamed the world, at length comes upon a hovel occupied by the De Lacey family, whose warmth and affection he envies. Observing their activities, the creature says:

I heard of the difference of the sexes; of the birth and growth of children, how the father doated [sic] on the smiles of the infant, and the lively sallies of the older child; how all the life and cares of the mother were wrapped up in the precious charge ....

But where were my friends and relations? No father had watched my infant days, no mother had blessed me with smiles and caresses. (199)

After being rebuffed in his attempt to enter this family circle, he becomes embittered and vows revenge on his creator. So begins the killing spree that will mark the rest of his career, in which he murders a number of people whom Victor Frankenstein holds dear, beginning with Victor's little brother William, and then William's beloved caretaker Justine (whom the creature frames and who is executed for William's murder), Victor's best friend Creval, and finally Victor's cousin and intended bride Elizabeth.

When the creature and Frankenstein once again encounter each other, the creature begs his creator to make him a female companion, just as repulsive as he is, but with whom he could find happiness and move to the wilds of South America. After extracting the creature's promise that he will leave Europe forever, Frankenstein sets about creating such a mate for his creature; but then he is overcome by second thoughts. First, he reasons, this new creature might reject the original creature because of his ugliness, and prefer a human partner, thus adding yet another rejection to his first creature's unhappy life and angering him still more. He then turns to another line of thought:

> Even if he were to leave Europe, and inhabit the deserts of the new world, yet one of the first results of those sympathies for which the daemon thirsted would be children, and a race of devils would be propagated upon the earth, who might make the very existence of the species of man a condition precarious and full of terror. Had I any right, for my own benefit, to inflict this curse upon everlasting generations? (255)

With these considerations in mind Frankenstein destroys the female creature he has been creating, and as he predicted incurs still further the murderous wrath of the original male creature. The latter takes his grisly revenge by strangling Victor's beloved cousin and bride on their wedding night, as a talionic response to Victor's destruction of his own intended mate. Thus both he and Victor are deprived of the possibility of progeny through marriage. In Victor's case, this means that neither his artificially created "species" nor any genetic children of his own will ever come into being. The antipathy of "culture" in the form of the artificial monster to "love" represented by the nuptial bed in which Elizabeth dies could hardly be more clearly enunciated than it is here. But here it is biological love that is valorized, and artificial reproduction that is seen as wrong—literally anti-life, that is, lethal.

In the conclusion of the tale, Dr. Frankenstein pursues his creature to the arctic region, intending to destroy him if he can catch him. But instead he dies onboard Captain Walton's ship, after first recounting his story. The creature finds him there, dead, grieves over his loss, and then flings himself into the ice floes to seek his own death. Thanks to Captain Walton's letters to his sister, the awful tale does not die with its two main protagonists, but is passed along to us, the readers, and has since undergone innumerable reincarnations, most notably on film. The influence and impact on Western culture of the figure of Frankenstein and his "monster" are beyond calculation (it is interesting to note that after the success of the film version, the name "Frankenstein" is more often associated in the popular mind with the monster himself than with his creator). Dr. Frankenstein and his creature have come to stand as signifiers (as does Faust) of the dangers implicit in the relentless pursuit of knowledge and technical mastery at any price. The latter, it is given to understand, will eventually stifle those desirable qualities of love, affection, and familial amity that should ideally accompany and grow out of the sexual mode of reproduction in marriage.

As Elissa Marder points out, the world of *Frankenstein* is one from which motherhood is all but erased (another echo of Mary Shelley's own sad history):

> The most striking feature of *Frankenstein* is that it attempts to conceive of an entirely immaculate conception, one in which there is no place for the mother or her body. But the figure of the mother, along with the attendant worries of the relationship between maternity, femininity, and desire, are doubly effaced in *Frankenstein*. The text provides us with a series of family units in which every mother is absent, either entirely unaccounted for or dead. ([1818] 2012: 204–5)

Thus the careers of Victor and his creature are set in direct opposition to the world of sexual reproduction. The happy families of Victor's youth, and of the De Laceys, are contrasted with the isolation of the creature, and of Victor himself, both when he cuts off relations with his natal family while working on his creature and as he ends up, with his mother dead and his brother, best friend, father, and bride all murdered, dying alone in a frozen lifeless world represented by the arctic wilderness. One cannot, as I have said, overlook the coinciding of this cautionary tale, which found such a receptive audience, with the rise of the modern technological-industrial world system, and the fear that it has already suffocated meaningful human relations just as Frankenstein's monster did his victims. These meaningful human relations take the form either of romantic (sexual) love between men and women or of the sort of amity that family relations, made flesh by means of marital copulation and maternal nurture, are supposed to embody.

R.U.R

I will skip over further nineteenth-century literary examples of the artificial creation or simulation of life, such as the enchanting female doll Olimpia in E. T. A. Hoffman's tale "The Sandman" (1816), another story that found further representation in art, specifically in the theater, the ballet, and the opera, or the enduring children's story of the carved wooden puppet Pinocchio, who eventually becomes a real boy. Instead, I will turn finally to a consideration of the work that, though probably less known in its original literary form than *Frankenstein*, at least to Anglophone readers, has had a cultural impact that equals or surpasses that of Mary Shelley's creation, namely the play *R.U.R.* by the Czech writer Karel Čapek. Written in 1920, this work, the title of which stands for "Rossum's Universal Robots" (the name of a fictional company that produces automated workers), bequeathed to the world both the idea and the name of automata (actually androids, in modern terminology) that would relieve humans of the need to perform onerous labor by being designed to carry out this work mindlessly. The word "robot" is a play on a Czech word for someone who performs onerous and menial labor. Čapek denied that he was at all inspired by the idea of the golem, whom his robots resemble in being mindless artificial humans who perform work that frees their masters from having to do it. But the fact that the most famous legend of the golem takes place in Čapek's own city of Prague makes one at least wonder whether the similarity is wholly coincidental (though of course the Prague golem was a benevolent creature). Reading *R.U.R.* today creates a very uncanny impression, since it anticipates such a wealth of the themes and ideas that have played a major role in the cultural imagination as well as in the lived reality of our times.

The play, which portrays with rather light-hearted insouciance the destruction of the entire human race by the products of its own technological genius, comprises a prologue and three acts. The prologue takes place, as does the rest of the play, on a remote island on which is located the vast industrial enterprise called "Rossum's Universal Robots," a factory that produces artificial workers and supplies them to Europe as cheap labor. The robots were first invented by an isolated eccentric scientist named Rossum, whose name suggests the Czech word for "Reason." His son and successor turned the father's invention into a mass-produced industrial commodity. Now the company is headed by Harry Domin (whose name intentionally recalls the Latin *dominus*, "master"). As the play opens, a ship arrives carrying 21-year-old Helena Glory, the beautiful daughter of the president of the Republic, who has come with the express humanitarian purpose of liberating the oppressed robots, but ends the prologue by wordlessly assenting to a marriage proposal from Domin.

In the course of their conversation leading up to Domin's proposal, we learn the history of the invention of the robot. Old Rossum, it seems, wrote in his journal one day that he had discovered another way of organizing living matter from the one Nature has employed, one that is simpler, more moldable, and faster.

> DOMIN: Imagine, Miss Glory, that he wrote these lofty words about some phlegm of a colloidal jelly that not even a dog would eat. Imagine him sitting over a test tube and thinking how the whole tree of life would grow out of it .... Man made from a different matter than we are. Miss Glory, that was a tremendous moment. ([1920] 2004: 6)

With this new form of organic life, which he could have molded into anything—"a jellyfish with a Socratic brain or a one-hundred-fifty foot worm" (7)—old Rossum set about creating an ordinary vertebrate. After producing something that looked like a mutant calf and died after a few days, he then tried to create a human:

> DOMIN: But do you know what isn't in the papers? (*He taps his forehead.*) That old Rossum was a raving lunatic. That's a fact, Miss Glory, but keep it to yourself. That old eccentric actually wanted to make *people*.
> HELENA: But you *do* make people!
> DOMIN: More or less, Miss Glory. But old Rossum meant that literally. You see, he wanted to somehow scientifically dethrone

God. He was a frightful materialist and did everything on that account. For him the question was to prove that God was unnecessary. (6, emphasis in original)

This passage reminds us that God was conspicuously absent in *Frankenstein*. The issue in that work did not relate to the question of whether humans should or should not try to "play God," or whether technology might dispose of the realm of the divine altogether. Likewise Erasmus Darwin's account of reproduction in the animal world was written in praise of nature, not God, and when it called upon the Greek gods rather than the Christian one, it did so in a poetic rather than any literal-minded way. But in Čapek's play, we may infer that the author attributes the ultimate demise of humanity that ends the play to an original act of hubris on the part of Old Man "Reason" that offends the Almighty (just as Jove reacted when a human tried to kill him when he paid a visit to earth during the degenerate Age of Iron).

When Domin tells Helena that everything in the robots is an exact replica of the human anatomy down to the "superfluous" parts, such as the appendix, and also the sexual organs, she tries to respond but is at a loss for words:

HELENA: But after all those—those after all …
DOMIN: Are not superfluous, I know. But if people were going to be produced artificially, then it was not—hmm—in any way necessary—
HELENA: I understand. (8)

Domin then goes on to relate how the younger Rossum took a very different approach to the production of artificial life from that of his father. Whereas old Rossum was "well suited to the university, but … had no sense of factory production," young Rossum was of the new age and saw that human anatomy could be vastly improved by a good engineer. He eliminated all human needs from the design of the robots, because, as Domin points out, they are to be machines, and "a gasoline engine doesn't need tassels and ornaments" (9). After all, the best worker is not the one who possesses honesty or dedication, as Helena naively suggests, but rather the cheapest. In order to perfect a worker with minimal needs, young Rossum

chucked everything not directly related to work, and in doing so he pretty much discarded the human being and created the Robot. My dear Miss Glory, Robots are not people. They are mechanically more perfect than we are, but they have no soul. Oh, Miss Glory, the creation of an engineer is technically more refined than the product of nature.
HELENA: It is said that man is the creation of God.
DOMIN: So much the worse. God had no grasp of modern technology. Would you believe that the late young Rossum assumed the role of God? (9)

There is an interval of ten years between the time of the prologue, at the end of which we witness Domin's business-like "courtship" of Helena, and Act I. In the interim, the continuing introduction of robots into the world has wrought havoc: first the human workers have rebelled over their loss of jobs to robots, and then the governments began to arm the robots to protect themselves, and thus turn them into fighting machines for the army. Predictably, the robots finally themselves rebel and turn against the humans. Domin, Helena, and the other human directors of R.U.R. are isolated on their island and, as Act I begins, have not heard anything from the mainland for a week. The men try to keep any intimation of impending danger away from Helena, but they have prepared a getaway boat for themselves as they await what they hope will be the next ship bringing relief. Meanwhile, Helena, unaware that there really is a revolt of the robots underway in Europe, tells her husband Domin that her aim in coming to the island was "to instigate a revolt among your abominable Robots" (19). Domin replies, "Haha, Miss Glory, good luck to you! A revolt among the Robots! You'd have better luck instigating a revolt among nuts and bolts than among our Robots!" (30). Helena responds to him by accusing him of never having had any doubts or anxiety, even when his plans have backfired. When Domin asks her what has backfired, she reminds him of the revolt of the workers, the arming of the robots, and the resulting terrible wars. To which Domin replies, in an eerily prescient way, "We predicted that, Helena. You see, this is a transition to a new system" (30). She begs him to shut down the production of robots for the good of humanity, but he refuses to listen.

However, while Helena is moved by sympathy and humanitarian benevolence toward the oppressed robots, her own overriding anxiety is that she herself has not had any children, despite ten years of marriage to Domin. Not only has she not gotten pregnant but, it seems, all of humanity has become sterile since the rise of the robots, who have freed them from the necessity of labor. We thus learn that, as in *Frankenstein*, the making of artificial humans, or androids, is somehow in direct complementary opposition to sexual reproduction, which its success cancels out. In Shelley's novel, it is only Frankenstein and his kin who are affected; but in Čapek's play, it is all of humanity. Helena's maid, Nana, who is the voice of the common sense of the people in the play, tells her that her infertility is a punishment from God for the blasphemous impiety of wanting to be like him. Helena then asks the company builder, Alquist, the only one of the directors with any sense, why humans have stopped being born, and he tells her it is

> because human labor has become unnecessary, because suffering has become unnecessary, because man needs nothing, nothing, nothing but to enjoy—Oh cursed paradise, this …. Helena, there is nothing more terrible than giving people paradise on earth! Why have women stopped giving birth? Because the whole world has become Domin's Sodom! … Hurry, hurry, step right up and enjoy your carnal passions! And you expect women to have children by such men? Helena, to men who are superfluous women will not bear children! (35)

The reference to Sodom reminds us of a devalued and criminalized kind of non-reproductive sex. And here too we seem to be back in the city of Amathus, with its shameless daughters (and feckless sons), and with Alquist voicing the horrified views of Pygmalion. The rise of the robots has enabled humans to dispense with marriage and reproduction, and use their sexuality only for personal enjoyment. This, as we saw, is an affront to Venus, the goddess of love for whom sex is a divine gift, and whom Erasmus Darwin celebrates in his poem, itself in an echo of the magnificent paean to Venus with which Lucretius began his book *The Nature of Things* (2007).

We are also reminded of the difference enunciated by Freud in "On Narcissism" between the different and often conflicting aspects of human sexuality:

The individual does actually carry on a twofold existence: one to serve his own purposes and the other as a link in a chain, which he serves against his will, or at least involuntarily. The individual himself regards sexuality as one of his own ends; whereas from another point of view he is an appendage of his germ-plasm [DNA], at whose disposal he puts his energies in return for a bonus of pleasure. He is the mortal vehicle of a (possibly) immortal substance—like the inheritor of an entailed property, who is only the holder of an estate which survives him. The separation of the sexual instincts from the ego-instincts would simply reflect this twofold function of the individual. (1914, 78)

Meanwhile, back on the island, we learn that Dr. Gall, the head of the physiological and research division of R.U.R., has given more brains to some of the robots in secret unauthorized experiments. When one of them, Radius, has a fit of rage and expresses his wish to be a master of people rather than the other way around, Dr. Gall is called in to render a diagnosis. He is baffled:

HELENA: What was it?
DR. GALL: God only knows. Defiance, rage, revolt—I haven't a clue.
HELENA: Doctor, does Radius have a soul?
DR. GALL: I don't know. He's got something nasty. (Čapek [1920] 2004: 38)

Helena then asks Dr. Gall to answer her question about why humanity has become sterile. He replies,

DR. GALL: Because Robots are being made. Because there is a surplus of labor power. Because man is virtually an anachronism. Why it's just as though—bah!
HELENA: Go on.
DR. GALL: Just as though nature were offended by the production of Robots.
HELENA: Gall, what will happen to people?
DR. GALL: Nothing. There's nothing we can do against the force of nature.
HELENA: Why doesn't Domin cut back—

DR. GALL: Forgive me, but Domin has his own ideas. People who have ideas should not be allowed to have an influence on affairs of this world. (39)

Taking matters into her own hands, Helena burns the papers containing the plans for producing robots. She thus interrupts the chain of the reproduction of robots by literally destroying the "instructions," in this case symbolic ones (rather than genetic ones) that enable their perpetuation over generations. Not aware of this, the directors of R.U.R. have learned that the robots of Le Havre have created a union of all robots and invited the robots of the world to join them, in a parody of the *Communist Manifesto*, and are exhorting their comrades to exterminate the human race and seize power for themselves. Meanwhile, it starts to become clear that the boat that has arrived carries not relief for the humans but armed robots.

In Act Two, besieged inside the main office of R.U.R. by vast numbers of rebellious robots, the directors squabble among themselves and try to imagine a plan to save themselves. Alquist denounces Domin and the Rossums for creating robots in the first place, but Domin is unrepentant. Gall confesses that he is at fault, since in his last experiments he began giving the rudiments of a soul to the robots, which led to their rebellion. Together, they decide that the only way to save themselves is to trade the instructions for the replication of robots to the robots themselves, in exchange for their own freedom. Robots have all been designed so as to last only twenty years, after which they run down and are destroyed in a "stamping-mill"; and they know that without the plans for their own construction, they will be unable to reproduce and will die out. The directors all urge Domin to get the plans and negotiate with the robots, who vastly outnumber them, but he soon discovers that the plans have been destroyed, and no one among the directors remembers exactly how robots are produced. Helena confesses to burning the instructions, to which Domin reacts surprisingly philosophically. Robots, led by Radius, suddenly burst in and end Act Two by killing all the humans except for Alquist, whom they spare because, like them, being a builder, he does physical work with his hands.

Act Three is set after the debacle, with Alquist, the sole surviving human left on earth, trying desperately at the behest of despondent robots to rediscover the formula for constructing them. Radius confronts him in his laboratory:

RADIUS: Sir, the machines cannot work. We cannot reproduce.
ALQUIST: Call in people.
RADIUS: There are no people.
ALQUIST: Only people can reproduce life. Don't waste my time. (73)

Later, more robots including their ruler, Damon, renew their demands:

FOURTH ROBOT: We will die out if you do not help us multiply.
ALQUIST: Oh, just go away! You things, you slaves, just how on earth do you expect to multiply? If you want to live, then mate like animals!
    ....
DAMON: We will give birth by machine. We will build a thousand steam-powered mothers. From them will pour forth a river of life. Nothing but life! Nothing but Robots! (75)

The robots assert that they have become beings with souls, that something gets into them and thoughts come to them.

THIRD ROBOT: Hear us, oh, hear us! People are our fathers! The voice that cries out that you want to live; the voice that complains; the voice that reasons; the voice that speaks of eternity—that is their voice! (75)

As Alquist tries to operate on Damon in an unsuccessful effort to reconstruct the secret of how they are made, two of the robots Dr. Gall has inspired with a soul appear on the scene. One is a male called Primus, the other a female designed to look exactly like Helena. They begin to act suspiciously like two humans in love. Alquist pretends to want to dissect Primus, to discover by this ruse whether the robot Helena, unlike most robots, is willing to intervene and sacrifice herself for her lover. When she volunteers to do so he reverses the procedure and lets Primus live. Convinced of the genuineness of their love, he pushes them out saying "Go Adam, Go, Eve—be a wife to Primus. Be a husband to Helena,

Primus" (84). Then he closes the play with a rapturous monologue in which he quotes the passage in Genesis about God creating Adam and Eve on the sixth day, telling them to be fruitful and multiply.

> Rossum, Fabry [the technical director of R.U.R.], Gall, great inventors, what did you ever invent that was great when compared to that girl, to that boy, to this first couple who have discovered love, tears, beloved laughter, the love of husband and wife? O nature, nature, life will not perish! ... Only you, love, will blossom on this rubbish heap and commit the seed of life to the winds. (84)

In the 1922 New York Theatre Guild production of *R.U.R.*, the director added a final tableau, not called for in Čapek's script, in which Primus and Helena are discovered standing in front of a pleasant little cottage holding their new infant. Most critics have scorned this as sentimental tripe, but it does seem in keeping with the tenor of Alquist's final speech, and probably Čapek's slim optimistic hope that the robot apocalypse would not be the end of all life (or of life worth living) and that human sexual reproduction and its attendant benign and life-affirming affects would somehow continue. We are a far cry here from the genetic program as one of inherent conflict and selfishness; it has been transfigured to the one source of human goodness in the form of love.

Conclusion

R.U.R. seems to foreshadow—and skewer—a great many of the phenomena that would dominate the twentieth century: capitalism, communism, industrialism, slave labor, the class divide, utopian totalitarianism, technocratic hubris, the corporate devaluation of human life, mechanized warfare, and many others besides. Two main lines of descent can be traced from its seminal themes. One of these is in the realm of the imagination: here one thinks of such cinematic elaborations on the theme of artificial or simulated life and intelligence as Blade Runner, 2001: A Space Odyssey, or that more recent entry into the field, Ex Machina, in which the intelligent robot able to pass the Turing test takes the form of a beautiful young women designed to be capable of copulation (though whether she can reproduce is left to the viewer's imagination).

The other line of descent is the development of actual technological ways to produce living beings, including humans, that bypass copulation. One may further divide this category into two, the wet and the dry. The wet forms involve creating new life through gestation, but with artificial insemination, in vitro fertilization, cloning, or some other new reproductive technology substituting itself for the sexual act. The dry form involves trying to make human-like beings out of inorganic matter, programming them to act like humans, and then claiming that there really is no important difference between them and ordinary humans begotten by sexual means. This category would embrace the thriving scientific fields of robotics, artificial intelligence, and the futurists' world of high-tech cyborgs.

I have shown in this chapter that this quest is not new; but that what is different now is that we actually have the technology to accomplish it and that this is yet one other example of the universal attempt of culture to eliminate its debt to nature, and undo the scandal (from culture's viewpoint) that we cannot make new versions of ourselves except in the way other animals do it. This problem, faced by any human society, is an inevitable consequence of the dual inheritance that is our unique system of reproduction.

Having now examined some ways in which the fact of dual inheritance and the conflicts inherent in it have found expression in Western culture, I turn my attention in the final section to how dual inheritance theory can help illuminate some of the central and lasting concerns of psychoanalytic theory and practice. I begin with a consideration of the phenomenon of incest avoidance, and turn next to the question of whether sexuality is a biological given or is culturally constructed; and I conclude with an investigation into the question why talking has therapeutic value as psychoanalytic practice assumes and demonstrates.

PART III

Our Two-Track Minds: A Dual Inheritance Perspective on Some Classic Psychoanalytic Issues

7

Incest Avoidance: Oedipal and Pre-Oedipal, Natural and Cultural

The prohibition of incest and the aversion to it which in some form or another are features of every human society, are continuing objects of fascination in psychoanalysis, anthropology, evolutionary biology and psychology, and many other fields, and the range of perspectives and the literature devoted to it are considerable. Here I limit myself to clarifying how psychoanalytic ideas regarding the Oedipal and pre-Oedipal dynamics that produce a subjectively felt aversion to incest can be understood in the light of recent trends in anthropological thinking about different kinds of incest. More specifically, my argument is about the relationship between aspects of human behavior that can be explained as conferring a Darwinian reproductive advantage and those that seem not to be determined by any gain in biological fitness from an evolutionary point of view; and between those aspects of human life that seem to be determined at least in part by an evolved genetic predisposition and those that appear to be largely or wholly cultural in their determination. I will not address such important topics as the causes and consequences of consummated incest, the treatment of incest victims, and other matters of vital interest to psychoanalysts, but will confine myself to a theoretical investigation of why most people refrain from committing incest—not only because there is an explicit prohibition against it, but because the idea in itself arouses an aversive reaction ranging from indifference to disgust, moral outrage, horror, and an indefinable sense of ineffable "wrongness."

What Is Incest?

Incest is generally taken to mean sexual relations between people related by kinship. Societies vary, however, in how inclusive that term may be. In almost every society, the strictest regulation is against sex between first-degree relatives: siblings, parents, and children. But whether cousins of various degrees are eligible or forbidden as sexual partners is far more culturally variable, and while some societies deem first-cousin sexual unions incestuous, others consider them the preferred form of marriage. In unilineal societies, distant relatives by a genealogical reckoning, but who belong to the same descent group—moiety, clan, or lineage—may be off-limits as sexual partners, depending on whether they are related through the mother or the father, while much closer genealogical relatives, whose connection is through the other parent, may be permitted as sexual partners or spouses. In short, socially defined incest prohibitions do not necessarily line up neatly with biological relatedness. Nonetheless, we can say in general that incest is widely understood to be a matter of sex between relatives, however these are socially defined, and that the idea of "relatives" carries an implication of real genetic relatedness, even when this is not strictly speaking the case.

In contemporary society, some sexual unions that do not involve genuine genealogical relatives are also considered incestuous. The most notable among these are relations between step-parents and step-children. In these cases, it is the social role, and the responsibilities and norms that go with it, that override the consideration of real biological relatedness. A step-father is expected to observe the same boundaries on physical intimacy with a step-daughter as a biological father would in relation to a daughter, although the two are not biologically related. A particularly intriguing problem is the question of siblings-in-law: norms and legal jurisdictions vary in the extent to which sex between these "relatives in law" is considered incest. I will devote further attention to these phenomena in a later section of this chapter.

While some would maintain that only evolutionary considerations, or only cultural considerations, can account for the avoidance of incest in humans, it seems more plausible to posit that prohibiting incest, at least among first-degree relatives, confers a biological advantage that accounts both for its universality and its close connection to actual genealogical relatedness, while at the same time recognizing that social norms, embodied in symbolic form as cultural rules and values, can expand the range of those considered out of bounds as sexual partners in a variety of ways that, as in the case of step-parents or siblings-in-law, pertain even to people who are not genealogical relatives at all. It would follow that incest prohibitions, and the felt aversion that leads to the avoidance of incestuous sexual objects, are (like most, if not all, human phenomena) composites of biological and cultural factors in their formation. It is, however, no easy matter to tease out the contributions and interactions of what we call "biological" and "cultural" factors in human life. My effort here will be to clarify our thinking about the intersection of biological and cultural factors as these are conceived of in dual inheritance theory, and to demonstrate, applying this model to the case of incest, how it leads to insights into psychoanalytic understandings of the dynamics of incest avoidance.

Dual Inheritance Models of Human Phenomena

Among the most important contributions to dual inheritance theory is that of Richerson and Boyd when they hypothesize that

> people are endowed with two sets of innate predispositions, or "social instincts." The first is a set of ancient instincts that we share with our primate ancestors ... shaped by the familiar evolutionary processes of kin selection and reciprocity, enabling humans to have a complex family life ... The second is a set of "tribal" instincts that allow us to interact cooperatively with a larger, symbolically marked set of people, or tribe. (2005: 196–7)

"These new tribal instincts," they hold, "were superimposed [in the course of evolution] onto human psychology without eliminating those that favor friends and kin. Thus, there is an inherent conflict built into human social life. The tribal instincts that support identification and cooperation in large groups are often at odds with selfishness, nepotism, and face-to-face reciprocity" (215).

The tribal instincts to which they refer are largely supported by the cultural "road" of human evolution, which has favored altruism; shared symbolic systems such as language; rules for the conduct of human affairs, such as the regulation of sexual behavior, mating, and marriage; and the ability through the evolution of the pre-frontal cortex to inhibit impulses for action and to reflect on possible consequences of one's acts before deciding to carry them out—a process whereby biological evolution adapts to a culture-saturated niche. By contrast, the selfish and nepotistic instincts following the genetic "stream" are derived from our pre-human primate days and were designed by natural selection to maximize genetic reproductive advantage. In what remains the most ambitious attempt yet to integrate the perspectives of evolutionary theory, sociocultural theory, and psychoanalysis into a comprehensive biosocial account of incest, Fox (1980), building on the prescient insights of Chance ([1961] 2004, 1962), emphasized the importance of self-regulation, and how the expansion of cultural life provided the evolutionary milieu in which altruism, cooperation, and adaptive "ego functions" might evolve. And in what is the most comprehensive biosocial and psychoanalytic account of incest since Fox, Ingham and Spain (2005) have stressed the same point, linking the evolution of cortical self-control as well to the evolution of pair bonding. In modern humans, uniquely among primates (and indeed among most mammals), relatively stable pair bonds are integrated into a wider group affiliation, much as Richerson and Boyd would have it. In the human pair bond itself, sexual and affiliative impulses are amalgamated; in the wider "tribal" bonds, affiliation generally operates without overt sexuality. This raises the question, central to current psychoanalytic debates, whether attachment is affiliative, and becomes sexualized only in deviant or pathological situations (however frequent), or whether it starts out combining affiliation and sexuality, and separates these out only in the later course of development.

Is the Mother-Infant Bond Sexual or Not?

One of the most divisive issues in the current discussion about the biosocial foundations of incest avoidance is the nature of the early mother-child bond. Almost all in the debate agree that this first social relationship is crucial to individuals' eventual success in regulating their sexual life. Failures at this stage are widely seen as leading to the sexualization of later relationships, including incestuous relations with kin. The point of contention springs from the assumption that Freudian theory posits that incest taboos rein in or otherwise regulate originally incestuous strivings, an assumption based in turn on the supposition that the early mother-child bond is sexual in nature, so that what is being regulated are erotic impulses and fantasies that in the first instance are directed at an incestuous first-degree object. Thus, Erickson, who falls into the camp that views affiliative and sexual strivings as separate and in fact mutually exclusive, and attributes only the former to the mother-child relationship, writes:

> Oedipal psychology assumes that all social bonds are ultimately sexual. This assumption forced Freud to explain how sexual behaviors are directed away from kin. Childhood castration fears were evoked .... Later psychoanalytic writers ... argued or inferred that a nonsexual form of affiliation emerges between kin under normal developmental conditions ... Yet, these authors lacked an explanation of how non-sexual bonds could exist. We now know that nonsexual, or familial bonds, can exist because evolutionary pressures shaping kin-directed behaviors (altruism, attachment, incest avoidance) are significantly different from those shaping sexual behavior. (2000, 219–20)

In psychoanalytic circles, Suttie (1935) can be identified as one of the original godfathers of the idea that family bonds are non- or even anti-sexual, along with Ferenczi ([1933] 1949); the idea has been taken up and developed by various object relations and self-psychological thinkers.

By contrast, Ingham and Spain (2005) maintain that the integration of sexual into wider altruistic and affectionate ties and feelings in the prototypical romantic or mating pair bond is the great human evolutionary achievement, and that it is the successfully negotiated early mother-child union, with sexual stimulation and satisfaction undifferentiated from tender love and care, mutuality, dependency, and altruistic idealization, that lays the groundwork for successful adult unions. Conversely, it is failure in this first relationship that leads later to pathologies including incestuous acting out.

Although this issue remains highly controversial, I favor the Freudian theory, which I contend is at times oversimplified or misrepresented by its critics (I have argued this in greater detail elsewhere [Paul 2008]). It seems quite clear to me that Freud's intention was to argue, with his libido theory and especially his later theory of the life drive, that the force that binds us pleasurably to fellow human beings originates as an undifferentiated Eros containing all the sorts of attraction between people, including the sensual and the sexual. Only as development proceeds does Eros get separated into overtly sexual and "aim-inhibited" affectionate strands. I believe that the ideal prototypical mother-child relation includes sexual as well as nurturant and tender elements and that the "nurturant" substances (oxytocin and vasopressin) associated with tender care in childbirth and nursing are also essential elements in the complex cocktail of adult human sexual love. Most important, the "sex" we are talking about in the case of small children is not primarily genital, but is focused on looking, hearing, touching, and, most of all, oral stimulation, occurring mainly around feeding, and this is perfectly compatible with the kind of tender care and dependency that characterizes kinship affiliation.

The Oedipus complex, by contrast, is a phenomenon associated with the later ages of roughly four or five to seven (except in Kleinian theory), and involves phallic wishes toward the parent, coming after considerable development of cognitive and interpersonal capacities has occurred with maturation. Thus, the two issues—infantile attachment in the maternal dyad and Oedipal dynamics in a triadic context—are not mutually exclusive, as Erickson's statement, for example, would imply. It is completely possible to argue that "attachment" is "contrasexual," as many theorists do, and still accept that there is a later sexual love of the parent that, repressed or otherwise sublimated or transformed, is the basis for later successful love relations. As Ingham and Spain note,

According to Freud ... the Oedipus complex, by adolescence, ordinarily undergoes more or less complete destruction; what remains is not an unconscious desire for the parent as a sexual object but only traces of the parental image as model for the ideal mate. Putting the matter this way, it becomes more comprehensible how the early parent-child relation might serve as a foundation for love relations even though the parent becomes an object of sexual avoidance. (2005, 689)

I do not wish, however, to leave the impression that I insist that the Freudian theory is right and that others are wrong; on the contrary, my effort here is to forge a synthesis. To tip my hand somewhat, I will argue that these two different dynamics—pre-Oedipal and Oedipal—line up with the two different "social instincts" identified by Richerson and Boyd and, furthermore, that they also correspond to what, as I now intend to argue, are two distinct kinds of incest avoidance. Before getting to that, however, I must address the matter, central to discussions about incest, of the Westermarck hypothesis.

The Westermarck Hypothesis

The Westermarck hypothesis is named for the British Finnish theorist of the early twentieth century, Edward Westermarck, who first proposed it. This evolutionary explanation of the phenomenon of incest avoidance and the prevalence of the incest taboo lay fallow until resurrected late in the twentieth century to become a cornerstone of contemporary evolutionary thought. The hypothesis is that incest taboos, far from being in place to prevent what otherwise would be an impulse to pursue incestuous sexual relations, simply codify as cultural norms an evolved human disposition to feel a lack of sexual interest in close relatives. It has been a firm conviction of most evolutionary theorists since Darwin himself that "too close inbreeding" has deleterious effects on reproductive fitness, because it multiplies the chances that harmful recessive genes will express themselves. It is therefore assumed that all sexually reproducing animals must have evolved some mechanism to prevent or at least discourage such unions. And while it was believed until relatively late in the twentieth century that humans alone observe incest taboos and thus largely avoid too close inbreeding, it is now recognized that animals other than humans do in fact have ways to avoid first-degree matings to a great extent (though like all things in nature there are of course exceptions).

Westermarck's hypothesis about how incest avoidance is accomplished in humans is that people with whom a child shares domestic space during a critical period in earliest childhood become objects of later sexual indifference, due to the principle stating that "familiarity breeds contempt." It is presumed that close childhood association leads to later lack of sexual attraction through a kind of imprinting that results in a numbing effect on sexuality. This theory, once all but forgotten, was brought back to prominence almost single-handedly by the anthropologist Arthur Wolf (1995), who analyzed extensive data from his field site in Taiwan to show that arranged marriages, called "minor marriages," involving girls brought into an intended groom's household at a very early age and raised there had a higher rate of divorce, childlessness, and other presumed indicators of lack of sexual compatibility than marriages contracted in the more usual way involving grown individuals. Together with the reports by Spiro (1958) and Shepher (1983) that age-mates raised in Israeli kibbutzim did not engage in much or any sex and rarely married each other, Wolf's findings have provided the basis on which many evolutionary thinkers now confidently assert that first-degree incest avoidance is produced during the early attachment phase of child development through an evolved mechanism that in the normal course of things renders genetic parents and siblings sexually unattractive, but that can produce the same result with non-related others who happen to be raised in shared domestic space, as in the "minor marriages" reported by Wolf or the collective age sets of the classic kibbutz. (It is surprising to me how rarely it is noticed that the Westermarck hypothesis does not at all explain incest avoidance on the part of parents, who of course are not raised in propinquity with their children.)

Wolf is of the opinion that his findings "disprove" Freudian theory, because, he argues, Freud believed that people have an impulse to engage in incestuous sex but that this is held in check by the incest taboo. On the contrary, Wolf argues, incest avoidance is an evolved behavior pattern with a genetic basis: infants avoid those raised in close proximity; the cultural norm against incest, far from being the agency that "represses" it, is simply an expression of the distaste naturally arising from being raised in the same house as one's parents and siblings.

What this argument, repeated by many who follow Wolf (e.g., Erickson), overlooks is that the Freudian theory of repression predicts the same behavioral outcome as the Westermarck hypothesis, namely, sexual aversion to first-degree relatives. But instead of seeing this as based on early imprinting or some sort of undefined "numbing" of sexual interest, the Freudian view is that aversion is the result of an earlier deep love, the sexual dimension of which has been subjected to repression out of fear of the danger to which these impulses might lead. As Greenberg has noted,

> The differences between these theories [i.e., Westermarck's and Freud's] may not be as great as first thought, and it may be possible for us to reconcile them by noting that Westermarck addresses the behavioural aspects of incest avoidance, whereas Freud illuminates the psychological aspects; at a high level of generality, therefore, boredom and familiarity might be the outward manifestations of repression, which result in incest avoidance. (1993: 5)

(I have commented at greater length elsewhere [1987b, 1988, 1991] on the relationship between psychoanalytic theory and the Westermarck hypothesis.)

It should be noted too that Ingham and Spain are not persuaded by Wolf's case for Westermarck, arguing that even by his account, the majority of minor marriages do in fact seem to work, so the avoidance effect can't be all that strong. They favor a kin recognition mechanism whereby early association leaves olfactory memories of early household mates, and that this, rather than propinquity itself, is the mechanism that induces avoidance by enabling one to recognize close kin by their odor. This hypothesis has some support in current research, as these authors show; I refer the reader to their contribution to the debate.

The case that the behavioral pattern of Westermarck's "propinquity theory" operates according to Freudian dynamics is, in my view, greatly strengthened by the discovery of "genetic sexual attraction," or GSA (Greenberg 1993; Greenberg and Littlewood 1995). Identified only recently thanks to legal and social developments that have facilitated the reuniting of first-degree relatives separated through adoption, GSA involves the unexpected arousal of overpowering erotic attraction between the reunited pair, often leading to consummated incest. While the data are as yet scanty, they are well documented and lead to the conclusion that without the Westermarckian experience of childhood association, close relatives often experience something they themselves describe as "falling in love" in the true romantic and sexual sense. This would seem to indicate that the "indifference" normally felt toward close kin indeed may be a flip side of sexual excitement, as the Freudian theory would predict. As Erickson (2000) points out, Oedipus himself is an exemplar of the GSA phenomenon: he fell in love (or at least consummated a union) with his birth mother, after having been raised by adoptive parents and then reunited with her (p. 220).

Another example, indicating that the Westermarck phenomenon might have been noticed in biblical times, is the injunction against incest with a man's sister in Leviticus 18:9: "Do not have sexual relations with your sister, either your father's daughter or your mother's daughter, *whether she was born in the same home or elsewhere*" (my emphasis). The italicized phrase suggests that the writer of Leviticus was aware that it makes a difference whether siblings are raised together or apart and, we might also infer, that the temptation to sibling incest might indeed be more acute when siblings are born and raised in separate homes. But while I am prepared to agree that close association in childhood plays a role in producing subjective incest aversion, I need to stress again the difference between the early attachment or "oral" phase, to which some writers ascribe the aversion, and the Oedipal phase. The dangers posed in these two situations are different and lead to two different kinds of incest avoidance: one Oedipal and one distinctively pre-Oedipal.

Incest of the Second Type

The great anthropologist Claude Lévi-Strauss ([1949] 1969) did not agree that the incest taboo has a biological dimension; he held instead that it represents the intrusion of cultural norms into the otherwise biological phenomenon of reproduction. His explanation for its existence as a universal in human society thus involves a social rather than selfish reproductive benefit. According to him, the incest taboo, or incest avoidance, is a way of ensuring that people marry outside the nuclear family, thus extending the range of social alliances among individuals to encompass a wider group than just the nuclear family. For him, then, incest avoidance serves not the interests of the reproducing individual, as the Darwinian theory has it, but rather the collective interests of the society as a whole, which indeed it helps found and maintain by providing rules for the regulation of marriage exchanges. These, in turn, create the ties that bind families together into larger communities.

One of the most interesting recent contributions to the theory of incest in this tradition has been made by Françoise Héritier, a student of Lévi-Strauss and his successor in the Chair of Anthropology at the Collège de France. In a provocative book, Héritier (1999) makes the case for the widespread (though not universal) existence of belief in a kind of incest that does not involve relations between genealogical relatives at all, but that instead is based on the idea that sexual relations between a person and two other people who are first-degree relatives are also incestuous. She calls this "incest of the second type." According to this second notion of incest, if a man has sexual relations with his wife's sister, or if a woman has sex with a man and his father, for example, this is regarded as incest even though the people having sex are not at all biologically related. Examining marriage regulations and sexual norms from biblical and ancient times, through history and across a wide range of ethnographic cases, Héritier shows that a prohibition of this sort does in fact exist in many eras and places, and, moreover, that while not explicitly recognized, it characterizes the Western cultural system as well, though in a covert way.

It seems immediately clear that incest of this second type could not be related to the dangers of inbreeding, or to the Westermarck theory, or indeed to any discernible reproductive fitness advantage. A man is not related genealogically to his wife's sister, nor has he been raised under the same roof, and the same goes for a woman and her husband's father (or perhaps his son by a previous marriage, as in the case of Phaedra). Except in the very general sense that any rule that provides for the stability of a social group through the regulation of marriage and sexual relations thereby provides adaptive advantage to individuals in that society, it is hard to see what similarity there is between sleeping with a sibling and sleeping with a spouse's sibling that would have them both classed as violations of the prohibition against incest.

And yet evidence abounds for the effects of this strain of thought in our own culture since early times. For example, while Leviticus 18:16 warns "Do not have sexual relations with your brother's wife. This would dishonor your brother," we find in Leviticus 18:18, which is a listing of sexual unions forbidden as incestuous, the prohibition, "Do not take your wife's sister as a rival wife and have sexual relations with her while your wife is living."

The latter injunction figures in a historically momentous case involving incest of the second type: Henry VIII was married to

Catherine of Aragon, the widow of his deceased older brother, Arthur. When he fell in love with Anne Boleyn and wished to marry her, Henry put forward the theory that Catherine had failed to deliver a living heir to the throne as punishment for the fact that her marriage to Henry was incestuous and needed to be annulled, basing his claim on Leviticus 18:16. (It is interesting that this verse does not add an exemption in the case of the brother's death, as Leviticus 18:18 does in the case of a man and two sisters.) To make his case, however, Henry had to disregard Deuteronomy 25:5, which makes exactly the opposite claim: "If brothers are living together and one of them dies without a son, his widow must not marry outside the family. Her husband's brother shall take her and marry her and fulfill the duties of a brother-in-law to her." Finding the latter passage inconvenient for his purposes, Henry mobilized his scholars to prove that Deuteronomy was in fact not an authentic scriptural text, but a later interpolation. This case had wide ramifications both for the establishment of the Reformation in England and for the history of critical biblical scholarship.

In Gilbert and Sullivan's *Iolanthe*, the hero Strephon, who is half fairy and thus endowed with supernatural powers, enters Parliament for reasons typical of Gilbertian plots. The Queen of the Fairies announces that he will be able to accomplish there achievements impossible for mere mortals: "He shall prick that annual blister,/ Marriage with deceased wife's sister" (Gilbert 1882). Presumably Gilbert knew he could count on both understanding and a laugh with this couplet, which refers to the fact that throughout much of the eighteenth and nineteenth centuries, a controversy simmered in parliament as to whether it ought to be legal for a man to marry his wife's sister after his wife has died. (The matter was settled in 1907 in favor of such marriages.)

The plot of *Hamlet* is likewise propelled by the marriage of Gertrude, widow of the deceased Hamlet Senior, with her late husband's younger brother Claudius—a relationship that in the play is referred to as "incestuous." Even in *Oedipus Rex*, Héritier argues, the chorus implies that in addition to the incest involved in marrying his mother, Oedipus has committed incest of the second type by "plowing in the same field as his father"—thus causing his mother to commit incest of the second type as well.

According to Héritier, Woody Allen's affair with the adopted daughter of Mia Farrow, his (unwed) partner at the time, was tantamount to incest of the second type, since he had sex with a mother and her daughter (in addition, he also committed incest by violating the boundaries supposed to prevent sex between step-fathers and step-daughters). As Héritier argues, Allen's defense that none of the people in this case were related by either blood or marriage was neither here nor there—the odor of incest hung about the case nonetheless, since the people involved formed a social family of parents and child.

The principle involved in incest of the second type explains why sexual relations between a step-father and a step-daughter, for example, are considered incestuous even though there is no biological relationship between them: the step-daughter is a first-degree relative of the man's new sexual partner. Therefore, by copulating with his wife's (or partner's) daughter, the man is committing incest of the second type with a mother and her daughter. The Allen case is of course complicated by the fact that Mia Farrow's daughter Soon-Yi was adopted and not her biological offspring; in the more usual case, on which this one is a complex and quite ambiguous variation, the step-parent commits incest of the second type based on the real genetic relationship between the child and his or her biological parent.

Finally, the recent resurrection of the claim that Freud himself had an incestuous liaison with his wife's sister Minna, put forward by Maciejewski (2006, 2008), would constitute yet another case in which the covert paradigm of incest of the second type is evoked. Maciejewski argues that if any such thing occurred it would be incestuous by extension in fantasy from sibling incest. But I would argue that it seems more elegant to assume that the reason for labeling such a possible affair incestuous derives from the second type of incest. (I want to stress that I am not taking any position at all on the question of whether this happened, but only on the question of why we would deem such a union incestuous.)

The Identical and the Different

So then why should this second type of incest be forbidden, and why should it qualify as "incest"? Héritier's argument, following Lévi-Strauss's structuralist line of thinking, is that there is a widespread, perhaps universal, cultural logic according to which a fundamental distinction is posited between the identical and the different. Agreeing with Freud on this point, she claims that the reason this distinction is so common and so influential is that its original instantiation is the existence of the two sexes, the members of each of which are like each other and unlike those of the other sex. This primary duality has the consequence that it enables distinctively human cultural, symbolic thought, which, as structuralism holds, rests on the kind of binary oppositions found in the linguistic phenomenon of the phoneme. The first distinction we make, then, is important not only because it relates to sex, but because of what that difference exemplifies: the very idea of sameness as contrasted with difference. The latter allows us to create perceptions of separate things and people in the world and categories and ideas in our minds so that we can perform distinctively human thought. It is in this sense that we can follow Lacan ([1966] 1985), who in his own structuralist way, influenced by Lévi-Strauss ([1949] 1969) and Roman Jakobson (Jakobson and Halle [1956] 1971), suggests that infantile fantasies about the phallus and castration, based on the (erroneous but common) presumption that the two kinds of people are defined by the presence or absence of the phallus, are also the basis of the human capacity for signification because of its binary logic, and thus lie at the root of our cultural capacity.

In further exploring the basis for the conception of incest of the second type, Héritier argues that in a wide array of cultures in the ethnographic record there exists some version or other of a theory about the flow and circulation of life-giving substances, of which the most commonly employed are blood, semen, vaginal fluid, milk, marrow, and cerebrospinal fluid. Cultural systems around the world elaborate the notion that these substances either must or must not come into contact with each other for the orderly functioning of the social world. We can see this for ourselves in our own folk belief that people who are related by "blood" should not have sex or there will be dire consequences (i.e., there will be a monstrous birth as a result). It is clear in this example that "blood" is used here in a symbolic sense, since we know perfectly well that relatives do not share the same blood in any literal way.

The logic of incest of the second type, then, is that if a man sleeps with two sisters, for example, he causes the identical substances of the two sisters to come into forbidden and dangerous contact with each other through the intermediary of himself, the man who carries some trace of the substance of the first sister, which he transmits when he has sex with the second. The fundamental idea here is that sex should be an act between people whose substance is optimally "different," and thus that too much "sameness" of substance, whether or not literally true at the genetic level, is the essence of incest. Héritier shows on the basis of her fieldwork among the Samo people of Burkina Faso that this sort of logic is explicit in the local discourse, and she bolsters her argument with other strong ethnographic examples. She is of course well aware that the contact of identical substances may in some instances not be forbidden, but actively encouraged or even mandated. For example, in the case of the widespread practices of the levirate and sororate, according to which a man should marry his dead brother's wife, or a woman her dead husband's brother, the sibling is the ideal substitute for the deceased mate precisely *because* they share an identical substance. Indeed, we have just observed the conflict of these two beliefs within the same cultural milieu in the inconsistency between Leviticus and Deuteronomy on this subject.

For Héritier, each culture seeks to achieve a balance between the identical and the different, and different cultural systems represent different "grammars" in which the dialectic of the same and the different is elaborated, with an emphasis on one or another, perhaps, but never with the complete domination of one over the other. This is expressed not only in marriage rules, but also in ritual, where symbolic representations of the sexual substances, as well as these substances themselves, are often manipulated.

The Classical Psychoanalytic Perspective on the Incest Prohibition

Having outlined some of the anthropological context of current thinking about the incest problem, I turn first to a brief exposition of the classical Freudian theory of incest avoidance, and then, in the next section, to more recent developments in psychoanalysis. Why, according to Freud and those who have followed him, should sex, which is supposed to be pleasurable, evoke such negative responses when engaged in with a close relative one presumably loves?

According to Freud (1924), a passionate erotic attachment to a parent in early childhood has fallen victim to repression in the Oedipus complex, thought to occur around ages five through seven. In many if not most cases, "dissolution" of the Oedipus complex is incomplete, and unconscious fantasies continue to have a fixation on the Oedipal object, which has never been completely abandoned. Along with this impossible love comes guilt before the internalized angry parent or punitive superego, as well as shame at the failure to succeed in the Oedipal project. For Freud, the ideal outcome of the Oedipal phase should be the relinquishing of the Oedipal object in unconscious fantasy, paving the way via symbolization and displacement for the later search for an appropriate love object, enough like the abandoned object to arouse desire, but different enough not to arouse too much anxiety. This ideal is, of course, not always achieved.

Given the assumption of infantile sexuality, the infant's relationship with the good-enough mother who loves, feeds, and cares for it could be thought of as the original prototype of consummated incest (although the sexual dimension of consummation is of course not genital but oral and, in Freud's famous phrase, "polymorphously perverse"). Noting that mothers treat infants with elements drawn from their own love life—they kiss them, fondle them, give them the breast to suck, and so on—Freud (1905) proposes that far from being scandalous, this behavior prepares the child for a satisfying sexual life in adulthood, when the ideal of sexual love will be based on the suitably sublimated memory of the early maternal relationship. In subsequent developmental phases, this love of the mother (which in girls is said to be later redirected to the father) is, through the mechanism of retrospective re-imagining, transformed into phallic and finally genital terms in unconscious fantasy, for the first time in the Oedipal era, for the second during adolescence.

This positive dimension of the primal "incest" can appear in sublimated form either as the basis for more mature relationships, or as the unconscious allure of transgressive sex. The repression that is supposed to take place fits the paradigm of Freud's understanding of that process, described in *The Interpretation of Dreams*, whereby what was once wished for and associated with pleasure now leads instead to a negative attitude: "The fulfilment of these [infantile sexual] wishes would no longer generate an affect of pleasure but of unpleasure; and *it is precisely this transformation of affect which constitutes the essence of what we term 'repression'"* (1900: 604, emphasis in original).

As for why this reversal of affect occurs at this turning point in childhood, Freud (1924, 1925) proposed several hypotheses, including the one that today seems to me the most probable, namely, that this is an evolved developmental process like the falling out of milk teeth and their replacement by permanent teeth. Freud proposes, as psychological forces arrayed against earlier wishes, the emerging emotional psychological and social phenomena of disgust, shame, and morality.

For Freud, the culminating blow is delivered in the threat of castration as a talionic revenge for erotic wishes directed toward the Oedipal object (though with differing responses in boys, who fear it, and girls, who fear it has already happened). Castration anxiety (whether anticipatory or retrospective) restrains the Oedipal-age child from continuing on the path of the first incestuous love and leads to either dissolution or, more usually, repression of the Oedipus complex. (I must leave to one side any exploration of the important questions of homosexual developmental paths and the negative Oedipus complex.) While the original paternal prohibition pertains to the mother, our symbolic capacity allows us to extend the prohibition to siblings, cousins, and indeed to almost anyone.

While the status of the castration complex has become more contentious in recent years within psychoanalytic circles, the anthropologist in me has to mention that the ethnographic literature, replete as it is with instances of ritual genital surgery associated with the maturation of children, and of many other ritual and mythic or symbolic references to phallic gain and loss, provides ample grounds for assuming, as Freud (1916–17: 358–77) did, that this widely distributed fantasy syndrome has an evolved phylogenetic basis. The evolutionary reason for this, as I discussed in Chapter 3, would be the descent of *Homo sapiens* from a presumed primate ancestor whose social life was marked by male hierarchy and the related distinction between senior males with mating privileges and junior males whom the former excluded from mating. The ultimate feared sanction (short of death) in a struggle for reproductive advantage among males would be castration, that is, permanent exclusion from the possibility of reproducing.

As usual, Freud's theory seems to us to reflect a male bias. However, in *Inhibitions, Symptoms and Anxiety* (1926), Freud realized that his focus on castration as the feared punishment didn't really apply to women; therefore he introduced the danger of the loss of the object's love as an equivalent feared retaliation for Oedipal wishes as an alternative to castration.

Later Psychoanalytic Formulations

Much of the revision of Freud's work in the years following his original formulations has entailed filling in the wide gap in the developmental interval between birth and the Oedipal phases, that is, the pre-Oedipal phase, which Freud glimpsed, as from Mount Pisgah, only toward the end of his career (1931). We might generalize by saying that the Oedipus complex, insofar as it is still accepted as a definable entity by psychoanalysts (and this is by no means universal any longer), is now understood as the final act of a long drama that covers the whole period of dyadic relations between mother and infant, with its vicissitudes seen as influencing or determining the success or failure with which the Oedipal phase will be negotiated. The main story line in this period revolves around the emergence of a discrete self out of a primary encompassing dual unity, a process that is profoundly affected by the mother's ability, or lack of ability, to empathize with and be attuned to the infant's selfhood and to tolerate its differentness while not creating so great an emotional distance as to arouse excessive abandonment anxiety.

Without the original establishment of an unconditional affectionate attachment, it is thought, the necessary separation will not proceed without distortion that will compromise optimal maturation. Thinkers as different from one another as Ferenczi, Suttie, Klein, Balint, Winnicott, Fairbairn, Bowlby, Kohut, Mahler, Loewald, and Lacan, not to mention an array of more contemporary writers, have contributed to our understanding of the process of forming a self having good relations with acknowledged others (or not)—well before the melodrama of Oedipal passion, rivalry, and jealousy in a firmly established three-person field is even possible.

The developmental trajectory of humans is thus understood as moving away from an undifferentiated state into a differentiated one, in which the other is understood as really different from, as opposed to somehow identical with, oneself. The push toward autonomy is counterbalanced by the difficulty of making the break and mourning the loss of the symbiotic relationship with its implied security and cozy dependency. From this point of view, we might say that the incest barrier, warning against the allure of the pre-Oedipal mother, as opposed to the Oedipal mother, is the electric guardrail that prevents and counters the attraction of such tempting but ultimately futile backsliding. From the point of view I have just outlined, the danger that fuels the aversion to incest, as well as the societal prohibition that backs it up, is not the fear of punishment for sexual wishes, as in the classical view, but rather the more primitive, elemental dread of reabsorption and loss of a separate self through an ambivalently wished-for union with the engulfing mother. Lacan (Harari 2001) was particularly insistent on this point. Freud (1919) pointed in this direction too, when he derived anxiety aroused by the "uncanny" from too close an approach to the mother's body. At this early stage, the mother is the object of attachment for both sexes so this explanation for fears about incest is not gendered.

Whereas the classical view attributes the dread underlying the anxiety that accompanies and inhibits incest wishes and fantasies to "terror," in the face of an expected intolerable punishment in retaliation for transgressive wishes, the pre-Oedipal view would characterize the dread rather as "horror" at the attraction/repulsion of maternal re-engulfment. Both positions emphasize that the anxiety arises from fear of the possible success of repressed or otherwise disavowed incestuous wishes. It is my view, further, that we need not feel obligated to choose between these hypotheses: human mental life is complicated enough to allow us a "both/and" approach rather than an "either/or" one in this matter.

Discussion and an Attempt at a Synthesis

I have now presented a number of different perspectives on the aversion to incest from various theoretical and disciplinary perspectives. Let me try to begin integrating these by looking at human society in long-range evolutionary terms. Two important dualities in human existence come to the fore. One is the fact that human society manages to combine pair bonding for sexual reproduction in domestic units with the uniting of such units into a wider social grouping held together by affiliative ties of both kinship (consanguineal and affinal) and fellow-feeling. This led Richerson and Boyd, as we have seen, to propose that evolved human psychology involves a predisposition for two different kinds of social behavior, one "familial" and one "tribal."

The other duality I want to highlight here, related to the first, arises from the fact noted by various co-evolutionary theorists that humans have evolved a second channel of information transfer across generations, in addition to the genetic one, in the form of cultural signs and symbols capable of operating to some degree independently of the work of natural selection on genetic variation. This new realm of information transfer has made possible the sublimation into symbolic form of the sexual and aggressive impulses and behaviors that prevailed among our pre-human primate ancestors. Through shared cultural rules and norms, made public along the generally available symbolic road of information transmission, stable social arrangements could be established to contain and channel the conflict that implicitly arises among what Fox (1980) identified as the three social "blocs" constituting generic primate society: females, senior males, and junior males, with the latter two in competition for mating opportunities with the first.

Thus, the adaptive value of the Oedipus complex for humans, generally speaking, would on this view be to serve as the dynamic social and psychological process whereby such equilibration, inhibition, and sublimation are enabled through the mechanism of unconscious guilt, that is, aggression turned against the self to achieve self-control, internal discipline, and submission to the rules of the group as Freud (1930) proposed in *Civilization and Its Discontents*. Through the operation of the symbolic cultural channel in human society, the succession of generations and the competition for breeding success are largely redirected to symbolic and ritual arenas rather than physically violent ones. This enables humans to carry off the otherwise nearly impossible feat, achieved infrequently elsewhere in nature, of long-term cooperation among unrelated adults, especially the highly rivalrous males. Insofar as the Oedipus complex is enforced by the real or fantasied threat of castration, it serves the purpose of managing conflicts posed by the genetic program, with its overriding goal of inclusive reproductive fitness. We may thus say that the Oedipus complex, which analysts see clinically mostly when it is not working optimally, and thus deem to be pathological, is at a more fundamental level the adaptive mechanism whereby nuclear family members are turned outward from the family hearth, through the prohibition on erotic love within the family (except of course between the parents), and thus enabled to form the larger cooperating communities that constitute human society over and above the domestic unit—much as Lévi-Strauss had argued.

The incest prohibition of the first type, whereby young individuals are required to repress and sublimate their primary desires and aggressive impulses, not only prevents too close inbreeding, as the Darwinian perspective insists, but also provides for the division of society from an actor's point of view into appropriate and inappropriate sexual and marriage partners, thus regulating the reproductive life of the individual and of society as a whole, just as the structuralists would have it. Incest prohibitions of the second type do not seem to provide any Darwinian selective advantage from the genetic reproductive point of view, but they do, like the first type, serve to demarcate who is and who is not a potential suitable mate, operating in this way to organize and manage mating competition. To do these things, these incest beliefs mobilize a language composed of bodily fluids—blood, semen, milk, etc. But, as our own ideology that speaks of "blood" relations illustrates, these substances are mobilized not as "real" material biological things, but as symbols demarcating the degree of supposed shared substance among kin and non-kin. Through this language of symbolic fluids, and the ritual substances that often substitute and stand for them (as for example rice substitutes for semen in American wedding rituals), a system of thought can be built in which excesses, lacks, and balances of sameness and difference can be imagined and then elaborated as the foundation for the self-regulation of the group.

I have argued, following Héritier, that the second form of incest rests on the fundamental principle that, while undifferentiated unity remains an impossible goal for humans, except perhaps in the goal of death as nirvana that Freud (1920) struggled to comprehend, there is a process whereby difference, emerging out of sameness, once achieved, allows for the possibility of the subsequent reconnection of what has been differentiated, forming higher entities that come as close as humans can to the long-abandoned ideal of blissful merger. Infants break out of symbiosis with the mother to become separated, individuated, gendered persons, who in latency learn the necessary social and cultural skills so that after puberty they can seek a mate and, in unconscious fantasy, re-create the lost maternal bond. We know that this process is imperfect; but so is everything else in human life.

Lévi-Strauss's view of the incest prohibition as forcing marriage exchange through the rule of exogamy, or marrying out, forms part of a larger picture of society in which goods, symbols, and marriage partners are all put into circulation in a way that contributes to the overall integration of society. He saw the inward turning of incestuous wishes within the family as leading to involution and isolation, even as it remains a primordial dream. This view is interestingly parallel to that taken by Freud (1914) in his attempt to use the libido theory to understand the phenomenon of narcissism. Whatever one thinks of that theory as an actual hypothesis about the clinical phenomenon of narcissism, the underlying metaphor seems to be this: libido, whatever it is, can like a "substance" either be held within the individual, in which case it turns malignant and produces isolation, or be put into productive circulation. In object love, on the other hand, as Freud argues in *Group Psychology and the Analysis of the Ego*, "the ego becomes more and more unassuming and modest, and the object more and more sublime and precious until at last it gets possession of the entire self-love of the ego" (1921: 113). What is implied, if not stated, is that the self-regard that is lowered in lovers as they pour their libido into the object (or really the object representation) is replenished by the object's reciprocal investment of libido in the lover. Love relations, in this view, thrive on the exchange of libidinal energy, rather than its being held back in the self. The same idea is implied as well in the otherwise puzzling passages in *Beyond the Pleasure Principle* that describe how single-celled organisms die if left to themselves or mingle only with their own kind, but prolong their lives if instead of being inundated with their own waste products they exchange substances with other kinds of microorganisms. The idea behind this seems to be that exchange among living beings that have been differentiated from each other is vital and creative, while the hoarding of anything, such as libidinal energy, or the keeping of it only among those who are "identical," leads to stagnation and death.

From these considerations, then, perhaps we can say that incest is sex with a person with whom one shares too much "substance," and thus is too much like oneself—whether that shared substance is genetic (i.e., the DNA in the gametes that actually lead to procreation) or cultural and symbolic. It would be the very prototype of a developmental movement that runs backward against the stream of growth toward differentiation and complexity and then on toward reunion. Other examples might be fetishism, regression, and compulsive masturbation. What all of these share is stasis or backward flow that inhibits the circulation and exchange of libido, or Eros, that sustains life. The societal norms that prohibit or condemn these various activities are thus society's protection against allowing individuals to be governed by the wish for merger with the fantasied pre-Oedipal mother without negotiating the narrow and treacherous straits of Oedipal development that should lie ahead. The dilemma for individuals is that as they try to grow, incest avoidance of the first type, in the form of Oedipal guilt and dread of castration (or some other feared retaliation), constitutes one obstacle to conflict-free forward movement. But one cannot go backward either, because of fear of the pre-Oedipal mother of merger that fuels the second type of incest aversion to excessively close contact with "sameness."

Conclusion

I have argued that there are two different kinds of incest and incest aversion. One of them, at least in part the product of genetic evolution through natural selection acting on real biological reproduction, is implicated in regulating our lives as organisms who must mate to reproduce in a society of others with whom we must compete for mating opportunities even as we cooperate in many other ways. We may say, then, that this first type of incest aversion ensures that we avoid too close inbreeding and forces us into the condition of social adaptation that will allow us to compete successfully according to the rules in play in the society in which we find ourselves.

The second type of incest also concerns itself superficially with biological matters of sexual substance, but on closer inspection does so in a symbolic way, acting as a mechanism for ensuring that society operates with the proper measure of differentiation, exchange, and circulation, in a dialectic involving identity and sameness, to produce social cohesion and functioning. While the first kind is enforced by the threat of retaliatory punishment, the second is enforced not by anxiety stemming from fear of separation but, on the contrary, by the lure of regression to the primal dual unity and the obliteration of hard-won differentiation and individuation. One kind makes it frightening to move forward in development; the other makes it equally frightening to go backward. Both serve the social function of defining the range of acceptable sex, mating, and marriage partners.

The strategy of the first type of aversion is to control, inhibit, and sublimate sexual (and aggressive) impulses that were evolved in our primate past for mating competition. The strategy of the second type is to construct a cultural logic built up out of combinations of sameness and difference. The first kind aligns with the Oedipal phase, in which sexual rivalry is central, while the second aligns with the pre-Oedipal period, during which the emergence of difference out of sameness, and the learning of cultural symbols systems encoded in binary logics that this enables, is paramount. Both, working together, produce beings who can live in and contribute to the ongoing re-creation of a social order in which most of them will engage in both sexual mating and asexual social affiliation. For this task, our evolution has created a psychology predisposed to operate with both a Darwinian, genetic program designed to maximize reproductive fitness and at the same time a cultural program that to a certain extent runs counter to the sexual program. But it is this countering of the evolved Darwinian program by culture that, as Ingham and Spain argue, optimally leads not to unproductive conflict but to a viable social system that encompasses both sexual love for reproduction between mates and friendly affiliation with neighbors and kin.

A Parthian Shot

In his early theorizing on sexuality, Freud (1905) put forward the idea that childhood sexual curiosity revolves around the question

"Where do babies come from?" (and its implied correlates "How can I make one?" and "How can I prevent my parents from having another one?"). Later in his career (1925), he decided he had been wrong about that, and that the fundamental issue on which childhood sexual researches focus is rather the question "What is the difference between the sexes?" with its implication for the castration complex insofar as the fantasies of the phallic phase imagine the difference between the sexes to be the presence or absence of a penis.

In the light of the present analysis, we can see that in fact both answers are right, but they pertain to two different realms of human experience, the genetic and the symbolic, which in turn correspond to the two kinds of incest and the aversion to them. The question of where babies come from is a question about the "facts of life" and refers to the Darwinian imperative in us. The question of the difference between the sexes is, on the other hand, involved with our ability to form cultural logics out of binary oppositions, first and foremost that of sameness and difference themselves, presented to us in the perception of the difference between the sexes. Sex is central to both, but in one case in its dimension as the means of biological reproduction and also as a source of sensual pleasure and attachment, while in the other case it is present in its dimension as something that is not only good to do, but good to think. These considerations lead directly into the next chapter, dealing with the question of the relative parts played by biology and culture in human sexual life.

8

Sexuality: Biological Fact or Cultural Construction?

Introduction

The Western world has unquestionably undergone a major upheaval in its thinking about sex and sexuality over the course of the long twentieth century. While the contemporary system, from its own perspective, can certainly be represented as a story of the liberation of a natural human capacity with many variants (such as same-sex orientation, or non-genital practices) from the shackles of needless restriction, seeing the matter this way simply restates our own contemporary implicit premises and values, and achieves little by way of self-consciousness and thus intellectual purchase on what is actually going on and why. In this chapter, I offer an analysis of what has changed at the fundamental level and why, and what implications this has for psychoanalytic theory and practice. My argument will be that the shift from the preeminence of the stream of biological reproduction to that of the road of cultural reproduction that I have identified and explored in previous chapters can be seen at work in the transformations that our attitudes about sex have undergone and are still undergoing. On the basis of this analysis, sexuality will be seen to be both biologically grounded in observable fact and at the same time subject to widely varying cultural constructions, in understandable ways that I will spell out.

The Demographic Transition

The "progress" story, upon examination, necessitates the implication that our forebears in an earlier, benighted era, however high their IQ's, just didn't, couldn't, or wouldn't see things as they ought to be, but that now we can see things the right way. But a bit of reflection persuades us that as individuals we are no smarter or ethically wiser than were our ancestors, and the fact that they didn't see things our way is not necessarily evidence of a failure of intelligence or a faulty moral compass on their part. Rather, it is more useful analytically to assume that what has happened is that a new cultural episteme, or paradigm, has emerged, in a way that, as Foucault (1971) has argued, has very little to do with anyone getting smarter or more ethical. For the anthropologist looking at the metamorphosis of our ideas and practices regarding sex, something in social reality must have changed to which the cultural shift we have all experienced corresponds. That change, I will argue, is the demographic transition.

A demographic transition occurs, according to the generally accepted model, when the pattern of high birth rates balanced by high mortality rates, leading to population equilibrium, or steady state, is disrupted. Classically, the mortality rate goes down first, leading to a rise in population; this leads to a situation of population pressure and crisis, and subsequently to a drop in the birth rate, which leads either to a new equilibrium, or else, as has happened in the Western world (though not in much of the rest of the world), to an overall ongoing decline in population growth rates. This process is associated with the transition of the affected society from a "traditional" mode of life to "modernity," as that concept is widely understood. Western Europe underwent its momentous great demographic transition in the years between 1880 and 1910. In those years, as mortality declined, thanks to improved nutrition and living conditions, the birth rate also declined very rapidly, so that a steady decline in population in Europe, and latterly in other modern industrialized nations including the United States, has been unevenly taking place ever since. Those same years were also the years during which Freud developed the theory and practice of psychoanalysis. Coincidence? I don't think so.

As McLaren (1979) has shown in considerable detail, there is a direct correlation between Freud's early theorizing about the role of sexuality in the neuroses, both "actual" and psychogenic, and the effects of the demographic transition. The circumstances that are usually understood to have contributed to the demographic transition in Europe are the result of the shift from a predominantly agrarian society to an industrialized, urban dominated society (Handwerker 1986). In the latter situation, the economic value of children went from being an overall asset, as it had been in agrarian society, to an overall cost. In the agrarian world, children as potential workers on the farm from an early age gave their parents economic value, and thus gave the greater number of offspring per family greater economic benefit, whence the high birth rates of "traditional" society. In the newly emerging "modern" world, a number of factors converged to reverse the situation: more women entered the industrial work force, and thus had less time to devote to child-rearing; women began to be educated, and were less willing to bear children one after the other; and children, to succeed in the new economy, required a great deal more investment in education and much lengthier care before entering the work-force than was the case in agrarian society. The overall result was that for both personal and economic reasons, children came to be an economic burden rather than an asset, so that far smaller families than the traditional ones came to be the valued norm in the upper ranks of urbanized society, including in the emerging middle class.

The Effect of the Demographic Transition on Freud

The question then arises of how this reduction in reproductive rate could have been achieved. The answer is the widespread use of contraceptive methods. It was to the inadequacy of these now-requisite methods, as he saw it, that Freud attributed the great frequency of sexual dysfunction that characterized his early practice as a neurologist in Vienna. The reader of Freud's letters to Fliess (Masson 1985) will be struck, first, with how many of the men and women who called on him suffered from impotence, premature ejaculation, frigidity, and other related pathologies of sexual function; and second, as McLaren has amply documented, how convinced Freud was that these maladies as well as neurasthenia, anxiety neurosis, hysteria, and other disorders were the result of unsatisfactory sexual experiences. As is well known, his first theory of anxiety (prior to his publication of *Inhibitions, Symptoms, and Anxiety* in 1926) rested on the view that the sexual substances, by which he meant then as yet unknown chemical stimulants that led to sexual arousal, if not released adequately in a "specific action," would cause the symptom of anxiety, while masturbation, primarily in men, would lead to neurasthenia. The psychoneuroses too arose from the effects of unspent sexual excitations banished by repression from consciousness and operating indirectly through seemingly meaningless symptoms (such as Dora's famous cough).

For Freud, sexual arousal acts as a stimulus in the same way an itch or a tickle in the throat might act, leading to an evolved physiological "specific action" designed to discharge the excitation. The itch leads to scratching, and the tickle in the throat to coughing. Likewise the specific action designed for the release of sexual arousal Freud (1895) assumed to be heterosexual genital intercourse leading to mutual orgasm. The evolutionary advantage of this—self-evident to someone in Freud's era—would be that people would be motivated to undertake the one thing—copulation with an opposite sex partner—that had the capacity to lead to biological reproduction. Therefore, for Freud, interference with this function through the use of condoms, the rhythm method, *coitus interruptus*, or the practice of sexual acts other than heterosexual genital intercourse, was unsatisfactory deviation from the normal specific action, and the result would be undischarged libido and hence anxiety. Therefore, for Freud, the wave of sexual dysfunction and neurosis that he saw in his practice could be laid at the feet of the demographic transition and its requirement that sexual reproduction be curtailed; but in the absence of fully satisfactory methods of contraception, most sexual activity did not in fact allow for full sexual release.

Normative Sexuality Then and Now

Freud (1914) understood that human sexuality serves two masters: on the one hand, it is a source of (potentially) pleasurable experiences for an individual, while on the other hand, insofar as it leads to fertile intercourse, it is the means by which the genome perpetuates itself into future generations, and is therefore not, strictly speaking, serving the interests of the individual whom it impels to undertake the specific action, acting instead for the benefit of the "germ plasm," or DNA as we would now say. Since he viewed all contraceptive methods available in his time as interfering with the sexual function in a pathogenic way, he also held that the development of a truly safe, cheap, and non-interfering means of contraception would alleviate the malaise, or "discontent," our civilization imposes on its members by the restrictions on sexuality it requires. These restrictions, which delimit legitimate sexual activity to heterosexual intercourse within the bounds of marriage—a standard against which Freud railed (1908)—are necessitated by the means of family planning necessary for adaptation to the demands of modern middle-class urban life. Since for him all available means of contraception are unsatisfactory, it follows that

> whoever fills in this lacuna in our medical technique [the absence of a contraceptive device that is "certain and convenient" and would not diminish pleasure in coitus and would not "wound women's sensibilities"] will have preserved the enjoyment of life and maintained the health of numberless people; though, it is true, he will also have paved the way for a drastic change in our social conditions. (1898: 277)

What, we may ask, is the drastic change in social conditions to which Freud's final caveat refers? Well, now we know, because between 1952 and 1960, just such a device as Freud envisioned was finally invented. This made possible the "raising of the responsible act of procreating children to the level of deliberate and intentional activity and in freeing it from its entanglement with the necessary satisfaction of a natural need" (*Loc. Cit.*). The device in question is the female birth control pill, and it is indicative of its centrality in the sociocultural upheaval that it inaugurated that among all the myriad pills available to us moderns, it is the only one that needs no further designation than simply "the Pill." It did, as Freud foresaw, certainly make possible rational family planning without any diminution in the pleasure of genital intercourse; but it also did much more than that; it decoupled sexual activity from the procreation of children in a way that has now become definitive.

Freud had viewed procreation, and therefore sexual intercourse, as a "responsible act" because, as we have seen, the demographic transition required that people (of a certain class, at least) needed to postpone marriage, limit the period of fecundity for women, and devote precious economic and mental and physical energy resources to the rearing of a few children who would be primed to flourish and to sustain their class position. He saw other forms of sexual activity—oral, anal, or manual sex, same-sex activity, and the "perversions" or paraphilias—as not serious, robbing sexual experience of its risks, namely those of pregnancy as well as venereal disease and the high-cost offspring imposed on the woman and on the family unit. Masturbation, for example, he saw as deluding people into accepting a cheap and effortless method of achieving orgasm that ill-prepared them for the self-control and renunciations that responsible family planning would impose on them.

In the new world ushered in by (relatively) certain, effective, non-pleasure-inhibiting birth control, then, the "drastic change" Freud anticipated meant that all sex, the heterosexual genital kind and all others, could be pursued for individual "recreational" purposes without the risks entailed by the service of copulation to the reproduction of the genome. What were the sequelae of this shift? The Pill was approved for public use in the United States in 1960; and one obvious result was "the '60s," a period characterized by a radical change in sexual norms, first among adolescents and young adults but spreading throughout the population; and then by the feminist and gay liberation movements that challenged not only existing sexual and gender norms but also the existing structure of the nuclear family. The family had, in the previous sociocultural paradigm, existed as the institution designed to promote legitimate reproduction through the restriction of sex, as heterosexual coitus, to the marital pair. That norm was no longer required once coitus no longer carried the risk of pregnancy. We now live in the aftermath of that drastic change. With sex effectively divorced from procreation, there was and is no longer any reason for the onerous renunciations civilization had, in Freud's formulation, imposed on itself. The careful control and reduction of fertility consistent with the conditions that produced the demographic transition could be managed without them.

What this meant, in short, was that whereas concerns about sexual reproduction had been central to the social institutions surrounding sexuality in the era in which Freud lived, they withdrew to the background once it had been possible to manage them effectively. It is diagnostic that influential psychoanalysts at mid-century, just before the sexual revolution ushered in by the Pill, such as Fenichel (1945) or Erikson (1950), continued to stress the requirement of mutual complete orgasmic release in heterosexual intercourse for genuine psychological health. This consideration began to wither and eventually die in the years that followed the critical year 1960, as the various object relations schools (as formulated by Greenberg and Mitchell 1983), which generally dispensed with the drives and the central importance of sexuality altogether, began to take off in the United States at the expense of more traditional Freudian theory and technique. Freudian conflicts around sexuality gave way, both in theory and in the patient population, to disturbances in the intersubjective, interpersonal, and/or relational field. Biology gave way to an emphasis on the cultural and social dimensions of life.

Dual Inheritance and the Cultural Shift

Dual inheritance theory, as I have been presenting it in the present volume, pictures a cultural, symbolic system seeking to establish harmony and therefore to minimize the problematic selfish and competitive aspects of the genetic reproductive program, and therefore standing in opposition to the pursuit of maximal individual fitness, the unchecked pursuit of which would lead to destructive competition. This picture of human nature struggling with conflict between the urgings of sex and the forces of society opposed to sexuality closely approximates to the Freudian picture. What the Freudian picture does not include are the ways in which sociocultural symbol systems that resolve the inherent tension between the two imperatives can vary greatly, now favoring one side of the conflict, now another. One can find examples in world ethnography in which the cultural system largely encourages maximal reproduction, and others in which it opposes biological procreation to the point where the reproduction rate barely sustains the ongoing existence of the group, and everything in between.

Nonetheless, despite quite radical variations in the degree to which copulation is valued or devalued in different sociocultural settings, in only the rarest instances and only under certain well-defined and restricted conditions is copulation or even overt discussion of copulation something that can be carried out in the public arena, that (now predominantly virtual) world in which the cultural symbol system is sustained and enacted.

Freud of course understood that sex and public social order are inherently at odds; but it is evident on the basis of dual inheritance theory that this opposition is not just something that the benighted society of our forebears dreamed up for no good reason. One of the most startling remarks Freud made about sex reflects this realization on his part. When he comes finally to a direct discussion of the nature of sex in his *Introductory Lectures in Psychoanalysis*, he has this to say: "First and foremost, the sexual is what is improper, what must not be talked about" (1917: 304). That is, sex is that which must be excluded from the realm of the public arena, unless it is solemnized by the cultural rules regulating marriage or theorized in the sober chambers of science.

However, over the last fifty years, we have seen the erosion of this principle; nowadays everything that is sexual is freely available to us, in virtual form at least, with the click of a computer key. Nor is any sexual behavior, with the exceptions of pedophilia and some of the paraphilias such as necrophilia, regarded as strictly off limits. One could hardly imagine a more radical shift in cultural premises and norms. The difference makes sense, however, when it is understood that Freud lived during the era in which the high seriousness of sex in the cultural system arose from its necessary connection to procreation, whereas we now live in an era in which that connection is no longer necessary, in which the "seriousness" of sex has been undermined by technological interventions, and in which that side of sex that is the personal possession of the individual as a potential source of pleasure, rather than as a function primarily in the service of reproduction, has been emphasized in the public arena. (I forgo here a discussion of the new risks that HIV and STDs pose to the newly valorized modes and practices of sexuality.)

Nothing could make this cultural shift clearer than the very dramatic and sudden acceptance in many parts of the United States of the concept of gay marriage. (I have commented further on the dispute over gay marriage in Paul [2017].) This entailed that the fundamental premise of what "marriage" is change completely. While in Freud's day it was an institution that was defined by its inseparable connection to the process of sexual reproduction, and thus the interests of the gene pool, today marriage is seen as an institution whose primary purpose is to provide for a legitimate intimate sexual relation leading to personal and shared satisfactions for the partners. The emphasis has shifted from a situation in which the importance of sex for reproduction outweighed its role as a source of pleasure for the individual, to the opposite. This represents a process whereby the cultural road has gained the upper hand over the biological stream; and, as I have shown, the social and historical roots of this can be found in the demands of the demographic transition necessitated by the emergence of modern industrial urban life, and in the possibilities opened up by the invention of a means of contraception that met the requirements Freud laid out for it.

Sex vs. Gender

In contemporary usage, "sex" usually refers to aspects of physiology and anatomy, while "gender" refers to the sociocultural concomitants of those aspects. Gender is socially constructed (as Freud well knew), but this "social construction" must be understood in a particular way. Some things like a "touchdown" or a "political election" are entirely culturally constructed, in the sense that they only exist within a certain sociocultural system, and only make sense within it. There are no touchdowns or elections, for example, in aboriginal Australian society, just as there are no corroborees in American culture. This does not mean, however, that such things are arbitrary, meaningless, or in any sense less real than anything else in the world. Very real consequences follow from each of these; but they have no correlate in the natural world beyond the sociocultural system in which they play a part.

But other aspects of human social life are culturally constructed in the more restricted sense that something that actually has a real-world, extra-cultural reality, especially in the life of the human as a physical organism, is also endowed with particular meanings within a particular cultural context that go beyond its given nature. Thus, for example, death as something that happens to all living humans is not itself culturally constructed; it is a fact of life. But funeral rites that accompany death, religious ideologies that contextualize it in a particular way, and indeed the criteria for establishing that death has occurred *are* culturally constructed. "Gender" is, then, the socioculturally constituted range of meanings associated with the anatomical and physiological facts about sex, most importantly that only one variant of it leads to procreation.

From the point of view of dual inheritance theory, while the socially created cultural meanings of sex and gender vary greatly among and within different societies, it remains the case that the life trajectory of human organisms is no different from that of other organisms, which must accomplish two tasks: developing and maintaining themselves for their allotted lifespan, via nutrition, metabolism, avoidance of predation, and so on; and reproducing viable offspring that will carry forward their genes and pass them on in turn. As T. S. Eliot put it in *Sweeney Agonistes,* "Birth, and copulation, and death. That's all the facts when you come to brass tacks" ([1930] 1971: 80). While there are numerous physiological concomitants of sex in the human body, only one fact is determinative of the actual sex of a particular individual in a biological sense: that is whether it is able to produce fertile gametes that will result in the creation of a new organism and deliver them to an opposite sex partner in an act of genital copulation. This is the biological bedrock that grounds sexuality and gender in nature beyond culture. Everything else about sex, however, is to some degree culturally constituted in the sense I have given that phrase.

In the sociocultural milieu in which Freud wrote, the struggle between genetic and cultural reproduction was played out starting from the fact that heterosexual intercourse was inexorably linked to the creation of children; this made it a brute reality with which the sociocultural system had to deal. It did so by prescribing legitimate sexual activity as intercourse in opposite-sex marriage, and sequestering it in the marital bedroom so that it would not intrude, even in verbal form, in the public arena. Deviations from this norm, however widely practiced in actuality, were (in theory at least) severely sanctioned and the necessity of copulation to the perpetuation of society was given sacred status in the cultural construction of marriage as a union before and blessed by the deity.

Once sex was separated from the high risk of reproduction, however, this social formation became unnecessary. The goal of the cultural system, because unregulated sex threatens social cohesion, is generally to reduce the importance of the genetic system as much as possible. And whereas before the advent of effective contraception, and more recently of reproductive technology, this could only take the form of accepting the centrality of sexual reproduction and managing it through various sociocultural regulations and constructions; with the erasure of reproduction as the central factor of sexual life, gender became almost entirely autonomous and in a certain sense gratuitous. In the public arena in which sociocultural reality is enacted and transmitted, it usually makes no difference what genitals one has or whether one can produce sperm or eggs; these aspects of one's embodied existence play almost no role in whether one can do the jobs of modern industrial and post-industrial life. Only when it comes to sexual reproduction do those particular facts take on paramount importance—and of course this is no wholly longer true either since the advent of new reproductive technologies (Mann 2014).

The social results, at least within certain social strata, have been myriad: the decline of the married household, the rise of single parenthood, the recognition that women and LGBTQ people can occupy almost all social roles on an equal footing as heterosexual men, the acceptance of gay marriage, and the current focus on various "trans" phenomena both in the professional therapy and medical worlds and in the wider public arena, to name only a few. The speed with which all this remarkable change has happened demonstrates the power of social and cultural norms to adjust to new realities much more quickly than could be achieved via genetic evolution: this, indeed, is one of their great adaptive advantages for our species.

It is, thus, quite undeniable that sex and gender are culturally constructed, gender in the strong sense that applies to touchdowns and corroborees, sex in the weaker sense that an (until now) unavoidable biological fact is given cultural elaboration in a particular sociocultural context. But it must be stressed that all of this is far from arbitrary; what I have described is rather a particular moment in the always ongoing equilibration that human societies, and the people who live in them, must accomplish between the imperatives of the genetic program and those of the cultural program. So the answer to the question "is human sexuality biologically determined or culturally constructed?" is, as it is with most such antinomies: yes. It is both biologically determined and culturally constructed.

What Is the Relevance of All This for Psychoanalysis?

The theory of dual inheritance, which arose at the intersection of the fields of evolutionary biology and anthropology, provides a scientific grounding for the Freudian world picture, and suggests that it was this insight that Freud intuited and attempted to theorize with his two formulations of mental organization, the topographic and the structural. The self-interested, nepotistic, and competitive urgings of the genetic program we share with other animals are held in check, regulated, and transmuted via sublimation into the symbolic realm by our capacity for culture, which enables us to form cooperative groups and to change with the rapidity required by history (as this chapter has demonstrated). Freud's language of id, ego, and superego, and of the drives, now strikes many as dated or inadequate precisely because he did not, as later object relations theorists did, recognize sufficiently and theorize an autonomous social realm, or the pathologies arising from problems of life as a self in society. Thinkers from Sullivan, Horney, and Fromm to Mitchell, Aron, and Stolorow (to mention only a few in the US context) have added to psychoanalytic theorizing those dimensions of life that arise from our being social animals. But too often such thinkers, instead of supplementing the Freudian view, have simply replaced Freud's biological formulations with social ones, ignoring or downplaying the fact that while it is true that we are *social* animals, we are at the same time social *animals*. In my view, a unified psychoanalytic theory of human life can and should be built on the "both/and" formulation arising out of the dual inheritance model.

Implications for Clinical Practice

I have so far written from the perspective of a cultural anthropologist looking from a disengaged observer's vantage point (insofar as that is possible) at the shift in ideas and practiced regarding sex and gender in the industrialized West over the course of the past century or so. But when I enter the clinical situation with an analysand, I must act and speak not as a disinterested observer but as an engaged listener and interlocutor, and also as a citizen of one particular segment of the contemporary social and intellectual world. In that role, I inevitably respond to the analytic process as it unfolds in a way that is both evaluative and influenced by the current cultural and social climate. It is evaluative because insofar as I and my analysands agree that they need treatment, I hold out for them, as they do for themselves, a vision of something different that they have the potential to become; and this evaluation is in turn embedded in the social reality and cultural norms and values that constitute our present world.

Thus in the United States up until the 1960s, it was widely taken for granted that homosexuality was a "perversion" that was in itself shameful and unacceptable in the public arena, and therefore that a therapy ought to aim to "cure" it. Likewise, it was generally accepted that the normative gender roles were those defined by the structure of the typical middle-class single family. And the treatment of men and women (and children) took that norm as given.

The radical shifts within psychoanalytic thought and practice on both these counts did not arise as a result of any new psychoanalytic scientific discoveries about the nature of sex or anything else. On the contrary, these shifts arose first of all in the public arena in the form of political and social movements led by activists from the LGBTQ and feminist communities. The change in the official stance of psychoanalysis in the United States regarding homosexuality and the more general change in the sense of "what women want" were responses to new external social realities. Not only did most psychoanalysts as citizens of the modern world alter their own views about sex and gender issues, but gay people and women who came for analysis no longer accepted the former set of norms, affirming instead an alternative sexual orientation or gender identity and role as a given. They could not be treated effectively under the old rules anymore.

These considerations raise the question of the status of psychoanalysis as a scientific endeavor based on an accurate understanding of the structure and function of the human mind, in the same way a cardiologist, say, understands the structure and function of the heart. The heart does not alter its structure and basic physiology in response to external social shifts (though of course it may respond to new stressors or nutritional or environmental factors in new ways). If the preceding analysis is taken as at all valid, then it would seem that the structure and function of the mind are so influenced by social and cultural externals that they could not in principle be the subject of an objective theory of the way things are outside experience. If what is taken as "given" can change so dramatically between 1950 and 2020, then how could it be that any of our theories "carve nature at the joints," so that they accurately correspond to a ground external to themselves? And if psychoanalysis cannot stand on any such foundation, then on what can it rest and what validity can it have?

The work of the "culturalist" analysts in the United States had, as I mentioned, already shifted the emphasis of psychoanalytic theory away from Freud's biologically based metapsychology and toward social and cultural factors. This tendency was marginalized within organized American psychoanalysis for many decades in favor of ego psychology, but in 1976, works by George Klein and Roy Schafer, writing from within the ego psychological camp, quite definitively rejected the metapsychology in favor of a clinical theory that was phenomenological and eschewed any attempt to divine the essential nature of the mind in itself. The waning of the hegemony of ego psychology in US psychoanalysis opened the field to other theoretical systems that either had previously been neglected or rejected, such as British object relations theories or were newly developed to fill the void and address the changing face of society and of patient populations, as with self-psychology or the relational turn.

However as Busch (2015) has pointed out, while these differing schools may have incompatible grounding premises, there also seems to be emerging a clinical approach that is shared across school lines. Avoiding interpretive formulations heavily grounded in one or another theory, the lighter touch of this approach is theoretically unsaturated, designed to allow the analysand creative space within which to represent and express thoughts, memories, and affects previously inaccessible to conscious awareness. This raises the question of whether it really matters whether psychoanalysis as a whole field has a unified underlying psychology that could be said to correspond to a supposed hard reality. Of course, the sociocultural milieu changes over time; but it is still as "real" as anything else in the world, and it is with this and within this that we work. We rely on our clinical method in the here-and-now of analytic process to help guide analysands where they need or want to go; and our treatment successes, when we have them, assure us that the method is effective even if we can't explain on the basis of general and demonstrably "true" underlying principles exactly how or why it has worked.

A further grounding for us in our practice is the treasure trove passed down to us in the literature and in our training and ongoing involvement in the profession that contains a record of the range of fantasies, many of them touching on sexual matters, that our predecessors have observed, beginning with Freud. Like the ethnographic record of world cultures, the psychoanalytic catalogue gives us a sense of what kinds of fantasies have been encountered by previous explorers of the unconscious mind, in the context of which we can then place and evaluate our own observations and hypotheses. The question of whether these fantasies are universal, or timeless, or even genetically transmitted, as Freud supposed was true of primal scene fantasies, for instance, while interesting, is clinically irrelevant.

The question also arises of just how elastic the fantasies that shape and accompany sexual behavior are. After all, the sexual program is stubborn, as one would expect from a function that evolved to ensure our survival as a species. Most of the core conflicts around which a neurosis and therefore its analysis revolve, and the fantasies engendered to deal with them, are traceable to often sexualized interactions with the same key personnel of childhood experience no matter what the cultural surround. At the same time, changes in norms, such as the recent greater acceptance of single motherhood or homosexual parenthood, affect both what we observe and how we think about and evaluate it. But just as we can successfully treat people with whom we disagree about such matters as politics or religion, our evaluation is of use only insofar as it helps us understand what will be right for this patient, and that itself can vary.

When I treat people who are firmly set in a same-sex orientation, I take this as a given, not as the problem to be treated; there is always plenty else to talk about. On the other hand, there are others who are conflicted about their orientation or identification, or anxious about warded-off desires contrary to their official ones. Then the task is, as usual, to help the analysand disentangle defensive constructs and unhelpful fantasies from real and achievable wishes and desires.

The difference that the social surround makes is that "achievable goals" have changed, in sex along with other social changes: thus gender transition is relatively much more feasible and socially acceptable (at least in some circles) than was the case not very long ago. Or, in earlier times, one can suppose that many analysts did not support a patient's felt homosexual orientation not (only) out of homophobia but because the social stigma and disruptive fallout that would predictably result if the patient came out as gay in that era could not be defensibly construed as a wholly good outcome for the patient. That has clearly changed, at least in some sectors of contemporary society. In the end, the American predilection for pragmatism allows us to deal with these matters on a case-by-case basis without having to worry too much about how the human mind actually works at a more general abstract level. Physicists, after all, don't really know what gravity is either, but they work with it pretty well.

Conclusion

I have argued that matters such as gender role and sexual orientation are socially constructed, as the self-evident observation that these have changed so much in the course of less than the lifetime of some of us attests. However, the concept of social or cultural construction should not be misconstrued as license. As I have also argued, social construction is itself not free, arbitrary, or unconnected to reality, whether biological or cultural and historical. The changes in sexual values I have discussed follow from the shift in values from a system giving pride of place to sexual reproduction to one in which this consideration can be effectively sidelined. Often social construction is taken to mean we could recreate society along any lines we would like; but history has, I think, made short work of that seductive but dangerous fallacy. Of course, it is true that some large-scale sociocultural changes like the change in attitudes toward women and LGBTQ people were achieved by the hard efforts of real men and women. But they were also working in the direction that society was of necessity moving as the result of larger forces. Efforts to construct society against the tide have generally been less successful and usually a lot less pleasant.

Then too, it must be stressed that sociocultural construction is only one half of the human equation. The other is genetic construction, and that continues to operate in the old-fashioned way, carrying with it a suite of values and imperatives that can be quite incompatible with organized society. To achieve some level of cooperation and internal peace, human society must, with the help of the cultural code, contain, control, and otherwise manage the promptings of the genetic code, including through sublimating them by translating them into the symbolic code. Although social mores vary enormously in the ethnographic record, they always do so within limits set by having to cope with our being as biological organisms.

It was central to Freud's initial insights that we are greatly determined by our creatureliness, and that our highest values find their roots there. At the same time, he recognized the importance of how our real life experience with others in the arenas of family and society transforms us (usually) into social beings whose sexual, destructive, and narcissistic strivings can be shaped in prosocial ways—while also making us prone to neurosis and worse. In asserting that sexuality and gender are socially constructed, then, I do not wish to be understood as overlooking the dual nature of human existence, and the paradox that we are at once both free and highly determined from within and without. Psychoanalysis as a procedure is poised at the crux of this paradox, whatever the present sexual and other norms may be, and sustains itself as a method even while theory changes to accommodate new social realities.

9

Consciousness, Language, and Dual Inheritance

Psychoanalytic treatment aims to make the unconscious conscious; but this statement raises some important questions: What is consciousness, and why should becoming conscious of previously unconscious thoughts be therapeutic? This chapter addresses those questions.

Oddly, while psychoanalysis since Freud has had a lot to say about what is unconscious, it has had less to say about consciousness. The by-now quite vast contemporary literature on consciousness studies in fields ranging from cognitive science and neuroscience to philosophy and even anesthesiology has thus far made little impact on psychoanalysis, and vice versa. In the short compass of this chapter, there can be no hope of addressing the wide range of that literature and still less of solving the fundamentally insoluble mystery of consciousness. What I hope to do is illuminate the question of consciousness, and its role in clinical psychoanalysis, from a dual inheritance perspective. It is, after all, in the human mind that the two tracks of inheritance, the cultural road and the genetic stream, and their distinctive agendas must come together and reach some sort of more or less operative arrangement with each other.

Freud pictured for us the mind as prone to conflict between drive and defense, id and ego, libido and repression. His "economic" model saw these as quantitative forces pitted against each other, with the victory going, as he put it in his wry way, to the side with the big battalions. His picture of the drives allots to these ultimately biologically derived forces quotas of psychic energy (whatever that might be) which must, accordingly, be kept in check by psychic expenditures of equal or superior strength. He also understands thought as a process demanding only small quantities of energy, so that it can perform "trial runs" of planned action and take into account difficulties posed in external reality as well as internal sources of unpleasure, without the psychic costs that would result from committing one's full quotas of psychic energy to an action before thinking it through.

Here at once is a seeming paradox: if thought involves small quotas of energy, how could it control the powerful forces of the id, of the drives, as we expect it to do if we believe that making unconscious thought conscious is a part of effective psychic therapy? Freud clearly thought that consciousness is not where thought takes place; it is only an organ of perception by means of which thought, which is in itself unconscious, attaches itself to perceptions. Mark Solms (1997) has shown definitively that this was Freud's view. But this doesn't really solve the problem, because thought, even in the unconscious, operates at a lower level of psychic expenditure than we would imagine the drives to possess. So how could it successfully manage them?

In *The Ego and the Id* (1923a), Freud writes that the ego, like a rider on a horse, often has to "decide" to go where the id wants to go. As he makes clear, the horse is much stronger than the rider, just as the id is much stronger than the ego, and so it seems the ego must generally bow to the urgings of id impulses. But he revised this view a few years later in *Inhibitions, Symptoms and Anxiety* (1926). There he writes that the ego can control the id by producing signals of anxiety, drawing on an already existing reservoir of the capacity to generate anxiety dating back to the trauma of birth. Like a horse that can be guided by skillful application of reins, bit, and spurs, the id can be managed by the ego through manipulation of its fear of generating unacceptable unpleasure if it persists in pursuing its own wishes. Freud likens the situation to that in which a small minority opposes a measure favored by the majority of the populace, and through its access to perception can control the power of the press. By thus effectively influencing public opinion, it can thwart the stronger will of the many despite their greater numbers. This reference to the power of the press—symbolic communications in the realm of perception—gives us a key to addressing the problem: The whole matter of the conflict in the mind may perhaps better be addressed not as a problem involving the physics of opposing energies, or the economics of quantities of libido, but rather as a semiotic, and therefore, cultural problem.

I will therefore approach the issues at hand by proposing that we set aside the concepts of the id and the ego, and the "forces" of the drives and of repression that oppose them, and substitute concepts suggested by the dual inheritance model of human life. According to this view, the phenomena that are in conflict or opposition are not psychical forces pictured as quanta of energy, which as Freud admits cannot be measured, pushing against each other. Rather, the theory of dual inheritance lets us imagine the mind as trying to obey two differing sets of instructions from two different sources. One of these sources, originating in the genes, urges the person to obey the genetic program, while the other source, the external system of symbolic forms in use in the social environment, presses for the performance of the priorities of the cultural program. These programs and the instructions they call for are each transmitted in the form of a code: the genetic material in the one case and the cultural systems of symbols, especially including language, in the other.

The genetic program is guided by the biological imperatives that humans share with all other organisms: to maintain themselves as metabolizing systems for their allotted lifespan and to reproduce themselves during the course of that lifespan. The cultural program needs to control, manage, and transform the physical and mental resources evolution has made available to the organism for the execution of the genetic program in the interests of allowing prosocial cooperation and social stability, maintained by bonds of shared trust, friendship, and amity.

With this picture of the human predicament in mind, let us return to the question of consciousness. To begin once again with Freud, we recall that he saw a critical link between consciousness and language. In his essay "The Unconscious" (1915b) and in other writings, he distinguishes between "thing presentations" and "word presentations," arguing that only by attaching words to the thing presentation can that "presentation"—that is, a thought, feeling, memory, or idea—reach consciousness. As Ana-Maria Rizzuto (2015) points out, the word "thing" (*Sache*) in this context is rather misleading; what is being referred to more often is a "scene," that is, the total image of a situation or experience, usually involving one or more others, that is known or remembered unconsciously but is prevented by repression from becoming conscious. There are certainly non-verbal ways in which a scene or experience can be communicated in the clinical encounter, such as via enactments of transference fantasies or projective identifications; but for the purpose of psychoanalytic treatment, the key effective medium of communication is speech. What is it that makes speech the key factor in the so-called talking cure?

Students of consciousness distinguish between consciousness itself and reflective consciousness. The former, it is assumed, is to be found in all living organisms, insofar as they are in some way or other aware of their surroundings or their inner states or both, and can act on this awareness. What that awareness "is like," to use the widely cited phrase coined by Thomas Nagel (1974), is not something we can know or describe, but we can assume it implies subjectivity and agency. Even a single-celled organism "knows" to flee from its predators or approach its sources of nutrition. Humans, of course, being organisms, have this sort of consciousness. But what distinguishes them from other species is a higher order of what we call "reflective" awareness, that is, knowing that one knows something. This situation necessarily implies that the mind can divide itself into what Rizzuto calls the "subject ego" and the "object ego," or what Sterba (1934) had called the observing ego and the experiencing ego, so that one part of the mind is aware of what it itself has experienced or is experiencing or is going to experience. This is consistent with Freud's view that the ego "can take itself as an object, criticize itself, and do Heaven knows what with itself. In this, one part of the ego is setting itself over against the rest. So the ego can be split" (1933: 73). He gives some good examples of this in ordinary speech, such as: "When *I* think what *I* have done to this man"; or "When *I* think that *I* too was a child once" (1923b: 120; emphasis in original). In these phrases, the two uses of the word "I" refer on the one hand to a subject who thinks and on the other to the representation of the self as the one who did something or was a child, now the object of the subject ego's knowing (see also my further remarks on this subject in Paul [2011]).

Recent cognitive theorists recognize the distinctiveness in humans of this sort of meta-cognition, or "re-representation," and explain it by the human capacity for "semiotic mediation" (Valsiner 1998), which is the ability to "name" our experiences, that is, to attach a word or words to the experience. As Gillespie (2007) writes, "In order to obtain dinner one must first name one's hunger ... The naming, which is a moment of self-reflection, is the first step in beginning to construct, semiotically, a path of action that will lead to dinner" (678). In this example, I must know that I know I require nutrition and be able to report it either to myself or to an other or others, or both. Kastrup (2019) says it clearly: "*Direct* insight into one's conscious inner life is limited to those experiences one's ego can access through introspection and then report to self or other" (156; emphasis in original). And Shanks and Newell (2014) write that "awareness should be operationally defined as reportable knowledge" (45).

The phrases "reportable knowledge," "naming," and "semiotic mediation" alert us to the fact that it is by means of words that reflective consciousness, as opposed to simple consciousness, comes about. The same report that I can give of my thought to another or to others is also one I can also report to myself as "inner speech." Even if I do not actually silently form the words "I am hungry" in my mind, I know that I could do so, and in fact might want to do so, for example in preparation for informing a companion of my hunger and suggesting that we have dinner. To report something means to be able to state it in words, rather than for example to communicate it by screaming, as a baby does—or as a cat does by mewing. In these cases, the non-self-reflective being is emitting a symptom of its hunger, rather than reporting it, so that its reflective caretaker can respond with the appropriate action. In analysis, we aim to get patients to be able to report on their inner states rather than to simply express them as symptoms, enactments, or feelings they induce in us by non-verbal means; and we often provide interpretations that restate as verbal reports communication we have received non-verbally or only indirectly through obfuscated or distorted speech.

There is a division of opinion in the literature about how the self-reflective ability develops. Some, such as Piaget or Chomsky, see this is a cognitive process that takes place internally. In contrast, I myself think there is more plausibility to the view of such thinkers as Rochat (2009), Prinz (2012), and Tomasello (2019) who, following in the footsteps of earlier writers like G. H. Mead ([1934] 1997) and Vygotsky (1978), regard the inner speech that constitutes self-reflective awareness as the secondary development of a capacity initially experienced in interaction with another, more mature person. Reporting to the self is thus a skill developed as a gradual internalization of the originally real dyadic situation of perceiving and learning to interpret the response of a mature other to one's own communications.

Herbert Terrace, the psychologist who attempted to teach human language to the famous chimpanzee he named "Nim Chimpsky," admits in his recent book *Why Chimpanzees Can't Learn Language and Only Humans Can* (2019) that his experiment was a failure. He therefore concludes that there is an unbridgeable gap between animal communication, even that of our close relatives among the great apes, and human language. While his experience led him to a partial acceptance of the views of Chomsky about a universal language and an innate language acquisition device, he also came to diverge from Chomsky's view that language ability is an internal cognitive achievement. Taking a cue, ironically, from Chomsky himself, Terrace notes that in an unguarded moment Chomsky had alluded to the "stimulating loving environment" in interaction with the mother that prepares the way for an infant to learn to use words, that is, to "name" things.

Terrace writes:

Two non-verbal relations between an infant and her mother—one emotional, the other cognitive—have been shown to be critical for the development of language. Both occur during an infant's first year, before the infant speaks her first words. The first, a dyadic relation called intersubjectivity, is based on sharing affect. The second, a triadic relation called joint attention, is based on the ability of an infant and her mother to share their perception of an external object. (134)

Thus Terrace falls into the camp of those for whom the first social relationship is the necessary matrix in which the learning of language can occur; and only in humans do the two processes he mentions take place during the very prolonged period of post-natal immaturity and dependence on a loving parent. No other animal has anything comparable to these experiences.

Tomasello (2019), whose work Terrace cites, has brought together what has been learned about the difference between chimpanzee and human ontogeny. Going beyond Terrace's emphasis on the first year, he identifies not only joint intentionality but also a second step, "the emergence of collective intentionality at around three years of age" (8). At that age, the child engages in interactions with "knowledgeable and authoritative adults" as well as with co-equal peers. From the adults, three-year-olds begin to learn language and culture in a serious way, while with peers they learn through experience about collaboration and communication. Three-year-old human children (unlike three-year-old chimpanzees) begin the process of self-regulation of thoughts and actions "socially through their constant monitoring of the perspectives and evaluations of social partners of the self. ... [They] socially self-monitor the impression they are making on others so as to maintain their cooperative identity in the group" (9). They make joint commitments with others to monitor themselves and others as well as making "collective commitments to the group's social norms to which 'we' make sure that both self and others conform" (9).

Tomasello calls his approach "neo-Vygotskyian" in that it follows Vygotsky (1978) who more than many other thinkers emphasized the role of the entire community—the "collective"—in the socialization and enculturation of the child. But it is "neo-" in that it brings to bear an evolutionary viewpoint that was unavailable to Vygotsky. By emphasizing the two-step development of maturation, Tomasello recognizes that there are two kinds of socialization processes involved in learning language and thus enabling conscious, rational thought. The first is the dyadic interaction between the mother and the infant; the second is the interaction of the slightly older child with the collective community, through its representatives in the form of both elders and peers. It is in the context of the later experience that the function of reporting one's thoughts to self and others emerges in importance, since it is only through such reports that "we"—possessing what Tomasello calls joint intentionality—can determine who is or who isn't conforming to the norms of the group and to the commitments that we have made among ourselves.

In an earlier paper (Paul 2018), I called attention to what I there identified as a key difference between human culture and all other purported forms of animal "culture." While acknowledging the ability of other animals to communicate, to cooperate, to learn socially, and so on, I focused on the unique ability of human societies to form what I referred to as the "public arena." As I wrote there, "The public arena is that space, partly real, partly virtual ... in which social activity is carried out" (63). I continued:

> In this public arena, individuals are on public display in roles, assigned or assumed, that give them a part to play in the larger sociocultural system and its constituent institutions ... These roles they may perform well or badly, and publicly recognized value is assigned to their performance. (63–4)

This public arena, in which the emotions of pride, shame, honor, disgrace, resentment, and many other "social" feelings are felt and enacted, is very likely not to be found in the social lives of any other kind of animal besides humans (though I cannot be sure about porpoises or killer whales). It is in this arena that the symbolic systems—the "semiotic mediators"—of the culture are constantly enacted and thus made available for any individual to perceive, evaluate, participate in, and be judged by. It is here, according to my account of dual inheritance, that language resides, as the continuous stream of speech that is uttered and can be heard in any human community. Through its initial preparation via interaction with the mother in the early stages of development, and thanks to its evolved capacity to learn language and to speak, the developing child thus becomes a participating member of a speech community. This distinction meshes with dual inheritance theory in that the tie to the mother is a genetic as well as an incipiently cultural one, whereas the tie to the collectivity is only cultural. Tomasello's two stages of joint attention, first with the mother and then with the community, correspond to Richerson and Boyd's distinction, discussed earlier, between genetic or "family" social instincts and what they call "tribal" social instincts.

But the speech community into which the child is introduced is also always simultaneously a moral community. Language is not learned in a social vacuum; it is absorbed in the context of actual interactions with others. These interactions always have an evaluative dimension, as Tomasello stresses: the mother not only teaches the child the words to say things and the beginnings of the syntax to form more complex and recursive thoughts but she also begins the process of letting the child know what is and what is not appropriate, right, permitted, or acceptable to do and say. First the mother, and then the wider community of others, reflects back to the child the effects of its behavior by way of their responses, approving or otherwise, which in turn elicit in the child evaluations of its self and its actions as good, bad, or whatever so that it begins to feel pride, or shame, or anger, or pleasure, depending on the success or failure of its public, that is, perceivable, performance. This reminds us of Freud's remark, which I cited in the previous chapter, that sex is what cannot be talked about in public.

Wolfgang Prinz (2012) goes so far as to argue that "language has evolved for the sake of control, or more specifically, for the sake of control of individual willing and acting" (249). By "control," he means not just the imposition of someone's more powerful will on someone else's will, which has a negative connotation, but a more neutral general interactive process: "We may speak of social control if a given individual's action is modulated by others' actions—be they past, present, or future" (250). The implication is that there is a moral, judgmental dimension inherent in speech, insofar as it is an essentially social process, and society is an essentially moral entity. Indeed, it would not be a society unless it had some sort of widely understood moral code for conduct (whether or not members actually live up to it).

Summing up, speech may be thought of as the medium for reporting on one's inner states to self or others. Furthermore, one not only is able to report one's inner states, but must be at least potentially ready to account for them or, still more forcefully, to justify them, in the first instance before the mother or parents, then later before the collective judgment of the public arena, or before our internalized representation of these others. We need not wholly accept Prinz's assertion that language evolved primarily to enable social control; but his phrase, that language serves the purpose of the social control "of individual willing and acting," certainly resonates with the theory of dual inheritance as I have been expounding it. Not only does the collective society mold and channel the originally inchoate impulses of the new human organism but it must actively oppose or sanction at least some of them. This is because the genetic program, while it does certainly provide a foundation for prosocial feelings and actions, also urges some self-aggrandizing, sexual, and aggressive wishes that are in opposition to the moral norms of any functioning social group.

Jonathan Haidt (2012), a leading theorist of social morality, comes to a similar conclusion. Human beings, he writes, are the "world champions of cooperation beyond kinship, and we do it in large part by creating systems of formal and informal accountability. We're really good at holding others accountable for their actions, and we're really skilled at navigating through a world in which others hold us accountable for our own" (87). Societies, if they are to sustain themselves and provide to individuals the enormous adaptive advantages and other benefits they can provide, must hold themselves together in the face of the antisocial tendencies and impulses that spring from the genetic program. But, citing research by Lerner and Tetlock (2003), Haidt asserts that people are often "trying harder to *look* right than to *be* right," and he concludes that "conscious reasoning is carried out largely for the purpose of persuasion, rather than discovery" (89). Individuals as often as not have to persuade themselves as well as others of their own conformity to social expectations by means of the process of rationalization—the concoction of socially acceptable cover stories for inherently unsocial thoughts or acts.

The psychoanalyst and philosopher Jonathan Lear reaches much the same conclusion about accountability when he likens free association to the Socratic method of inquiry:

> When we state our beliefs or ask others to do something for us, we implicitly acknowledge that there is room for the question *Why?* ... We take ourselves to be *answerable* both to others and to ourselves. This helps us understand how it could be that the Greek word for *Reason*—"logos"—also means *language*. We need to give reasons why we believe what we believe and why we want what we want—and language is the vehicle in which such expressions occur. (2019: 1105)

From a psychoanalytic point of view, we are vulnerable to the interpellation whereby the collective society demands an answer from us, precisely because we carry a reservoir of guilt owing to the fact that the genetic program has induced us to wish for things of which the public arena would not approve and would negatively sanction. The answer we are prepared to give in order to be understood by the other to whom it is addressed must be in words that we both understand. It is a unique "design feature" of human language (Hockett 1960) that speakers can hear the words they themselves are speaking to another at the same time the other hears them and we may regard this as the basic mechanism whereby self-reflection is enabled. Consciousness, materialized as speech, is thus necessarily an interaction taking place in an interpersonal situation (Fonagy and Allison, 2016). One says something *to somebody,* and both parties hear what is said.

With all these considerations in mind, let us now return to the questions with which we began, and first of all address this one: what is consciousness? Before saying anything about that mysterious problem, we may recall the caveat that Freud offers: "There is no need to discuss what is to be called conscious: it is removed from all doubt" (1933: 70). What this comment seems to mean is that on the one hand, what is conscious is self-evident to each of us, as was first enunciated in philosophy in Descartes's *cogito.* We all know from our own incommunicable experience that we have conscious awareness, because even if we doubt its existence, it itself would be the one doing the doubting, and so it affirms its existence even by its doubt about whether it exists. But on the other hand, alongside this certainty, there is the ultimate unknowability of what this consciousness is, precisely because it itself is the means by which we know things at all. In the same way that a flashlight in a dark room can illuminate all the objects in the room except itself, so too consciousness can make us aware of other objects but not itself. For this reason, as the Buddhists say, "The self is not found." Shakespeare makes the same point in *Julius Caesar:* in answer to Cassius's question "can you see your face?" Brutus responds: "No, Cassius, for the eye sees not itself/But by reflection, by some other things" (I, ii, 56–8).

Since we cannot say anything useful about consciousness as such, then, we can at least say something about the kind of consciousness we value in ourselves: self-reflective consciousness. This skill is made possible by language; language is the medium in which we formulate our thoughts so that they can be reported to ourselves and to others. It is the medium in which we "understand" something; we can put it into words that fit it into our generalized knowledge about our inner reality and our social world. And language is that which marks the difference between what is unconscious and what is or can be made conscious. Repression, therefore, is the process of depriving a thought, memory, or wish of a connection to words. There are certainly also plenty of thoughts, memories, wishes, and scenes in our minds that have never had word presentations attached to them for one reason or another, as for example Levine et al. (2013) and Donnell Stern (2018) have emphasized, though in different ways. For the thoughts that exist in the unconscious, the only avenue to expression in the public arena is via the medium of communication in that arena, that is, language. This is the process of symbolization, naming, semiotic mediation. It may also be thought of as the essential condition of the process of sublimation.

But language, as I have argued, is first of all a collective phenomenon existing as the ongoing speech of the members of the community in the society, in which any new learners are immersed and from which, via the sense of hearing, language makes its way into their individual minds. We may therefore come to the unexpected conclusion that consciousness, which has most frequently been treated as a matter of individual psychology—which it undoubtedly is—is at the same time in a very real way a social fact. Just as the cells in our bodies all contain the genetic code within themselves, and in this way are able to constitute an organism that encompasses them all, so too normally developed individual persons carry the linguistic code inside themselves, and this fact enables them to form a society that encompasses them all and that operates as its own emergent organization over and above the individuals composing it. Self-reflective consciousness is therefore social before it becomes psychological, and is thus in a genuine sense an aspect of the presence of the cultural program inside the minds of each of us.

Nor is this external, collective consciousness entirely neutral or benign; as we have seen, it implies that because individuals have the means to represent their thoughts in the code society has given them, they may be called upon to be accountable to the collectivity as a whole, as it exists in external reality and as it is represented in the individual's ego and superego. The linguistic code is not only a moral code, however. It is a moral code that the individual is incapable of living up to for the simple reason that he or she also answers to another master, the non-social imperatives of the genetic program.

When one undoes a repression by putting what was only a thing-presentation into connection with a word-presentation, this mental act should itself be seen as preparatory to a social act: one does not just say words, one says them to someone else, who by her reaction indicates not only comprehension but also approval or disapproval. As G. H. Mead (1967/1934) argued, a complete act of meaningful communication arises when the person who makes a gesture, such as a verbal utterance, registers the response that her gesture has induced in the addressee. To take a famous example, consider the actual moment when the idea of the "talking cure" for hysterical symptoms originated in Josef Breuer's mind. When his patient Anna O. became mute, the meaning of this symptom dawned on him:

> Now for the first time the psychic mechanism of the disorder became clear. As I knew, she had felt much offended over something, and had determined not to speak about it. When I guessed this and obliged her to talk about it, the inhibition, which had made any other kind of utterance impossible, disappeared. (Freud and Breuer 1895: 25)

Because of his familiarity with the O. household, Breuer understood what Anna was communicating by her muteness (muteness is itself a negative spoken gesture, the zero-signifier): that she was very angry but was withholding saying anything about it. When he communicated that back to Anna, she perceived his comprehension of her meaning, and was then able to speak to him about her feelings—to add words to what had been up until then repressed thing-presentations. She was able to do this because instead of the angry response she expected to get had she made her feelings known to the members of her household, she knew that in responding Breuer would make no judgment or give any sort of disapproving (or approving) response. (In all likelihood, this bad response she anticipated was not conscious, but had taken the form of an internal inhibition over the course of many previous such experiences.)

Anna knew this about Breuer's response because, as Rizzuto (2015) points out, for the very first time in the history of psychotherapy, he listened to his patient with a totally new mode of listening, the precursor of psychoanalysis: he saw her in an ongoing continuous treatment, in which he expressed true interest in the patient's private world, and asked only that she tell him everything (18). Anna could have confidence and trust in her interlocutor because over the course of their sessions together he had consistently acted with patience and non-judgmental interest. Of course it helped that she was in the beginnings of a positive transference, the sexual aspects of which eventually outweighed the helpful ones and put an end to the treatment, as we know. She also, as Rizzuto remarks, happened to have an acute intelligence and, even in the middle of her hysterical attacks, was capable of a degree of self-observation and thus self-reflection while she was acting in pathological psychosomatic ways.

These considerations prepare us now to answer our second question: why does talking have a beneficial effect in the clinical setting? The patient has repressed or otherwise defended against certain wishes, memories, thoughts, and feelings because of the anticipated negative response from the others in the environment. These are the "danger signals" that Freud (1926) argued the ego generates to initiate a defense so as to avoid anxiety. This "other" may be a single other, such as a parent, or it may be Mead's "generalized other" in relation to whom the individual is answerable. In terms of dual inheritance, this generalized other, the equivalent of Freud's "superego," is the individual's internalization of the "voice" of the public arena, Lacan's "big Other," which demands an answer to the questions "What are you up to, what do you want, and what are you thinking?"

The technique of psychoanalysis, then, depends on the analyst successfully conveying to the patient that she may indeed say anything and everything, and there will be no retaliations, responses in kind, or repercussions from the analyst. This is as true of positive things as well as negative ones: the analyst no more responds in kind to the patient's apparently loving erotic transference than she does to the patient's rage at her. In analysis, there is only one expectation for which the patient is accountable, and that is that she do her best to say everything without self-criticism. Certainly the patient will resist, and fail to keep to the agreed upon bargain. The analyst does not criticize, but tries to help the patient understand the roots of the resistance. Needless to say the analyst sometimes fails in this, and enters into a collusion or enactment with the patient, or responds from an internalized projection or projective identification. But presumably, she eventually comes to recognize the situation and interprets it to the analysand. She thereby indicates that the analysand is not accountable to her as an imagined stand-in for the group or the superego.

Many analysts have recognized the importance of accountability in analytic technique. To cite just one example: Stephen Mitchell, following Loewald (1960), notes that the analyst must be organized and responsible in a "parental" way that the patient must not be; but in contrast the patient should not be "responsible"—that is, answerable or accountable. If the analysand in free association holds herself accountable to her internalized others, she will in this way "be resisting the precious opportunity the analytic situation provides for a freedom from conventional *accountability,* as surrender to unintegration" (2000: 51, my emphasis). And later in the same work Mitchell writes:

> We [analysts] try to help make it possible for analysands to surrender themselves to their passions, outside and within the analytic relationship, partially so that they may learn more about [their] unconscious intentions. We try to cultivate in the analysand a kind of analytically constructive *irresponsibility.* (131, my emphasis)

To unpack these comments briefly: the analyst must strive to be responsible—accountable, answerable—to the practice of the technique, to the expectation that the boundaries are firm, and to the enabling of free association according to the fundamental rule. That is, she answers to the ideals and norms of the profession, her relevant reference group, and to the pursuit of free inquiry. But the patient, who brings to the situation all the repressions and other defenses that have accreted in response to the reactions, real or imagined, anticipated from the public arena, exhibits these defenses in the form of resistance. The aim, then, is to allow the patient to become persuaded, as Anna O. was with Breuer, that the analyst can be trusted when she says that anything may be said no matter how it might violate the expectations current in the discourse of the public arena. (Of course it must be recognized that there are certain exceptional circumstances, such as accounts of child abuse or plausible threats to self or others, in which case mandatory reporting is required.)

What the analyst does, in short, is to construct with the analysand a new tightly enclosed and protected "public arena" consisting of just two people, the analytic couple. We might refer to it as a "private arena" in contrast to the outside public one. This new little society, a special self-contained linguistic and moral community of two, will in the course of the treatment come to replace the former, more restrictive one. This is what Mitchell means when he says that the patient must learn to be irresponsible, that is, no longer answerable or accountable to the conventional strictures of the big Other out of deference to which the patient has unnecessarily restricted and inhibited herself in the past. In the closely guarded enclave of the consulting room, the patient's only answerability, ultimately, is to the fundamental rule and, through it, to herself and her wish to be well and to realize her best self.

The analyst's words—her interpretations and other interventions—serve as the reflective consciousness of which the patient is, at least at the beginning of the treatment, incapable. The analyst does not respond in kind to the expressions of the patient's impulses and intentions, but rather points them out: "You speak as if you see me as a punitive parent," or "you are made anxious by your emerging sexual feelings toward me." In phrases like this, the analyst occupies two positions: one as the new object who makes the observation and one indicated in her speech as the object representation of the patient's transference. The analytic situation is thus itself an enactment of self-consciousness, in which the analyst stands to one side of the patient's constructed imaginary dyad with the analyst in the transference and reports what she observes to the patient. We assume that one key dimension of improvement in an analytic treatment is the patient's growing ability to do this for herself, as she identifies with the analyst's role as auxiliary observing ego. By observing aloud the patient's resistances and their sources, the analyst allows the patient greater and greater latitude to herself say what had previously been quite literally unspeakable, and models how to do it.

Freud spoke of "lifting the repressions." This image conjures up the removal of a counter-force keeping down the thought that is struggling to emerge. The metaphor implies two forces in opposition, as when we keep a beach ball under water from popping up to the surface by the continuous counter-pressure of our hands. But if repression is viewed rather as depriving a thing-presentation of a word-presentation, then the "lifting" involves no interplay of force and counter-force. Instead, the image is more like one of giving someone a password that allows her to access previously restricted content. It is thus, as I proposed initially, to be thought of as a semiotic, symbolic activity, not an energetic one.

When Freud says that analysis is a cure by love, or that the real curative factor is the relationship with the doctor, what this means, in the light of the foregoing discussion, is that the analyst, like Breuer in the example I cited with Anna O., creates a new, private arena in which the rules that pertain in the wider public arena do not apply. She does this by consistent, continuous, interested caring, listening, and observing—a form of loving. The interpretations she offers do not themselves cure: the patient does that herself thanks to the non-accountability she experiences with her analyst in their sequestered domain. No longer fearing archaic dangers, she issues herself an entry ticket to consciousness in the form of permission to attach word-presentations to the previously repressed thoughts. And the repressions and defenses, no longer felt as necessary, are then able to dissipate in the course of the treatment.

The ability of the patient to say what is really on her mind, in the presence of the analyst as non-judging target of accountability, is thus the effect, not the cause, of the "lifting of repression." The talking cure works not because the patient has somehow talked away the symptom, or because the analyst's interpretations have been so very persuasive, or because the analyst lends her energy forces to the weaker ones of the patient to enable her with their combined force to overcome the counter-force of repression. Rather, the inhibitions and symptoms have been rendered superfluous through the analysand's immersion in a new and transformative social surround, in which she becomes capable of full speech through having become accountable only to the fundamental rule of analysis embodied in the non-judgmental analyst. The patient's freer talk in the talking cure is thus the evidence, not the agency, of the success of the treatment.

The self-centered and asocial dimensions of the mind, the promptings of the genetic stream, have been allowed access to words and thus to reflective consciousness; and the path is open to better use of them via their redirection into the cultural road through sublimation via the symbolic medium of words. Replacing mute impulses with thoughts available to consciousness is indeed a work of culture, like draining the Zuyder Zee. After all, when the Zuyder Zee was drained, what had previously been inaccessible ocean floor became useful and productive soil.

Seen in this light, psychoanalytic treatment emerges as yet another example of the process I have explored throughout this book of the cultural program superseding the genetic program in an interpersonal and psychological arena parallel to the same process as it occurs in evolution, culture and culture change, history, and literature.

REFERENCES

Boehm. C. (1993). "Egalitarian Society and Reverse Dominance in Human Nature." *Current Anthropology* 34 (3): 227–54.

Boehm, C. (1999). *Hierarchy in the Forest: The Evolution of Egalitarian Behavior*. Cambridge: Harvard University Press.

Boehm, C. (2012). *Moral Origins: The Evolution of Virtue, Altruism, and Shame*. New York: Basic Books.

Boyd, R. and P. J. Richerson (1985). *Culture and the Evolutionary Process*. Chicago: University of Chicago Press.

Busch, F. (2015). "Our Vital Profession." *The International Journal of Psychoanalysis* 96 (3): 553–68.

Campbell, D. T. (1975). "On the Conflicts between Biological and Social Evolution and between Psychology and Moral Tradition." *American Psychologist* 30: 1103–26.

Čapek, K. ([1920] 2004). *R.U.R. (Rossum's Universal Robots)*. Trans. C. Novack. New York: Penguin Books.

Cavalli-Sforza, L. and M. W. Feldman (1981). *Cultural Transmission and Evolution: A Quantitative Approach*. Princeton: Princeton University Press.

Chance, M. R. A. ([1961] 2004). "The Nature and Special Features of the Instinctive Social Bond of Primates." In S. L. Washburn (ed.). *Social Life of Early Man*. 17–33. London: Routledge.

Chance, M. R. A (1962). "Social Behaviour and Primate Evolution." In A. Montagu (ed.). *Culture and the Evolution of Man*. 84–130. New York: Oxford University Press.

Chapais, B. (2008). *Primeval Kinship: How Pair-Bonding Gave Birth to Human Society*. Cambridge: Harvard University Press.

Cooley, C. H. ([1902] 1956). *Human Nature and the Social Order*. Glencoe: The Free Press.

Darwin, C. ([1871] 2007). *The Descent of Man*. New York: Penguin.

Darwin, E. (1804). *The Temple of Nature: Or, the Origin of Society: A Poem with Philosophical Notes*. New York: T. and J. Swords.

Dawkins, R. (1976). *The Selfish Gene*. New York: Oxford University Press.

Dawkins, R. (1986). *The Blind Watch-Maker: Why the Evidence of Evolution Reveals a Universe without Design*. New York: W. W. Norton.

Dennett, D. C. (1995). *Darwin's Dangerous Idea: Evolution and the Meanings of Life*. London: Simon & Schuster.

Des Chene, D. (2001). *Spirits and Clocks: Machine and Organism in Descartes*. Ithaca: Cornell University Press.

Durham, W. H. (1991). *Co-evolution: Genes, Culture, and Human Diversity*. Stanford: Stanford University Press.

Durkheim, Émile ([1915] 1967). *The Elementary Forms of the Religious Life*. Trans. J. W. Swain. New York: Free Press.

Elias, N. ([1939] 1982). *Power and Civility*. Trans. E. Jephcott. New York: Pantheon.

Eliot, T. S. ([1930] 1971). Sweeney Agonistes. In T. S. Eliot (ed.). *The Complete Poems and Plays 1909–1915*. 74–85. New York: Harcourt Brace.

Erdal, D. and A. Whiten (1996). "Egalitarianism and Machiavellian Intelligence in Human Evolution." In P. Mellars and K. Gibson (eds.). *Modelling the Early Human Mind*. 139–50. Oxford: Oxbow Books.

Erikson, E. H. (1950). *Childhood and Society*. New York: W. W. Norton.

Erickson, M. T. (2000). "The Evolution of Incest Avoidance: Oedipus and the Psychopathologies of Kinship." In P. Gilbert and K. G. Bailey (eds.). *Genes on the Couch: Explorations in Evolutionary Psychotherapy*. 211–31. East Sussex: Brunner-Routledge.

Fenichel, O. (1945). *The Psychoanalytic Theory of Neurosis*. New York: W. W. Norton.

Ferenczi, S. ([1933] 1949). "Confusion of the Tongues between the Adults and the Child (The Language of Tenderness and of Passion)." *International Journal of Psychoanalysis* 30: 225–30.

Fonagy, P. and E. Allison (2016). "Psychic Reality and the Nature of Consciousness." *International Journal of Psychoanalysis* 97 (1): 5–24.

Foucault, M. (1971). *The Order of Things: An Archaeology of the Human Sciences*. New York: Pantheon Books.

Fox, R. (1980). *The Red Lamp of Incest: What the Taboo Can Tell Us about Who We Are & How We Got That Way*. New York: E. P. Dutton.

Fox, R. (1993). *Reproduction and Succession: Studies in Anthropology, Law, and Society*. New Brunswick: Transaction.

Freud, S. (1986). *The Standard Edition of the Complete Psychological Works of Sigmund Freud*. Ed. and trans. James Strachey *et al.*, 24 Vols. London: Hogarth.

Freud, S. (1895). "Project for a Scientific Psychology." *S.E.* 1: 281–386.

Freud, S. (1898). "Sexuality in the Etiology of the Neuroses." *S.E.* 3: 259–85.

Freud, S. (1900). "The Interpretation of Dreams." *S.E.* 4/5: 1–627.

Freud, S. (1905). "Three Essays on the Theory of Sexuality." *S.E.* 7: 123–243.

Freud, S. (1908). "'Civilized' Sexual Morality and Modern Nervous Illness." *S.E.* 9: 177–204.

Freud, S. (1913). "Totem and Taboo." *S.E.* 13: 1–160.

Freud, S. (1914). "On Narcissism: An Introduction." *S.E.* 14: 67–103.

Freud, S. (1915a). "Instincts and Their Vicissitudes." *S.E.* 14: 109–39.

Freud, S. (1915b). "The Unconscious." *S.E.* 14: 166–204.

Freud, S. (1915c). "Thoughts for the Times on War and Death." *S.E.* 14: 273–300.

Freud S. (1916–17). "Introductory Lectures on Psychoanalysis." *S.E.* 15-16: 1–463.

Freud, S. (1917). "Mourning and Melancholia." *S.E.* 14: 237–57.

Freud, S. (1919). "The 'Uncanny'." *S.E.* 17: 217–52.

Freud, S. (1920). "Beyond the Pleasure Principle." *S.E.* 18: 1–64.

Freud, S. (1921). "Group Psychology and the Analysis of the Ego." *S.E.* 18: 65–143.

Freud, S. (1923). "The Ego and the Id." *S.E.* 19: 1–59.

Freud, S. (1924). "The Dissolution of the Oedipus Complex." *S.E.* 19: 173–82.

Freud, S. (1925). "Some Psychical Consequences of the Anatomical Distinction between the Sexes." *S.E.* 19: 241–60.

Freud, S. (1926). "Inhibitions, Symptoms and Anxiety." *S.E.* 20: 77–174.

Freud, S. (1930). "Civilization and Its Discontents." *S.E.* 21: 57–145.

Freud, S. (1931). "Female Sexuality." *S.E.* 21: 225–43.

Freud, S. (1933). *New Introductory Lectures on Psycho-analysis. S.E.* 22: 7–182.

Freud, S. (1939). "Moses and Monotheism: Three Essays." *S.E.* 23: 1–138.

Freud, S. and J. Breuer (1895). "Studies on Hysteria." *S.E.* 2: 1–306.

Fukuyama, F. (2011). *The Origins of Political Order: From Prehuman Times to the French Revolution.* New York: Farrar, Straus and Giroux.

Geertz, C. (1973). *The Interpretation of Cultures: Selected Essays.* New York: Basic Books.

Gibbon, E. ([1776–1789] 1962) *Gibbon's Decline and Fall of the Roman Empire.* Ed. M. Hadas. New York: Capricorn.

Gilbert, W. S. (1882). *Iolanthe.* Available online: http://www.sullivan-forschung.de/html/e3-libretti-iolanthe.html.

Gillespie, A. (2007). "The Social Basis of Self-Reflection." In J. Valsiner and A. Rosa (eds.). *The Cambridge Handbook of Sociocultural Psychology.* 678–91. New York: Cambridge University Press.

von Goethe, J. W. (1932). *Faust.* Trans. George Madison Priest. New York: Covici Friede Publishing.

Goldschmidt, W. (2006). *The Bridge to Humanity: How Affect Hunger Trumps the Selfish Gene*. New York: University of Oxford Press.

Goodall, J. (1986). "Social Exclusion, Rejection, and Shunning among the Gombe Chimpanzees." *Ethnology and Sociobiology* 7 (3/4): 227–36.

Greenberg, J. R. and S. A. Mitchell (1983). *Object Relations in Psychoanalytic Theory*. Cambridge, MA: Harvard University Press.

Greenberg, M. (1993). "Post-adoption Reunion: Are We Entering Uncharted Territory?" *Adoption and Fostering* 17: 1–5.

Greenberg, M. and R. Littlewood (1995). "Post-adoption Incest and Phenotypic Matching: Experience, Personal Meanings and Biosocial Implications." *British Journal of Medical Psychology* 68 (1): 29–44.

Groark, K. P. (2019). "Freud among the Boasians: Psychoanalytic Influence and Ambivalence in American Anthropology," *Current Anthropology* 60: 559–88.

Haidt, J. (2012). *The Righteous Mind: Why Good People Are Divided by Politics and Religion*. New York: Vintage Books.

Hamilton, W. D. (1964). "The Genetical Evolution of Social Behavior I and II." *Journal of Theoretical Biology* 7: 1–16 and 17–52.

Handwerker, W. P. (1986). "Culture and Reproduction: Exploring Micro/Macro Linkages." In W. P. Handwerker (ed.). *Culture and Reproduction: An Anthropological Critique of Demographic Transition Theory*. 1–28. Boulder: Westview Press.

Hanly, C. (2006). "Pragmatism, Tradition, and Truth in Psychoanalysis." *American Imago* 63 (3): 261–82.

Harari, R. (2001). *Lacan's Seminar on Anxiety*. New York: Other Press.

Héritier, F. (1999). *Two Sisters and Their Mother*. Trans. J. Herman. New York: Zone Books.

Hockett, C. (1960). "The Origin of Speech." *Scientific American* 203: 88–111.

Hrdy, S. B. (1981). *The Woman That Never Evolved*. Cambridge: Harvard University Press.

Hrdy, S. B. (2009). *Mothers and Others: The Evolutionary Origins of Mutual Understanding*. Cambridge: Belknap Press.

Ingham, J. and D. Spain (2005). "Sensual Attachment and Incest Avoidance in Child Development and Human Evolution." *Journal of the Royal Anthropological Society* 11 (4): 677–701.

Ingold, T. (2016). *Evolution and Social Life*. London: Routledge.

Jakobson, R. and M. Halle ([1956] 1971). *Fundamentals of Language*. 2nd rev. ed. The Hague: Mouton.

Kastrup, B. (2019). *The Idea of the World: A Multi-Disciplinary Argument for the Mental Nature of Reality*. Winchester: Iff Books.

Klein, G. (1976). *Psychoanalytic Theory: An Exploration of Essentials*. New York: International Universities Press.

Knauft, B. M. (1991). "Violence and Sociality in Human Evolution." *Current Anthropology* 32 (4): 391–428.

Lacan, J. ([1966] 1985). "The Meaning of the Phallus." In J. Mitchell and
J. Rose (eds.). Trans. J. Rose. *Feminine Sexuality: Jacques Lacan and
the École Freudienne*. 74–85. New York: W. W. Norton.

Lear, J. (2019). "Encountering and Speaking to the Unconscious."
International Journal of Psychoanalysis 100: 1102–16.

Lerner, J. S. and P. E. Tetlock (2003). "Bridging Individual, Interpersonal,
and Institutional Approaches to Judgment and Decision Making: The
Impact of Accountability in Cognitive Bias." In S. L. Schneider and
J. Shateau (eds.). *Emerging Perspectives on Judgment and Decision
Research*. 431–57. New York: Cambridge University Press.

Levine, H. B., G. Reed, and D. Scarfone (eds.) (2013). *Unrepresented
States and the Construction of Meaning: Clinical and Theoretical
Contributions*. London: Routledge.

Lévi-Strauss, C. ([1949] 1969). *The Elementary Structures of Kinship*.
Ed. R. Needham. Trans. J. H. Bell, J. R. von Sturmer, and R. Needham.
Boston: Beacon Press.

Lévi-Strauss, C. (1967). "The Structural Study of Myth." In C. Lévi-
Strauss (eds.). *Structural Anthropology*. Trans. C. Jacobson and B.
Grundfest Schoepf. 202–28. Garden City: Doubleday Anchor.

Loewald, H. (1960). "On the Therapeutic Action of Psycho-Analysis."
International Journal of Psycho-Analysis 41: 16–33.

Lucretius. (2007). *The Nature of Things*. Trans. A. E. Stallings. New York:
Penguin Books.

Lumsden, C. J. and E. O. Wilson (1981). *Genes, Mind, and Culture:
Coevolution*. Cambridge: Harvard University Press.

Maccoby, E. (1998). *The Two Sexes: Growing Up Apart, Coming
Together*. Cambridge: Belknap Press.

Maciejewski, F. (2006). "Freud, His Wife, and His 'Wife'." *American
Imago* 63 (4):497–506.

Maciejewski, F. (2008). Minna Bernays as "Mrs. Freud": What Sort
of Relationship Did Sigmund Freud Have with His Sister-in-law?
American Imago 65 (1): 5–21.

Mann, M. (ed.) (2014). *Psychoanalytic Aspects of Assisted Reproductive
Technology*. London: Karnac.

Marder, E. (2012). *The Mother in the Age of Mechanical Reproduction:
Psychoanalysis, Photography, Deconstruction*. New York: Fordham
University Press.

Masson, J. M. (ed.) (1985). *The Complete Letters of Sigmund Freud to
Wilhelm Fliess, 1877–1904*. Cambridge: Belknap Press.

Maturana, H. R. and F. Ayala (1980). *Autopoiesis and Cognition: The
Realization of the Living*. Boston: D. Reidel.

Mauss, M. ([1925] 2000). *The Gift: The Form and Reason for Exchange
in Archaic Societies*. Trans. W. D. Hall. New York: W. W. Norton.

McLaren, A. (1979). Contraception and Its Discontents: Sigmund Freud and Birth Control. *Journal of Social History* 12 (4): 513–29.

Mead, G. H. ([1934] 1997). *Mind, Self and Society: From the Standpoint of a Social Behaviorist*. Chicago: University of Chicago Press.

Mitchell, S. A. (2000). *Relationality: From Attachment to Intersubjectivity*. New York: Routledge.

Nagel, T. (1974). "What Is It Like to Be a Bat?" *Philosophical Review* 83: 435–50.

Newman, W. R. (2004). *Promethean Ambitions: Alchemy and the Quest to Perfect Nature*. Chicago: University of Chicago Press.

Nietzsche, F. ([1872 and 1887] 1956). *The Birth of Tragedy and the Genealogy of Morals*. Trans. F. Golffing. New York: Doubleday Anchor.

Opie, K. and C. Power (2008). "Grandmothering and Female Coalitions: A Basis for Matrilineal Priority?" In N. J. Allen, H. Callan, R. Dunbar, and W. James (eds.). *Early Human Kinship: From Sex to Social Reproduction*. 168–86. Malden: Blackwell.

Ortner, S. (1974). "Is Female: Male as Nature: Culture?" In M. Z. Rosaldo and L. Lamphere (eds.). *Women, Culture, and Society*. 67–87. Stanford: Stanford University Press.

Ovid. (1964). *Metamorphoses*. Trans. R. Humphries. Bloomington: Indiana University Press..

Oyama, S. (1985). *The Ontogeny of Information: Development Systems and Evolution*. Durham: Duke University Press.

Paul, R. A. (1976). "Did the Primal Crime Take Place?" *Ethos* 4 (3): 311–52.

Paul, R. A. (1987a). "The Individual and Society in Cultural and Biological Anthropology." *Cultural Anthropology* 2 (1): 80–93.

Paul, R. A. (1987b). "Comment on David Spain's "The Westermarck-Freud Debate." *Current Anthropology* 28 (5): 636–7.

Paul, R. A. (1988). "Psychoanalysis and the Propinquity Theory of Incest Avoidance." *Journal of Psychohistory* 15 (3): 255–61.

Paul, R. A. (1991). "Psychoanalytic Theory and Incest Avoidance Rules." *Behavioral & Brain Sciences* 14: 276–7.

Paul, R. A. (1996). *Moses and Civilization: The Meaning behind Freud's Myth*. New Haven: Yale University Press.

Paul, R. A. (2008). "Comment on Yoram Yovell's 'Is there a Drive to Love?'" *Neuropsychoanalysis* 10: 170–3.

Paul, R. A. (2011). "On the Observing Ego and the Experiencing Ego." In J. Lear (ed.). *A Case for Irony*. 164–70. Cambridge, MA and London: Harvard University Press.

Paul, R. A. (2015). *Mixed Messages: Cultural and Genetic Inheritance in the Constitution of Human Society*. Chicago: University of Chicago Press.

Paul, R. A. (2017). "Changing Attitudes About Sex: A Dual Inheritance Perspective." In V. Tsolas and C. Anzieu-Premmereur (eds.). *A Psychoanalytic Exploration of the Body in Today's World: On the Body*. 28–40. New York and East Sussex: Routledge.

Paul, R. A. (2018). "Culture from a Dual Inheritance Perspective." In N. Quinn (ed.). *Advances in Culture Theory from Psychological Anthropology*. 47–73. Cham, Switzerland: Palgrave Macmillan.

Pinker, S. (1997). *How the Mind Works*. New York: W. W. Norton.

Plato. (2000). *The Republic*. Trans. B. Jowett. New York: Dover Press.

Prinz, W. (2012). *Open Minds: The Social Making of Agency and Intentionality*. Cambridge: MIT Press.

Reilly, K. (2011). *Automata and Mimesis on the Stage of Theater History*. New York: Palgrave Macmillan.

Richerson, P. J. and R. Boyd (2005). *Not by Genes Alone: How Culture Transformed Human Nature*. Chicago: University of Chicago Press.

Rizzuto, A.-M. (2015). *Freud and the Spoken Word: Speech as the Key to the Unconscious*. New York: Routledge.

Rochat, P. (2009). *Others in Mind: Social Origins of Self-Consciousness*. New York: Cambridge University Press.

Sanday, P. (1981). *Female Power and Male Dominance: On the Origins of Sexual Inequality*. Cambridge, NY: Cambridge University Press.

Sarnoff, C. (1976). *Latency*. New York: Jason Aronson.

Schafer, R. (1976). *A New Language for Psychoanalysis*. New Haven: Yale University Press.

Scholem, G. ([1965] 1996). *On the Kabbalah and Its Symbolism*. New York: Schocken.

Shakespeare, W. (2008). *The Complete Sonnets and Poems*. New York: Oxford University Press.

Shanks, D. R. and B. R. Newell (2014). "The Primacy of Conscious Decision Making." *Behavioral and Brain Sciences* 37(1): 45–61.

Shelley, M. ([1818] 2012). *The Annotated Frankenstein*. Ed. S. J. Wolfson and R. Levao. Cambridge: Belknap Press.

Shepher, J. (1983). *Incest: A Biosocial View*. New York: Academic Press.

Smadja, É. (2019). *Freud and Culture*. London: Karnac.

Sober, E. and D. S. Wilson. (1998). *Unto Others: The Evolution and Psychology of Unselfish Behavior*. Cambridge: Harvard University Press.

Solms, M. (1997). "What Is Consciousness?" *Journal of the American Psychoanalytic Association*. 45: 681–703.

Spiro, M. (1958). *Children of the Kibbutz*. New York: Schocken Books.

Stanford, C. B. (1999). *The Hunting Apes: Meat Eating and the Origins of Human Behavior*. Princeton: Princeton University Press.

Stern, Donnell B. (2018). *The Infinity of the Unsaid*. New York and London: Routledge.

Sterba, R. (1934). "The Fate of the Ego in Analytic Therapy." *International Journal of Psychoanalysis* 25: 117–26.

Suttie, I. D. (1935). *The Origins of Love and Hate*. New York: Julian Press.

Terrace, H. S. (2019). *Why Chimpanzees Can't Learn Language and Only Humans Can*. New York: Columbia University Press.

Tetlock, P. E. (2002). "Social Functionalist Frameworks for Judgement and Choice: Intuitive Politicians, Theologians, and Prosecutors." *Psychological Review* 109 (3): 451–57.

Tomasello, M. (1999). *The Cultural Origins of Human Cognition*. Cambridge: Harvard University Press.

Tomasello, M. (2019). *Becoming Human: A Theory of Ontogeny*. Cambridge: Belknap Press.

Trivers, R. L. (1971). "The Evolution of Reciprocal Altruism." *The Quarterly Review of Biology* 41(1): 35–57.

Valsiner, J. (1998). *The Guided Mind*. Cambridge: Harvard University Press.

Virgil. (1980). *The Eclogues*. Trans. G. Lee. London: Penguin Books.

Vygotstky, L. S. (1978). *Mind in Society: Development of Higher Psychological Processes*. Cambridge: Harvard University Press.

de Waal, F. (1989). *Peacemaking among Primates*. Cambridge: Harvard University Press.

de Waal, F. (1996). *Good Natured: The Origins of Right and Wrong in Humans and Other Animals*. Cambridge: Harvard University Press.

Wiesel, E. (1983). *The Golem: The Story of a Legend*. New York: Summit Books.

Wilson, E. O. (2012). *The Social Conquest of Earth*. New York: Liveright.

Wilson, E. O. (2019). *Genesis: The Deep Origin of Societies*. New York: Liveright.

Wolf, A. P. (1995). *Sexual Attraction and Childhood Association: A Chinese Brief for Edward Westermarck*. Stanford: Stanford University Press.

Wrangham, R. (2019). *The Goodness Gene: The Strange Relationship between Virtue and Violence in Human Evolution*. New York: Pantheon Books.

Wrangham, R. and D. Peterson (1996). *Demonic Males: Apes and the Origins of Human Violence*. New York: Houghton Mifflin.

INDEX